The MX Decision

Westview Special Studies

The concept of Westview Special Studies is a response to the continuing crisis in academic and informational publishing. Library budgets are being diverted from the purchase of books and used for data banks, computers, micromedia, and other methods of information retrieval. Interlibrary loan structures further reduce the edition sizes required to satisfy the needs of the scholarly community. Economic pressures on university presses and the few private scholarly publishing companies have greatly limited the capacity of the industry to properly serve the academic and research communities. As a result, many manuscripts dealing with important subjects, often representing the highest level of scholarship, are no longer economically viable publishing projects—or, if accepted for publication, are typically subject to lead times ranging from one to three years.

Westview Special Studies are our practical solution to the problem. We accept manuscripts in camera-ready form, typed, set, or word processed according to specifications laid out in our comprehensive manual, which contains straightforward instructions and sample pages. As always, the selection criteria include the importance of the subject, the work's contribution to scholarship, and its insight, originality of thought, and excellence of exposition. The responsibility for editing and proofreading lies with the author or sponsoring institution, but our editorial staff is always available to answer questions and provide guidance.

The result is a book printed on acid-free paper and bound in sturdy library-quality soft covers. We manufacture these books ourselves using equipment that does not require a lengthy make-ready process and that allows us to publish first editions of 300 to 1000 copies and to reprint even smaller quantities as needed. Thus, we can produce Special Studies quickly and can keep even very specialized books in print as long as there is a demand for them.

About the Book and Authors

Focusing especially on the history of the MX program, this book examines the process of U.S. weapons procurement decision making. The authors demonstrate that strategic and general political factors (as opposed to bureaucratic concerns) play a far more decisive role in the decision-making process than is indicated in previous studies of weapons procurement. They also point to the significant contributions of congressional and public debate in influencing U.S. policy concerning weapons procurement. The authors conclude that the pattern of decision making with regard to the MX reflects a change that began in the 1970s and thus will be significant in explaining procurement policy in the decade ahead.

Lauren H. Holland is assistant professor of political science at the University of Utah. **Robert A. Hoover** is associate professor and chair of the department of political science at Utah State University.

To My Parents,
Marcie and Charles Holland,
With Love and Gratitude

To My Family,
Jeanne, J.J., and Suzanne Hoover,
With Love and Appreciation

The MX Decision

A NEW DIRECTION IN U.S. WEAPONS PROCUREMENT POLICY?

Lauren H. Holland
and Robert A. Hoover

with a Foreword by Wolfram F. Hanrieder

Westview Press / Boulder and London

OCT 85

Westview Special Studies in National Security and Defense Policy

Copyright © 1985 by Westview Press, Inc.

Published in 1985 in the United States of America by Westview Press, Inc., 5500 Central Avenue, Boulder, Colorado 80301; Frederick A. Praeger, Publisher

Library of Congress Cataloging in Publication Data
Holland, Lauren H.
    The MX decision.
    (Westview special studies in national security and defense policy)
1. MX (Weapons system)   2. United States—Armed Forces
—Procurement.   I. Hoover, Robert A.   II. Title.
UG1312.I2H67   1985   358'.174'0973   83-23468
ISBN 0-86531-993-6

Printed and bound in the United States of America

10   9   8   7   6   5   4   3   2   1

CONTENTS

LIST OF TABLES AND FIGURES

FOREWORD

In the nuclear age the idea of deterrence, which is as old as the use of physical force, embodies the conviction that the main purpose of military policy must be to avert war rather than win it. Consequently, a potential opponent must be persuaded that the anticipated benefits of initiating military action are incommensurate with its costs, and that it is likely that these costs will be inflicted. But one of the paradoxes of the nuclear age is that a viable deterrence posture requires that the opponent who is to be deterred must also be reassured. Once nuclear parity is reached, strategic doctrine as well as the nuclear force posture must express not only determination but also restraint. Both antagonists share an interest in stabilizing the existing balance of terror and in institutionalizing the inhibitions created by the prospects of mutual destruction: arms control becomes a way of expressing a military equilibrium and a shared will to avert nuclear annihilation. The need to deter the opponent with the prospect of unacceptable damage becomes meshed with the need to persuade the opponent of one's own restraint and sense of responsibility.

There are nuclear weapons — and in my view the MX is one — that are not suitable for the purpose of either deterrence or reassurance. The size, accuracy, and multi-warhead capability of the MX make it a supreme counterforce weapon, implying an American nuclear strategy that contemplates a first strike. As Henry Kissinger pointed out long ago, a counterforce strategy can suggest one of two situations: such superiority that we could win an all-out war even if we conceded the first strike, or a strategy in which we would win an all-out war but only if we struck first. The unsuitability of the MX as a deterrent force is further enhanced by the difficulty — some would say impossibility — of providing the MX with a sufficiently invulnerable basing mode. In short, the MX is likely to appear to the Soviet Union as both threatening and vulnerable — a dangerous combination of attributes that violate the imperatives of both deterrence and reassurance. As a consequence, the Reagan administration's intention to deploy 100 MX missiles in the old Minuteman silos has not only beclouded U.S.-Soviet relations and the prospects for superpower arms control agreements but raised serious misgivings among American allies and among the American people.

Alliance management is burdened by the assertive implications of the MX program (accompanied by the strident Cold War rhetoric of the administration) because the nuclear protector of an alliance, such as the United States, must convey to its partners as well as to its opponents that its deterrence policy is both responsible and credible, both firm and circumspect, governed by loyalty to the alliance as well as by the caution imposed by nuclear parity. This is not an easy task. Once the Soviet Union reached parity with the United States, Washington became obliged to accept Moscow as an equal in military-strategic matters — a necessity that was reflected in strategic doctrine as well as in the readiness to stabilize the nuclear balance through measures of arms control. Yet as long as Western Europe feels inferior in the area of conventional capabilities, the security of Western Europe can be convincingly assured only on the basis of an implied American nuclear superiority. A realistic American strategic relationship with the Soviet Union must rest on a balance of terror, whereas the guarantee of West European security rests, at bottom, on an implied imbalance of terror in favor of the United States — especially as long as the alliance contemplates the first use of nuclear weapons if deterrence should fail and the tide of conventional battle should turn against the West.

The MX program has proven divisive also in American domestic politics. Despite its technical complexity and political ambiguity, the MX aroused a good deal of public attention (especially in the states where the MX was to be deployed in its various basing modes); and the military-strategic, political, economic and ecological liabilities of the MX program occasioned a long and bitter debate in the Congress. The President, fearful that his negotiating stance in U.S.-Soviet arms control talks might be undercut by Congressional refusal to fund the MX, felt compelled to accept the proposal of the Scowcroft Commission to build a new small missile with a single warhead — a proposal that called into question the efficacy of the MX program and that required as well an adjustment of the administration's strategic arms control position.

The momentous implications of the MX program raise the question of why and how the decision — or, more appropriately, the sequence of decisions — to acquire and deploy the MX was reached. This is the question that Professors Holland and Hoover seek to answer. In tracing MX procurement decision making from the late 1960s to the present, the authors provide a detailed examination of the political and economic forces that accelerated or retarded the implementation of the MX program, but in so doing they present as well a panorama of the larger domestic and foreign policy issues that agitated the American political process of the last decades.

University of California, Santa Barbara   Wolfram F. Hanrieder

xii

PREFACE

As the U.S. Air Force was completing studies in 1980 to deploy MX in a multiple protective shelter basing mode (MX MPS) in the Great Basin of Utah and Nevada, people from that region were asking how and why it was that the newest and most massive U.S. nuclear weapon was coming to their mountains and deserts. About the same time, one of us, Bob, was beginning a manuscript on the strategic implications of MX while the other, Laurie, was initiating research with another author on the federal, state, and public law hurdles the air force faced in the deployment of MX in the Great Basin.

Although we teach at institutions that are only ninety miles apart and received our graduate degrees from the same university, we were unknown to each other and unaware that we were working on projects that were quite complementary. A fortuitous meeting at the American Political Science Association Convention in New York in 1981 precipitated a strong professional and warm personal relationship. After discussing the project and our concerns about the entire MX program, we realized that each offered the other a special knowledge that was necessary if the decision-making process for MX was to be explained. Thus, we joined forces.

As we explored the literature about procurement (i.e., design, research, development, testing, acquisition, and deployment of weapon programs), we discovered that the predominant approach, the so-called bureaucratic politics perspective most often associated with Morton Halperin and Graham Allison, was insufficient for describing and explaining the MX decision-making process. This motivated us to ask questions about the completeness and current utility of the bureaucratic politics perspective for explaining procurement decisions such as MX. Thus, we began our study of the procurement politics of MX with some trepidation, realizing that challenging the conventional wisdom was risky, and that in the end we could discover that the case of MX procurement was merely an aberration. It is not. In many ways, of course, the MX system is unique. However, the process by which critical MX decisions were made represents clear patterns in procurement politics that were also evident in the decisions concerning the antiballistic missile system, the Trident program, and the U.S. Navy's extremely low-frequency radio wave communication system. More importantly, given current trends in the economy, military technology, Congress, and the public discussion of weapons, we conclude that certain types of procurement decision making will conform in the future to the style of MX.

We thank the Departments of Political Science at Utah State University and the University of Utah for financial assistance tendered in support of the research for this manuscript. We are particularly grateful to the Milton R. Merrill Chair at Utah State University for providing financial aid for the research, editing, and typing of the manuscript. Many people, friends and colleagues, too numerous to identify individually, provided invaluable insights and critical comments during the writing of the manuscript. We offer special thanks to Robert Benedict, Dan Caldwell, William Furlong, Ron Hrebenar, Kent Kimball, James Kurth, Mark Lennon, Slava Lubomudrov, Dalmas Nelson, Carolyn Rhodes-Jones, and Larry Smith. In addition, we are deeply appreciative of the secretarial assistance provided by Cindy Nielsen, Craig Albiston, and Carmen Bullock, and the editorial assistance of Linda Speth, without whom preparation of this manuscript would have been virtually impossible. We also thank the nearly forty individuals associated with the MX project who in interviews with us provided information about the development of this controversial program. We have withheld specific identification of these individuals according to the ground rules of the interviews. Finally, a special thanks to Mark, Jeanne, J.J., and Suzanne — our spouses and children — for supporting us through the lengthy research and writing. We are, of course, solely responsible for the argument and content of the book.

Lauren H. Holland
Robert A. Hoover

INTRODUCTION

For the past several years, the United States has been embroiled in a political and strategic controversy over the feasibility of developing and deploying a new generation of intercontinental ballistic missiles (ICBMs) called MX (for missile experimental).[1] Strategic decisions about nuclear weapons are among the most important and far-reaching made by the human race. In addition to this awesome, ominous dimension, the potential size of the MX project created enormous financial incentives for industry, labor, chamber of commerce groups, and state governments, but held out the prospect of vast socioeconomic and environmental dislocation (e.g., boom town and desertification problems) for the region or regions in which it was to be deployed. The combination of these diverse factors produced several disputatious twists and turns in the MX story as it evolved during the 1970s and early 1980s.

The history of MX is a paradox. On the one hand, the scope of the MX project is unique; it is the most expensive weapon project contemplated, most extensive in resource consumption, most cogent in strategic significance since nuclear weapons and intercontinental missiles, and most expansive in environmental and socioeconomic implications. One of the proposed MX basing systems, the multiple protective shelter program, would have been the largest public works project in human history had it been initiated. The new ICBMs' proposed hard-target implications (i.e., the ability to destroy Soviet targets hardened in concrete), are so profound that enough of these weapons would provide a theoretical first-strike capacity for the United States against the Soviet Union's ICBM force. The MX decision has involved more private groups and individuals as well as elements of the U.S. government than any previously proposed weapon system. Furthermore, even after more than a decade of proposals and counterproposals, stops and starts, the final decision for acquisition and deployment of MX is still largely undetermined. Heretofore, nothing like this has happened.

And yet, MX is the clearest manifestation of the changes in the pattern of procurement decision making for major weapon programs that transpired during the past decade known as the post-Vietnam/Watergate era. Even though the history of MX is unusual in scope and certainly tumultuous, MX procurement decision making from the late 1960s through Ronald Reagan's narrow authorization victory in Congress in 1983 is also the clearest sign of the changes that have occurred in U.S. politics, particularly national security affairs, since Vietnam and Watergate. Hence the importance of this book rests on discovering and analyzing the reasons for MX's departure from the norm of procurement decision making in the 1950s and

1

1960s, and explaining why it is the harbinger of decision making concerning a certain type of major weapon programs.

These changes in procurement decision making are severalfold. Following the Vietnam War, the broad U.S. consensus about foreign policy objectives developed during the Cold War, and the U.S. public's trust in the presidency to promote those objectives, eroded. Vietnam left the United States divided over national security policy, a division that had vast implications for procurement. Watergate severely reduced the executive branch's power over national security affairs by provoking members of Congress to reassert influence over those activities. As a result of these changes, the foreign policy and strategic implications of procurement decisions are no longer viewed as the exclusive purview of the presidency. No foreign policy or strategic consensus seems likely to reemerge in the near future to reverse the direction of these trends. In addition, virtually all programs possessing a nuclear dimension have become highly visible and controversial issues. The nuclear freeze issue is just one of several politicized national security questions, and the freeze has had a significant impact on MX in the 1980s. Also, in an era of major budget deficits with corresponding pressures to trim fiscal items, the defense budget, and especially big procurement programs, are attractive targets for budget cutters. Deficits have been a problem for the past decade and are projected to continue as an even-bigger problem for much of the remainder of the 1980s. Finally, public opinion in the United States is far more divided about the pork-barrel benefits of military procurement than in the past. The often negative socioeconomic and environmental side effects associated with the deployment of weapon systems are now viewed as very important political questions, ones that cannot be ignored by the executive branch or Congress. Thus, while the sheer size of MX is unusual, its deployment implications will characterize decision-making activity for certain types of procurement decisions in the years ahead. Yet no theoretical framework currently exists capable of capturing this new pattern of procurement politics.

Conventional wisdom, embodied in theories of the process of military politics (Kurth, 1971:373-404), postulates that defense decision making, especially that of defense procurement, is characteristically dominated by the executive branch and is more hierarchical in nature than most other issue areas. Implicit in this contention is that factors important in domestic politics, such as Congress, interest groups, and public opinion, are less important and even peripheral in the defense process. However, the history of MX raises questions about the validity of the conventional argument. The MX policy debate and the decision-making process for MX have been and continue to be uncharacteristic of how the U.S. governmental system processed defense decisions for major weapons during the post-World War II period, at least until the 1970s.

In the following chapter, we examine the bureaucratic politics framework. It is the approach used most frequently by analysts to explain procurement decisions. Nevertheless, there exists no formal model of propositions and assumptions within the bureaucratic politics literature to explain decision making as it relates to procurement. However, we believe that the bureaucratic politics literature on procurement, found mainly in a vast number of case studies, suggests a number of cogent propositions and assumptions about decision making for major weapon programs. We formalize those propositions and assumptions by spelling them out. In effect, we present a descriptive model of procurement decision making derived from the bureaucratic politics literature.

The term procurement decision making is defined to include R&D (design, research, testing, and development), acquisition, and deployment. Although not an explicit feature of the bureaucratic politics literature, there seem to be two layers of decision activities: an inner and outer layer (see Figure 0.1). The inner layer focuses on decisions about the design, research, development, and testing of prototypes of weapons. The outer layer refers to decisions related to the acquisition and deployment of weapons. Although it is often difficult to distinguish when a prototype weapon system moves from testing to acquisition, as will become clear when we review the decisions about MX, the literature suggests a different set of propositions for each layer of activity to explain how the decisions are conducted.

We believe the outer layer of the MX decision-making process, which focuses on acquisition and deployment, is radically different from previous acquisition and deployment decisions, or at least those prior to the 1970s. To a much lesser extent, this has been also true for the inner layer, which focuses on design, research, development, and testing. For example, issues such as the strategic and foreign policy implications of MX have been far more instrumental in shaping the character of MX than previous weapon decisions discussed in much of the bureaucratic politics literature. Even more significantly, for the first time in the recent history of the procurement process (post-World War II), the ultimate power over such decisions was no longer the exclusive prerogative of the executive branch. New groups of interests materialized and intruded into the decision domain dominated previously by the military, defense contractors, key civilians in the Department of Defense, several important congressional actors, and the president and his presidential advisors for defense policy. These new groups brought to the procurement process a set of previously overlooked concerns: environmental impact, socioeconomic costs, fiscal and budget-

3

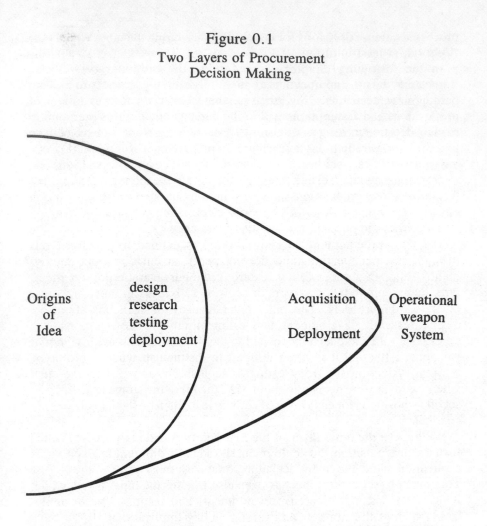

Figure 0.1
Two Layers of Procurement
Decision Making

Origins
of
Idea

design
research
testing
deployment

Acquisition

Deployment

Operational
weapon
System

ary demands, and strategic and foreign policy implications. In addition, these groups compelled state and local governments within the region targeted for MX deployment to become involved intimately in the decision-making process, thus activating previously unused governmental arenas .

Congress has played a pivotal role in the decision-making process on MX. It's concerns, traditionally limited to structural questions (i.e., porkbarrel) have extended to include strategic aspects of the system. Even the federal courts were brought into the MX fray as the public groups, who had organized to defeat MX, sought to use litigation in assisting arms control advocates in mobilizing public opinion against any ICBM with a first-strike capability.

After reviewing and questioning the utility of the bureaucratic politics paradigm, we turn in Part 2 to the prominent issues and actors that featured in the MX debate. An exploration of these issues offers the unfamiliar reader an introduction to the complexities of MX. More importantly, it provides insights into the complex and multifarious nature of the MX controversy.

MX decision making has focused on four substantive and interrelated issues: (1) the strategic requirements of the missile; (2) the strategic needs of an invulnerable basing mode; (3) the concern for compatibility between MX and the strategic arms limitation talks and other foreign policy considerations; and (4) the political and fiscal feasibility of its deployment in light of its vast socioeconomic and environmental implications. Although MX was promoted as a solution to the problem of ICBM vulnerability, it soon became apparent that any basing system had drawbacks. The multiple shelter protective mode (MPS), the mode chosen by the Carter administration in 1979, provided no clear-cut solution to the ICBM vulnerability problem confronting the United States by the mid-1970s. This was especially so after the apparent defeat of the Strategic Arms Limitation Talks II Treaty (SALT II) in the Senate in 1980. The defeat of the treaty opened up the basing mode question to considerable debate and controversy. It provided favorable conditions for the opposition that arose to MX on both strategic and nonstrategic (especially political) grounds.

In Part 3 we analyze in detail the character of the decision-making process for MX and compare and contrast it with the bureaucratic politics approach for procurement. We do not seek to write a history of MX. Rather we use available accounts of the MX process, our personal interviews with key legislative and executive actors, and public documents to reconstruct the pattern of procurement decision making for MX. The task of Part 3 then is to illustrate how MX differs from previous patterns of procurement decision making.

We begin by exploring the character of the decision-making process from the initial ideas about the new missile (late 1960s) to the acquisition decisions of the Ford and Carter administrations in 1976 and 1979, respectively. Here we review both the inner and outer layer activities during these two periods, particularly the factors leading to the decisions by both Ford and Carter to pursue the design, the research, the testing, and the development of MX while considering partially completed prototypes for its acquisition and deployment. During this period, strategic and foreign policy considerations were far more significant in influencing the character of MX than the bureaucratic politics literature suggests.

It is during the second period of the MX saga, 1979-83, that we find the bureaucratic politics literature even less informative. In analyzing the factors that caused the tumultuous reception of MX in the congressional and public arenas, we find evidence to substantiate the importance of these two realms in the decision-making process. By 1979 the Carter administration was involved in an organized effort with the Office of the Secretary of Defense (OSD) and the U.S. Air Force to build support in Congress and the regional areas cited for MX deployment. Support from the latter was especially important in light of the perceived socioeconomic and environmental disruption the deployment of MX in a MPS mode was likely to cause. The response of pressure groups, state and local officials, and senators and representatives in the region targeted for the deployment of MX MPS, the Great Basin of Nevada and Utah, was a critical factor in the MX story.

The role of Congress was crucial in the MX debate from 1979 through 1983, a role anticipated by attitudinal changes in the U.S. public and structural changes in the legislature during the late 1960s and early 1970s. Congress became the center of a storm of public pressure for political change in a variety of substantive areas during that period, including changing environmental attitudes, the nuclear freeze movement, and concerns over defense spending.

Congress was an active arena for both opponents and proponents seeking to influence the many and varied decisions about MX. As both a major public works project and weapon installation system, the MX issue was not just a national security policy decision. The scope of the financial rewards along with the tax burden and the social and environmental impact associated with the weapon were unprecedented. These implications brought into politics, especially into the governmental arena of Congress, groups formerly uninvolved and often uninterested in defense policy. The failure of MX to provide a definitive solution to the ICBM vulnerability problem only served to increase the legitimacy and intensity of citizen participation in the process and opposition to the system. These groups were instrumental in the government's conduct of this procurement decision.

Ironically, the access to weapon procurement decision making for newly activated public input was an unintended and unforeseen result of recent legislation for nondefense issues. MX antagonists creatively employed legislation such as the National Environmental Protection Act (NEPA) of 1969, the Federal Land Policy and Management Act (FLPMA) of 1976, and the Freedom of Information Act (FOIA) of 1965 to gain access to and influence on procurement decisions, access virtually unavailable previ-

6

ously to nondefense individuals and groups. NEPA, instituted in part to provide a hearing for environmental and social considerations for major federal projects by either the private or public sector, became one vehicle that anti-MX groups used to challenge the decision to deploy the missile system in the MPS mode in the Great Basin. The FLPMA requirement for state-federal cooperation and consultation in the land management process provided a legal basis by which dissenting state actors attacked the legitimacy of MX activities on public land. The FOIA allowed individual citizens and state and local actors to acquire information previously unavailable about the policymaking process for MX.

These new acts facilitate public input in the outer layer of the decision-making process for weapon procurement. The new ''defense'' interests actively pursued by these new groups when combined with the new access points to procurement decision making are the critical new ingredients of the MX saga. These new factors have vast implications for future large-scale procurement projects.

Finally, how the executive branch dealt with the pressures by other arenas to influence the decision process is quite important in understanding the relationships among the several arenas. For example, during his administration Carter was forced to modify three critical components of his planned MX MPS system: the North Platte Plains states were abandoned as possible deployment sites, the buried trench concept was discarded next, and the original racetrack format was replaced with the grid mode of the MX MPS system.

Ronald Reagan and Caspar Weinberger were ultimately compelled to adopt a compromise (the Scowcroft Commission Plan) carefully crafted by administration and legislative actors. The factors that produced these and similar concessions are identified and scrutinized. Of particular interest in this analysis are the political forces (e.g., the 1980 election), the legal issues (e.g., charges by special interest groups that NEPA and FLPMA had been violated), and the budgetary concerns that facilitated the MX system becoming the most politicized weapon program in U.S. history.

We also examine the relationships among foreign policy, arms limitation questions, and MX. During 1981 the modernization of theater nuclear weapons in Western Europe and public opposition became intimately linked to the MX debate and were influential in Reagan's MX decision in late summer of 1981. Concerns were raised about the the inability of the United States to project an united image on this issue for fear NATO allies would be reluctant to accept the Pershing II and cruise missiles.

Although the bureaucratic politics paradigm has much to recommend it, ultimately it fails to capture the complexity of procurement decision making for weapon programs such as MX. An alternative framework (which includes some of the propositions of the bureaucratic politics approach) is required to explain the MX decision-making process and to "predict" the probable nature of decision making for large weapon programs in the future. In the final chapter, we outline such an approach based upon the experience of MX. Our conceptual framework emphasizes multiple and active groups, multiple arenas, and feedback mechanisms among those arenas and the importance of the president within the executive branch arena.

One caveat is necessary, however. In explaining procurement programs that require relatively few resources and that have minor environmental or social costs, ones that do not have a nuclear dimension and/or raise strategic questions, the bureaucratic politics paradigm may still be appropriate. The decision-making activity will be relegated primarily to the executive arena. Nonetheless, with the growing sophistication of modern nuclear weapons, something that seems to translate into vast sums of money by the time of deployment, along with the often potentially significant environmental and social costs of many of those weapons, it is difficult to avoid the vision of the other governmental and political arenas playing important roles in procurement. Also, as MX demonstrates, Congress can be an active arena for even the strategic dimension of procurement. Ultimately, we conclude that for much of procurement decision making about weapons with these characteristics, the bureaucratic politics approach no longer provides an adequate explanation. It is our task to substantiate this claim and to suggest the outline of an alternative framework which captures the pattern of decision making for weapon programs that require considerable resources and have potentially significant environmental and social costs.

Endnotes

[1]For a representative sample of the debate, see Gray (1977), Scoville (1981), Snow (1981), Snow (1980), and Hoover (1982).

PART 1
THE BUREAUCRATIC POLITICS PARADIGM
FOR
PROCUREMENT DECISION MAKING

CHAPTER 1
BUREAUCRATIC POLITICS AND PROCUREMENT DECISIONS

A generation of national security analysts have agonized over who makes decisions about which weapons the United States should design, research, develop, test, acquire, and deploy. These are obviously important matters given the considerable resources the United States devotes to the procurement of weapons for the U. S. military. In addition, some of these decisions have profound implications for both the United States and the world given the enormous destructive power of nuclear weapons.

The framework most frequently used to analyze the procurement of weapons is the bureaucratic politics perspective or approach. Although a large body of literature about weapon procurement using this perspective has emerged, no one has explicitly delineated the assumptions and propositions of this approach.[1] Indeed, the literature constitutes a collection of case studies with an implicit framework of assumptions about procurement behavior; no explicit approach has been developed to explain the process.[2] Nevertheless, after an extensive review of the literature, it is clear that certain patterns of assumptions about procurement decision-making activities do exist in the many and varied case studies.

The first task of this chapter will be to specify the assumptions and propositions implicit in the literature on weapon decisions utilizing the bureaucratic politics approach. This entails developing an approach for procurement activities partially deduced from the general literature on bureaucratic politics along with extracting themes from the myriad case studies. Our second task is to determine whether or not this approach is an efficacious device for understanding the research, development, production, and deployment of large-scale weapon programs, such as the MX. In fact, recent changes in public attitudes and in the U.S. government about national security policy suggest that the bureaucratic politics approach as currently formulated no longer provides a viable tool for explaining certain types of procurement decisions. Thus, we conclude by refining and expanding that approach to better understand a decision like MX, i.e., one which requires extensive resources and portends vast socioeconomic and environmental disruption.

The Bureaucratic Politics Approach

In a watershed essay about the decision-making process for national security affairs, Graham Allison argued in 1969 that those who understood national security policy as the outcome of rigorous analysis of goals and strategies, would likely encounter significant difficulties in explaining much of U.S. foreign policy (Allison, 1969).[3] Analysts who assumed that the government was capable of rational behavior often attributed poor policy (i.e., results that did not seem to conform to the goals and strategy of U.S. interests) to poor conceptualization, poor management, or a combination of both.[4] After review of the Cuban Missile Crisis, Allison maintained that U.S. and Soviet behavior required more than just an examination of goals and strategies; rather behavior in that crisis could not be understood without an appreciation of how the governmental processes of the two superpowers affected the critical showdown over Cuba.

A decade before Allison's more thorough conceptualization of national security decision making, Samuel Huntington (1961:2) made similar assertions. "Military policy is not the result of deductions from a clear statement of national objective. It is the product of the competition of purposes within individuals and groups and among individuals and groups [in the executive bureaucracy]. It is the result of politics not logic, more an arena than a unity." Others, such as Roger Hilsman (1967), Warner Schilling (1962), Paul Hammond (1961, 1963), Richard Neustadt (1964), and Morton Halperin (1973, 1974), have since reiterated that proposition: policymaking is explained more effectively by examining how organizations and individuals within the executive bureaucracy influence decisions rather than by explaining it as the outcome of rational analysis by the U.S. government.

Allison separated the analyses by Huntington and these other scholars into two distinct explanations of how intra-governmental factors shape national security policy decisions. The first was the organizational process model (Allison, 1971:67-143), which described government as composed of a large number of semiautonomous organizations (i.e., the Department of Defense, the Department of State, and the Central Intelligence Agency, the CIA). In this framework, these organizations lead virtually an independent existence within the executive branch. Senior political officials occasionally influence these organizations, but do not directly control them. The relative permanence and unity of purpose of these organizations when compared to the ever-changing set and diverse interests of political leaders within the executive branch allows these semiautonomous organizations to dominate national security decisions. In the organizational process model, governmental policy outcomes can be understood "less as deliberate choices and more as *outputs* of large organizations functioning according to standard patterns of behavior" (Allison, 1971:67).

Allison labeled the second model the governmental politics framework (Allison, 1971:144-244). In explaining the model, he (Allison, 1971:144-45) suggested:

The apparatus of each national government constitutes a complex arena for the intra-national game. Political leaders at the top of the apparatus are joined by the men who occupy positions on the top of major organizations to form a circle of central players. Those who join the circle come with some independent standing. . . .[These] men share power. Men differ about what must be done. The differences matter. This milieu necessitates that government decisions and actions result from a political process. In this process, sometimes one group committed to a course of action triumphs over other groups fighting for other alternatives. Equally often, however, different groups pulling in different directions produce a result, or better a resultant — a mixture of conflicting preferences and unequal power of various individuals — distinct from what any person or group intended.

In this model, the skill of the individuals and power of their resources interact with the timing of events and issues to direct the various pieces of activity toward a policy outcome.

The bureaucratic politics approach employed by most analysts of procurement decisions is an amalgam of the two conceptual models described by Allison.[5] The key assumption of the bureaucratic politics literature is that what goes on inside the government, especially the executive branch, "counts" when explaining national security policy. The senior individuals such as the president and his appointees for national security affairs often interact with semiautonomous organizations and suborganizations within the executive branch. It is the interaction of these groups and individuals that molds U.S. foreign and military policy.[6]

As one might expect when dealing with any approach that is a combination of two other models, there are several layers of ambiguity in such a paradigm. Who are the major individuals or what are the major factors shaping national security policy? Is it the president, his major political appointees, the organizations, or the leaders of these organizations? Are their motivations personal ones, broad foreign policy considerations, electoral concerns, or organizational imperatives? The literature suggests that diverse groups and individuals with different motivations pull in different and often conflicting directions, and eventually this interaction produces a policy result different from that desired by any individual or organization. Although the specific outcome depends on the unique combination of actors, certain critical tendencies are apparent in this interaction.

Thus, a major dimension of the bureaucratic politics approach is that policymaking is the process of conflict and consensus building among the president, his national security and political appointees, and the individuals representing the national security organizations within the executive

13

bureaucracy. Both within organizations and within the executive branch, the advocates of a particular policy option must build support for that position. "Where there are rival advocates or rival policies, there is competition for support, and all the techniques of alliance appear — persuasion, accommodation, and bargaining" (Allison, 1971:158).

Another important premise of the approach is that each actor's stand on an issue is greatly influenced by the individual's organizational-institutional position, or more colloquially, "Where you stand depends upon where you sit." But, as Allison makes clear, "The propensities and priorities stemming from [the organizational] position. . .are filtered through the baggage that players bring to positions" (quoted in Krasner, 1972:166). This complex baggage includes conceptions of national goals and domestic interests as well as personal convictions (Allison and Halperin, 1972:40-79).

Each organizational position also carries with it certain resources, formal authority, and the power to compete in the policy game. Individual participants differ as to the skills they possess to exploit these positions in the competition over policy outcomes. And competition is inevitable given the diversification of interests and diffusion of power and authority. Again national security policymaking is the process of conflict and consensus building within the executive branch.

Bureaucratic politics analysts employ a set of concentric circles to graphically depict the set of relationships that exist in the national security policy process (see Figure 1.1).[7] Notice that national security power is concentrated around the president, his chief national security advisors (the National Security Council), the individuals and organizations in the Departments of Defense and State and the CIA, and sometimes key economic leaders within the executive branch. In the next circle are members of other organizations within the executive branch with significant interests but lesser responsibilities for national security policy. The next circle of actors includes members of Congress and the interested national security affairs public and interest groups. The outer circle is made up of the press and public opinion. The important assumption is that the farther one's distance from the core circle, the less influence one has over national security policy. Thus, the paradigm is executive branch centered. It is also hierarchical. Although the president is viewed as one player among a score of other "senior" ones, he "stands at the center," and his "role" and "influence" are "qualitatively different than those of any other participants" (Halperin and Kanter, 1973:6-7).

This does not mean that the president commands — "the president in riding boots" image. On the contrary, he is forced by the nature of this position to persuade — "the president in sneakers" image; and, thus,

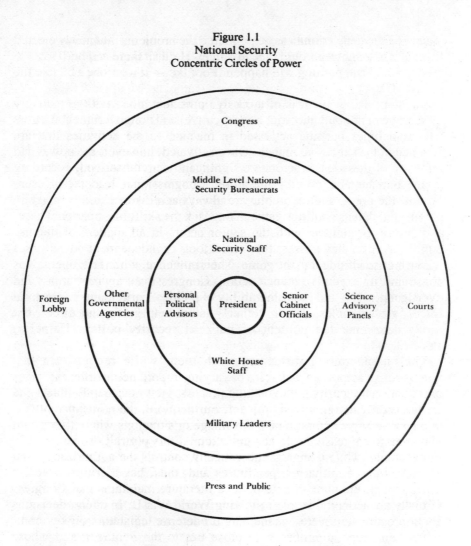

Figure 1.1
National Security
Concentric Circles of Power

Congress

Middle Level National
Security Bureaucrats

National
Security Staff

Foreign Lobby

Other Governmental Agencies

Personal Political Advisors

President

Senior Cabinet Officials

Science Advisory Panels

Courts

White House Staff

Military Leaders

Press and Public

sometimes even seek support from individuals outside the executive branch in building a coalition of support within the executive arena (Neustadt, 1964). In this way, the president is a critical fulcrum for linking the congressional and public arenas with the inner sanctum of the defense policy arena — the Pentagon. As a political figure, the president must be sensitive and responsive to certain public and private interests. As an administrative figure, the president must bargain and negotiate with technical advisors and career bureaucrats. As Dan Caldwell (1977:96) points out: "Bureaucratic politics analysts are fond of quoting the famous remark made by President Truman as he pondered the problems that newly elected President Eisenhower would face in office: 'He'll sit there and he'll say, do this! Do that! and nothing will happen. Poor Ike — it won't be a bit like the Army.' "

The impression, then, is of a passive president along with a relatively inert group of nonbureaucratic, nonexecutive, and nongovernmental actors who sometimes become activated in reaction to the activities that are centered in the executive branch. Once activated, however, the power and influence of these lesser actors are significantly circumscribed, according to the bureaucratic politics literature. Congressional leaders, pressure groups, the press, and the public are always at a distinct disadvantage in playing the defense politics game. They lack the skill, informational base, and access to compete with the senior actors in all matters of defense politics. Nor do they possess the formal tools or independent power bases with which to intrude into the game. Their influence, when felt, operates as constraints on executive branch action. Congressional appropriations and oversight powers, and the vulnerability of political participants to electoral forces, are examples. Thus, "other" actors help guide and direct, but rarely determine the content of national security policy (Halperin, 1974:73-74).

The bureaucratic politics approach then, while recognizing that nonexecutive actors can play roles of varying importance at different stages in the national security policymaking process, views these individuals and arenas as only marginally significant. Furthermore, the reluctance of certain nonexecutive actors to take advantage of situations where they could play a more aggressive role has underscored this portrait of marginality. For example, while Congress theoretically controls the authorization and appropriation of military expenditures and, thus, has a critical voice in procurement, the bureaucratic politics literature maintains that Congress virtually abandoned this role following World War II. In effect, decisions about procurement were "made" by prodefense legislators on key committees and subcommittees with close ties to the Pentagon and whose interests in procuring a particular weapon were nonstrategic such as porkbarrel. Other members of Congress were uninterested and uninvolved in defense politics, making Congress a peripheral arena for procurement decision making during this period (Halperin and Kanter, 1973:40-79).

Earlier advocates of the bureaucratic politics framework such as Huntington, Schilling, and Hammond actually accorded a much larger and more important role to individual members of Congress in national security decisions such as procurement.[8] For these analysts, Congress performed a critical lobbying function that brought legislators into the executive branch decision-making process.[9] Huntington (1961:134) described this role as that of prodder or goad of the Administration on behalf of specific programs or activities. With the executive decision-maker, Congress becomes the lobbyist. . . . The presence of dissenting agencies within the executive gives congressional groups a fulcrum for leverage. Just as in other areas the administration uses pressure and persuasion to move its legislation through Congress, so in military policy congressional groups often engage in sustained campaigns of pressure and persuasion to produce action on the part of the Administration. Congress as a whole, of course does not lobby with the executive, but particular groups within Congress do: committees, blocs, and/or even an entire house.

More recent analysts such as Halperin and Kanter suggest that the role of individuals and groups in Congress is more often secondary even as lobbyists. Nonetheless, both groups of scholars agree that the motivation for members of Congress to involve themselves with the executive branch was inextricably tied to porkbarrel, rather than to strategy (Huntington, 1961:134).

Although the policy process as described by the bureaucratic politics analysts may seem chaotic, it is not. Rather there are certain rules or procedures that either operate institutionally (e.g., standard operating procedures of organizations) or are determined by the players in the central circle (e.g., the rules of the game established by a president). This existence of "established channels" for processing policies regularizes the involvement of certain "important" and "influential" congressional and private-public actors in the game. These channels differ, just as the mix of players do, depending on the issue ("actions," "decisions," or "policies") and the decision stage (formulation or implementation) (Allison and Halperin in Tanter and Ullman, 1972:47-50).

Explanations of Weapon Procurement

As indicated above, the literature about how the United States decides and buys a weapon system predominately utilizes the ill-defined bureaucratic politics approach to both guide research about procurement and shape the eventual conclusions about the efficacy of the decision-making process. Guided by the wisdom of the bureaucratic politics approach, analysts of procurement have tended to focus on organizational factors and executive branch politics in explaining how and why a particular weapon system came into being. The normative conclusions of these studies have emphasized how changes or refinements in these organizations or in the consensus formation within the executive branch could produce better policy, i.e., weapon systems that would better support U.S. national security needs. As long as students of procurement continue to rely upon

17

the bureaucratic politics approach to guide their research, we contend their analyses may be incomplete, both in descriptions of the processes and in recommendations for improved efficacy. We base our assertions on descriptive and analytical accounts of the decision-making process preceding ABM, the refinement of U.S. counterforce capabilities during the 1970s, and Sanguine and MX. Determining whether the bureaucratic politics approach is flawed or whether MX is an aberration, is the central concern of this study.

If the bureaucratic politics approach is inadequate or incorrect in its explanation, then analysts who shape their studies with the assumptions of that approach will likely look for data in the wrong places and develop misleading conclusions about the effectiveness of the decision-making process. We suggest that critical changes in congressional and public attitudes about major national security decisions such as procurement programs, advances in nuclear weapon technology, and the democratization of the decision-making process have fundamentally altered the character of procurement decision making at least for certain types of weapon programs. This in turn has produced a decision-making process and policy results, from the perspective of the bureaucratic politics approach, that are neither predictable nor effective in achieving an efficient meld of weapon procurement and national security objectives. At the very least, national security analysts should recognize that the procurement process is different for weapons requiring large financial resources and threatening significant socioeconomic and environmental side effects. But it is also possible that these differences, while conceivably made in response to aberrant issues or forces, have permanently modified the decision-making process for procurement. This too needs to be demonstrated. Before turning to a discussion of recent developments in the procurement process, it is important to understand the critical propositions that the bureaucratic politics approach provides to explain procurement decisions.

The Assumption of the Two-Layered Decision-Making Process

Implicit in the almost endless number of case studies and analyses of procurement utilizing the bureaucratic politics perspective is the concept of two layers of decision-making activity. These two layers reflect the ambiguity in the amalgam of Allison's two conceptual models inherent in the bureaucratic politics literature. The first or inner layer of the procurement process encases those activities concerned with the origins of the idea, the design, and the research, development, and testing of a weapon system. The second or outer layer of procurement activities focuses on the decisions preceding the actual purchase (acquisition) and construction (deployment) of the system.

18

Although the outer layer of procurement activities is more visible and accessible to those concerned with weapon procurement policy, according to the bureaucratic politics perspective it is the activities in the inner layer that are important. However, this layer is barely visible and, in most cases, inaccessible to actors outside the inner sanctum of executive branch control. For these reasons procurement policymaking, like national security politics in general, is dominated by the executive and is hierarchical in nature. Although several additional arenas are given formal authority, and have acquired informal, access to the procurement process, they are only marginally important according to the bureaucratic politics approach. The states, nondefense interest groups, and the public are viewed as ancillary to the weapon process.

To bureaucratic politics analysts, executive branch preeminence over procurement activities in both layers derives primarily from institutional factors rather than constitutional ones. The executive branch is structured in ways that better insure secrecy and promote pragmatism and technical expertise. The hierarchical structure of the executive branch promotes dispatch, something not frequently found elsewhere in the government.

Within the constraints imposed by institutional factors, constitutional and statutory limits or guidelines shape the roles of other arenas in procurement. For example, the role of Congress in influencing activities in both layers derives from its constitutional powers: appropriations, lawmaking, oversight, and general Section VIII defense powers. Federal courts exercise general powers of constitutional interpretation and judicial review in determining the validity of executive branch and congressional activities, even for defense issues.[10] The nature of the U.S. political system creates a public role in defense policy as well. The press acts an an informational vehicle, the states exercise reserved powers, and the people "decide" elections.

These conventional notions of power in the public policymaking process suggest that the outer, more visible, layer of procurement decision making will be where participation is greater. This visibility is likely to create more interest in the direction of a weapon decision. It is also at this stage that the strategic implications, financial costs, and socioeconomic and environmental impacts of the system become publicly known. Too, the costs of acquisition and deployment of a weapon system are greater than that of research and development. All of these factors are likely to stimulate public and congressional interests and will activate people in both arenas to become involved in outer layer politics. The courts may even become a tool by which these actors can challenge a decision initiated by the executive branch.

However, it is *the key assumption of the bureaucratic politics approach that arenas beside the executive branch are rarely used and relatively unimportant, especially in the inner layer, but also in the outer layer of activities*. One need only examine decision-making activities within the executive branch arena to understand the design, research, development, testing, acquisition, and deployment decisions for new weapons.

The First Layer of the Procurement Decision Approach

What explanatory propositions are implicit in the bureaucratic politics analysis of procurement decision making? What propositions do these analysts use to explain the factors that determine which of the literally thousands of ideas about new weapons will enter the research, design, development, and testing phase of procurement and eventually emerge as one of the hundred or so weapons acquired and deployed by the Pentagon? According to bureaucratic politics scholars, the intra-governmental competition that characterizes procurement decision making calls into question the singular validity of either strategic [11] or technocratic[12] theory as the explanatory models for military policymaking. Because there is rarely an alternative that maximizes the technological or strategic benefits and minimizes the costs, the sphere of conflict is widened and intensified as organizations and individuals compete to secure the research, design, development, testing, acquisition, and deployment of their pet ideas for a weapon. Although the absence of a strategic or technological imperative will intensify competition over a weapon decision, the competition is by necessity still limited, falling short of the expectations raised by democratic theory.[13] Constitutional and legal assertions of power, as well as the practical considerations raised by foreign and defense issues, operate to circumscribe the nature of public debate.

The conflictual nature of the procurement process means that a weapon is deployed only after an extended process of research, design, and development. Therefore, the relationship between the appearance of a weapon in the inventory of the U. S. military and such things as "strategic doctrine, or estimates of enemy capabilities, or central governmental decisions is enormously complicated by assorted lags," which according to Graham Allison and Frederic Morris (1976:122) suggest a string of related propositions.

1. Major decisions about research are made ten to fifteen years before formulation of the strategic doctrine that will be official when the weapon enters the force posture.
2. Major decisions about research are undertaken ten to fifteen years before the actual Soviet capabilities against which the weapon will operate is known.

20

3. Major decisions about design and development are made five to ten years before formulation of the strategic doctrine that will be official when the weapon will operate is known.
4. Major decisions about design and development are undertaken five to ten years before the opponent's actual capabilities against which the weapon will operate is known.

Thus, the bureaucratic politics perspective suggests that factors other than strategic or technological imperatives, or adversary threats must be involved in the origin, design, research, development, and testing activities of weapon procurement. These factors are organizational and political in nature.

According to bureaucratic analysts (Allison and Morris, 1976:125), the genesis of most modern weapons is in the interaction of various groups within the executive arena. These include engineering groups within the Department of Defense such as the Director, Defense Research and Engineering (DDR&E), design labs of major defense industries, engineering elements of think tanks, and the subunits of the military services responsible for the development of new weapons. Each of these groups of actors is motivated by a different set of concerns. Effective bureaucrats evaluate procurement alternatives primarily as to how a particular weapon affects both their organization's essential mission and role in that organization (Halperin and Kanter, 1972:26-62). The military groups responsible for the weapon will bring into the fray their own set of goals and interests, which help shape the missions and strategic implications of the weapon (Allison and Morris, 1976:123-35). Allison and Morris conclude that

> weapon systems in the main line of a service's primary mission will be regularly improved by "follow-on," successive generations of weapons that make marginal improvements in principal performance parameters. . . .Weapon systems not in the main-line missions of a service or service subunit tend to develop slowly. . . .A mission to which a service assigns low priority (or to which it is not the primary mission of the service subunit) tends to be poorly performed. This is especially true if the performance of the mission is essential not to the service performing it but to a sister service.

Procurement decisions within the inner layer of decision-making activities are the result of the literally hundreds of separate decisions by the aforementioned groups. This causes the character of procurement decisions to be incremental rather than synoptic. Given the interrelationship of these literally hundreds of decisions, there is realistically no way that the outcomes of this set of activities would reflect any type of holistic logic except by chance (Allison and Morris, 1976:126).

21

Another key proposition of the bureaucratic politics perspective concerns the critical momentum that builds for a particular weapon in contrast to others that are unsuccessful. The small choices made at each point in the decision process have a cumulative impact. First, they continually narrow alternatives to virtually one by the time the second layer of activities begins — acquisition and deployment. Second, this narrowing of options enlarges the amount of resources, and thus the investment, devoted to this one alternative. These sunk costs in turn increase momentum toward that option in the weapon process. Consider a decision to enter into the engineering and testing stage of a weapon program. The evidence suggests that once testing has begun, and thus an investment initiated (i.e., contracts are let and jobs are committed), it is far more difficult to stop or delay such a program than another one that has not entered the engineering and testing stage. Such a commitment may permanently kill other programs that rival the favored weapon program (Greenwood, 1975:145-47).

The incremental nature of procurement decision making makes it difficult for oversight to be exercised by any one senior political official of the executive or legislative branches. Henry Kissinger (1982:266-67), former national security advisor and secretary of state for Presidents Nixon and Ford, suggests:

> It may seem strange that a decision [for procurement] of such consequence could be made by a department of the government without White House clearance. And technically they were not. But the White House faces a serious decision in determining at what point to intervene in the budgetary process. Our defense budget is larger than the entire expenditures of any European country. In early phases the Office of Management and Budget in the White House can have considerable influence — but only on the gross totals. . . .[The Department of Defense and the military services] are acutely sensitive about what they consider their prerogative in making the initial recommendation about how to divide up approved funds among the services. . . .The White House saw the outlines of the detailed defense program only during the summer before it was put into final form in October. By then the services had made their various trade-offs. Weapons considered obsolescent were the first to go, partly because as they disappeared they strengthened the case for entirely new systems. The unresolved issues were kept to a minimum and were usually highly technical, satisfying Presidential insistence on having the last word without enabling his staff to undertake a serious strategic review.

If these incremental decisions about the design, development, research, and testing of a new weapon are beyond the virtual control of the president, few outside the executive branch will be able to have an impact.

The president's inability to control procurement decisions at the inner layer stage is tied to his imperfect access to and knowledge of activities concerning weapon systems. Without information about alternative prototypes, it is most difficult to influence key decisions (Greenwood, 1975:145). This is exacerbated by the failure of the president's appointed senior national security officers to be better able to deflect the interests of career officials in bureaucratic wars. Thus, the president and his senior political officials may disturb decisions in this layer of procurement activity, but they rarely control them.

The Second Layer of the Procurement Decision Approach

The outer layer of the procurement process concerns two judgments: (1) the decision within the executive branch to acquire and to deploy a weapon system; and (2) the decision outside the executive branch to authorize the program and to appropriate funds for acquisition and deployment. The bureaucratic politics literature on procurement suggests that the number of participants in the decision-making process tends to significantly proliferate during these decisions. The arena of conflict expands from the narrow confines of the subunits of the military services and the Office of the Secretary of Defense (OSD), DDR&E, and the industry design laboratories to include bureaus and individuals outside the Pentagon. The weapon system will be thoroughly reviewed by OSD, the Joint Chiefs of Staff (JCS), and the Office of Management and Budget (OMB). Also, the White House/National Security Council (NSC) staff, the Department of State, and Arms Control and Disarmament Agency (ACDA) will consider the weapon's foreign policy and arms control implications and in some cases have an important impact on its future. However, as the bureaucratic politics literature suggests, these groups need not become *active* participants (Greenwood, 1975:145).

A weapon system facing an acquisition and deployment decision may also receive a more intensive and systematic examination in the subcommittees and committees of Congress than it received during the inner layer as lobbying activity begins in earnest. Important lobbyists may include the military services, industry contractors, labor organizations, state and local government officials interested in payrolls for their communities and larger tax bases for their budgets, senators and representatives with similar interests, and occasionally foreign governments interested in a particular weapon system. Thus, congressional engagement in acquisition and deployment decisions is usually motivated by porkbarrel (Huntington, 1961:134).

A weapon system, especially a potentially expensive one, may encounter competition at any point in the decision-making process from other weapon programs proposed as alternatives by individuals or groups outside the Pentagon. Although the alternative weapon may be designed for different tasks, it may also perform similar ones to the proposed weapon. Without adequate internal political support in the executive branch, and perhaps supportive lobbying from important members of Congress, and in the face of such competition, the previously attractive weapon system may not survive.

The more societal resources needed for the proposed weapon system, the greater the need for political allies and support. A weapon program requiring large financial expenditures threatens the resources allocated to other defense interests, and in some cases, domestic and foreign constituencies with their special interests as well as other governmental programs considered by the president. This generates intense political conflict, which in turn requires more allies and greater support if such a weapon system is to be deployed (Greenwood, 1975:144).

The "winning skill" of the bureaucratic players for promoting and protecting their interests in a particular weapon system is very significant in this competition. It is not enough to have credible justifications for a potential weapon system. Most bureaucratic politics analysts suggest that the success of a program also depends on the capability of the advocates both to promote and to protect their project. The key is garnering allies. Important friends might include prominent scientists with access to the president's advisors or to the president, media people who can give positive visibility to the weapon, and/or senators or representatives who might influence procurement decisions by influencing the president. In addition to promoting a program in Congress, advocates must protect the weapon system from other organizations within the bureaucracy. Inside the Department of Defense, there are always several other agencies that may lay claim to some form of jurisdiction over the weapon system. Thus, in both promoting or protecting the weapon system, bureaucratic skill constitutes an important factor in the success of a weapon program (Halperin, 1974:116-64).

The "rules of the game," particularly those established by the secretary of defense and the president, channel the competition in ways that shape *how* acquisition and deployment decisions are to be made concerning weapon systems in the executive branch. These rules dictate who has the "action" on a weapon procurement issue; that is, who has responsibility for raising the issue, responsibility for making the decision, and responsibility for implementing the decision. In some cases, the "rules" will prescribe the secretary of defense's involvement, OMB's, and perhaps the president's. These "rules of the game" also determine who outside the Defense Department, the White House, and OMB will be involved in acquisition decisions,[14] thus partially establishing the larger character of the decision-making process. For example, unless the rules prescribe their involvement, it is difficult for organizations, such as ACDA,[15] the CIA, and the Department of State to gain influence on a weapon project. Most administrations establish an intra-governmental committee that considers the various effects a weapon procurement decision would have for foreign policy, intelligence, arms control, budget, and taxes. However, these committees tend to be dominated by the organization with the most at stake concerning the issue at hand.

Regardless of the larger purview by others in the executive branch, the bureaucratic politics literature suggests that weapon programs in the outer layer of procurement decision making often develop an irresistible momentum once the Pentagon makes a positive decision about acquisition and deployment and if there is a conformity of support within the executive arena. There are few instances where weapon acquisition has been reversed after approval by the Defense Department.[16] In such instances, it took major action by the president to resist the considerable bureaucratic momentum behind the weapon system.[17] Again, Congress is not viewed in the bureaucratic politics literature as an important or effective arena for turning back a decision.

A weapon procurement decision undergoing scrutiny for acquisition and deployment in the executive branch, especially the Pentagon, is most likely to engender support if it has several important features. First, the mission of the organization responsible for the new weapon and the weapon's capabilities converge. Also, political support for a weapon system can be generated if technological opportunity dovetails with a perceived and widely held foreign policy dimension of national security policy. In addition, if larger strategic interests of U.S. national security policy match the capability of the weapon, the grounds for acquisition are improved. Moreover, if the costs of deploying the weapon system in domestic terms are low (i.e., money, land, and environmental impacts), then the chances for deployment approval increase. Finally, if there are significant benefits (such as patronage tools and jobs) to important interests in Congress and outside government, then support is broadened.

For the case in which a particular weapon alternative has not fared well in the outer layer of procurement decision activities, it may be resurrected by senior political decision-makers if they feel it meets a newly materialized threat. The president may force upon the Pentagon an entire design, research, development, testing, and acquisition program if a national consensus develops around a previously overlooked idea or underdeveloped research program. A corollary to this is that a particular weapon program that emerges from the first layer of decisions with considerable momentum may be overturned if a national consensus develops about a technological opportunity that converges with another alternative weapon system (Beard, 1976:153-213).

Explanatory Propositions of the Two-Layered Approach

We have gleaned from the bureaucratic politics literature two sets of propositions employed to explain the procurement decision-making process: one for the inner layer of procurement activities and the other for the outer layer. In the chapters that follow, these propositions are tested by evaluating the decision-making process for MX.

A. Propositions for the inner layer:

1. Ideas for new weapons or refinements of old weapons are seldom the result of deliberate strategic policy analysis. Rather they are the product of organizational doctrines, technological opportunities, perceptions of enemy threat, and/or incomplete and often vague strategic attitudes. More accurately, these ideas involve the interaction of engineering groups of the Director, Defense Research and Engineering (DDR&E), design labs in industry, engineering elements in think tanks, and the subunit of the military service with ultimate responsibility for the use of the new or refined weapon.

2. During the design, research, development, and testing stage, procurement decisions about weapon ideas continue to be determined by the interaction of engineering groups of the DDR&E, design labs in industry, engineering elements in think tanks, and the subunit of the military service with ultimate responsibility for the use of the new or refined weapon being the most significant actor.

3. The mission of the subunit of the military service with the ultimate responsibility in the military for the use of the new weapon along with the power of that subunit are more important factors in the success of a weapon system (i.e., the attractiveness of the weapon to draw support within the Pentagon as compared to other alternatives) than the larger strategic and force posture considerations of U.S. national security policy.

4. Senior political officials outside the Pentagon may disturb decisions at this layer of action on procurement but rarely control it.

5. Political officials outside the executive branch as well as extra-governmental individuals will seldom seek to influence the inner layer procurement decisions, let alone disturb or even control them.

6. The hundreds of interrelated yet individual decisions during design, research, development, and testing cause the character of

26

procurement decisions in this layer of activities to be incremental rather than synoptic.

7. The likelihood that a weapon idea will reach design, research, development, and testing depends on the effectiveness of its advocates to continually promote the economic and political well-being of their project, for the longer a new weapon system survives during this inner layer of procurement activities the greater the momentum that builds for the weapon. The repeated individual choices begin to establish an irresistible bureaucratic inertia.

B. Propositions for the outer layer:

8. When the decision for a weapon program reaches the point of acquisition and deployment, the number of participants with interests in a particular weapon system tends to increase significantly, especially inside the executive branch.

9. During the acquisition and deployment stage, more actors from the congressional and public arena are activated. However, the congressional and public arenas remain indirect and peripheral to the decision process for weapon procurement.

10. The principal factor for producing what congressional involvement there is in procurement is porkbarrel.

11. The acquisition and deployment of a weapon program continues to depend on the capability of its advocates to promote the economic, strategic, and political well-being of their project.

12. Those weapon systems being considered for acquisition and deployment most likely to engender significant support (i.e., that will be least controversial) are those where
   a) the missions of the organization responsible for the new weapon converges with the capability of the weapon;
   b) technological opportunity converges with a consensus on national policy;
   c) the strategic requirements or foreign policy needs converge with the weapon system's capabilities;
   d) the cost of deploying the weapon system in domestic terms (i.e., money, land, environmental impacts, and jobs) are likely to be relatively less than other alternatives; and
   e) the advantages of deploying the weapon system in domestic terms (i.e., contracts and jobs) are likely to be relatively greater than other alternatives.

13. Weapon programs are seldom slowed or overturned once initial approval of acquisition is achieved in the executive branch, and only a presidential directive is likely to slow or overturn that decision. However, the decision to modify, while executive based, may be made in anticipation of public or congressional resistance deemed threatening enough to warrant change.

14. The "rules of the game" introduced by the secretary of defense and the president shape how and by whom acquisition and deployment decisions will be made within the executive branch.

Criticism of the Bureaucratic Politics Approach

The bureaucratic perspective approach was a perceptive analytical device for explaining procurement decisions in the 1950s and 1960s as the plethora of case studies illustrates. In an era of broad national security consensus, fostered by a widely perceived Soviet threat, in an era where the environmental and social dimensions of weapon decision making were not major political issues, in an era where Congress was not an active arena for procurement decisions, the bureaucratic politics perspective offered the best explanation of why and how the United States chooses weapons. However, the characteristics of that era of procurement decision making are no longer representative of the present period, nor are they likely to be so in the near future. Times have changed. Unfortunately, no new consensus about how procurement policy is or should be handled has emerged to replace the bureaucratic politics perspective. For this reason, analyses of procurement politics continue to be characterized by critical attacks on the bureaucratic politics approach.[18]

Of the many concerns that students of weapon decision making have about the paradigm, three seem especially cogent to us when attempting to understand decisions such as MX. For one, issues such as strategic and foreign policy considerations associated with the procurement of a weapon, and the environmental and social impacts of that weapon, are understated as factors in procurement decision making. Second, the paradigm misconstrues the power of the president in foreign policymaking. Finally, it undervalues or ignores the role of the Congress, the public, interest groups, and the States. Consequently, the bureaucratic politics approach provides an inappropriate understanding for procurement programs that require relatively large amounts of resources (material and financial), have major environmental and social costs, have a nuclear dimension, and/or raise crucial strategic questions. These omissions are the heart of our critical appraisal of the empirical utility of the bureaucratic politics approach for explaining procurement decision making.

Changing Character of Procurement Decisions

The general pattern of executive branch dominance in matters of weapon procurement was changed by several developments in the late 1960s and the early 1970s. The Vietnam War ruptured the consensus for the need to contain the Soviet threat and the extensive military commitment to support containment. Watergate undermined the authority and credibility of the presidency. The rather stagnant economic conditions and the slow growth of the U.S. economy in real terms produced significant pressures on the U.S. government to reallocate financial resources from the military budget to social programs piquing the concerns of extra-defense and extra-executive individuals and groups. Finally, the enormity of several proposed new weapons, their vast resource needs, began mobilizing constituents to actively lobby their representatives and senators against the deployment of these systems.

The decline in executive branch power, the emergence of new groups interested in procurement, and the ascendance of Congress have combined to create a political process characterized by coalition building that transcends the traditional boundaries between the executive and legislative branches. These coalitions include senators, representatives, their staffs, journalists, and other lobbyists, as well as bureaucratic actors. Their initial targets were the president and important political advisors. However, these coalitions soon learned to exploit other spheres of decision-making activity such as Congress and the newly activated public arena.

Strategic, Foreign Policy, and Domestic Issues

Burcaucratic politics analysts maintain that strategic values are of secondary significance to bureaucratic participants in procurement decision making. Strategic issues operate only as a mechanism that reinforces the interest in a particular weapon system and supports the missions orientation of a military service subunit. In contrast, we believe that organizational disputes over weapon procurement are partially explained by *real* differences over strategic matters. This is especially true of weapon decisions in the outer layer of procurement activities, but may also be a factor during the design, research, development, and testing period as well. The foreign policy and/or arms control effects of alternative weapon decisions have become increasingly important factors in procurement. These are types of questions that are often inseparable from organizational motivations to protect one's turf, nevertheless, strategic and foreign policy differences over weapon procurement should not be discounted. Of significance in the strategic debate over MX both within the executive branch and also in the congressional arena was the uncertainty that evolved about the invulnera-

29

bility of various basing modes as well as the strategic utility of the entire system. Moreover, this uncertainty surrounding MX became linked to the growing public fears about nuclear war. The nuclear freeze movement and the uncertainty concerning the utility and purpose of MX produced the most extensive weapon debate in U.S. history. Finally, during the 1970s, questions concerning the financial costs and the socioeconomic/ environmental side effects of weapon programs were instrumental factors in many weapon decisions. These concerns will continue to be important.

The President

Despite being executive centered, the bureaucratic paradigm understates the power of the president, particularly his political authority. Although later bureaucratic analysts do attribute an ascendant role to the Chief Executive, Neustadt's "power of persuasion" theory (i.e., the image of the president in sneakers) prevails. The president is still viewed as only one among many players, albeit an important one. The framework needs to incorporate the reality that the president chooses most of the influential players and also determines how the policy game will be played. The president may of course choose not to take a predominant role, in which case power devolves to bureaucratic actors, and the approach is quite explanatory (Krasner, 1972:166). But, major defense and foreign policy decisions in the past twenty years have been presidential ones. It was Kennedy who killed the Skybolt missile program, Nixon and Ford who accelerated the cruise missile project, and Carter who cancelled the B-1 bomber. Dan Caldwell (1977:96-97) suggests that during the Cuban Missile Crisis

> the President's will prevailed and it was his preferences that influenced some of the players' positions; or to rephrase the Model III dictum: Where you stand depends upon whether the President allowed you to continue serving him. Cabinet members and presidential advisors serve at the pleasure of the President. Furthermore, the President is the only American official with a national constituency; as such, he stands above the members of the Cabinet and governmental bureaucracy all of whom are his *de jure* and *de facto* subordinates.

The bureaucratic politics perspective does anticipate preeminent presidential power, for the strengths of the presidency are the reverse of the handicaps of extra-executive actors: lack of formal authority, access, and information. In contrast, the president can act with unity of direction, has a superior informational base from which to work, and constitutes the central base to which access is sought.

In the end, the bureaucratic politics framework's oversights regarding presidential power are not serious since the understatement is merely a

30

matter of degree: The president is more powerful, but how much more? How dependent is he on those who advise him? To what extent do these people, when they disagree, as the paradigm suggests, circumscribe and, thus, predetermine what the president will decide?

Congress

A more serious shortcoming of the bureaucratic politics paradigm lies in its conceptualization of the role of Congress in defense politics. "One might search the entire body of the bureaucratic politics literature," note critics Nathan and Oliver (1978:88), "and find no analysis of Congress." On the one hand, the oversight is inherent in the approach's analytical focus on organizational behavior. However, Congress, during much of the post-World War II period, was seldom active in defense politics, particularly in weapon system research procurement decisions (Russett, 1970; Dexter, 1963). One analyst suggests that in the majority of cases "defense decisions functionally bypass[ed] the legislative segment of the process" (Laurence, 1976:217) except in cases where Congress was to decide structural issues: the management and operation of the armed forces, overall budgets, installations projects, and the like. Congress, guided by constituency interests, which were said to prevail, has always used its substantive legislative powers in defense, but generally in ways incidental to basic defense strategy. It has rarely decided defense policy, weapon system priorities, deployments, or strategic questions (Raymond and Dawson, 1962:42-50). In these latter areas, Congress has operated to "reinforce the prevailing inclinations of the executive branch rather than to temper them by exploring alternative policies" (Frye, 1975:2). In light of the rather different role Congress played in the MX decision, the bureaucratic politics paradigm is time-bound.

One can explain congressional inaction during this period in two ways. Some argue that Congress chose to be supportive of and deferential to executive prerogative in defense matters. Others contend that Congress, while always interested in strategic questions, has been limited by certain institutional-structural factors endemic to the federal legislature, most notably the extensive decentralization of power. In both cases, the need for dispatch, secrecy, and unity of direction, and the technological complexity of weapon systems, enhanced executive power. Whether one explains congressional inactivity during this period as voluntary or institutional, the fact that the last fifteen years has seen a resurgence of congressional interest and activity is enough to force a reevaluation of the bureaucratic politics perspective. And, as the case of MX illustrates, Congress can and is now willing to influence the content and direction of national security policy in ways not anticipated nor accounted for by the bureaucratic paradigm. What

31

the framework needs to incorporate, then, are the institutional-structural and behavioral changes that have been occurring in Congress since the Vietnam debacle.

Congress's national security powers derive from its control over appropriations, from its general legislative capabilities, from its authority to veto presidential appointees, from its oversight powers, and from its mandate to "provide for the common defense." The U.S. Constitution, then, assigns to Congress an integral role in the defense policymaking process. What has changed is the willingness of Congress to utilize the congressional arena in ways that challenge the executive branch on both structural and strategic grounds. Finally, Congress's "legal, structural and political capacity" to effect meaningful change has also increased (Haas, 1982:546).

At one time, the Defense Appropriations Subcommittees and Armed Services Committees in both houses provided cozy receptions to representatives of the military testifying about procurement. During the 1970s that changed. The promilitary, conservative monopoly on the leadership of these key committees and subcommittees was broken by a string of non-conservative replacements, thus introducing heterogeneity and conflict into a traditionally consensual environment.

This pattern of internal conflict has exacerbated the breakdown of the deference earlier paid to members of the Armed Services Committees by their colleagues. Debates, hearings, floor discussions, and amendments on defense bills are now more common. In addition, more committees outside the defense area have become interested and involved in defense issues and are holding hearings on the domestic aspects of weapon policies. The democratization of Congress during the 1970s, the increased stakes in nuclear arms development, the domestic consequences of the deployment of weapon systems, and the turnover in congressional membership have caused changes in the national legislature in the direction of heightened concern with procurement questions.

This heterogeneity was accompanied by an increase in the number and technical expertise of congressional staff than was the case in the 1950s and 1960s. There was a fivefold increase in congressional staff between the early 1960s and the late 1970s (Hamilton and Van Dusen, 1978:170-79). Although this growth of legislative assistants was not as spectacular in the Senate and House committees reviewing Pentagon requests, it was still significant. In the Senate, the legislative assistants attached to the Armed Services Committee remained rather constant for several decades prior to 1968. However, in the late 1960s and early 1970s, the number of legislative assistants on that committee expanded from twenty-seven to thirty-eight — a 25 percent expansion (authors' interviews with the Senate Armed Services staff). The legislative assistants in the House Armed Services

Committee expanded from about a "dozen" in the late 1960s to thirty-eight by the late 1970s — a 300 percent increase (interviews with House Armed Services staff). The pattern seems to be the same for the defense subcommittee of the Appropriations Committees for both Houses as well, although the records for those subcommittees are not as well maintained as those for the Armed Services Committees (authors' interviews with the Appropriations Committee staffs of both houses). It was not uncommon by the mid-1970s for legislative assistants on the committees and subcommittees to be just as experienced and in some cases more knowledgeable about defense policy issues than the governmental representatives testifying before Congress. As a result these committees and subcommittees have become forums where the government's national security positions are critically evaluated and alternatives frequently offered in contrast to the rubber stamp approach of the 1950s and early 1960s.

Congress is also better equipped to legislate in this issue area. For example, the Congressional Budget and Impoundment Control Act of 1974, which introduced coordination and direction into the authorization-appropriations process, has improved Congress's ability to use its money power to direct and affect procurement decisions. "The flow of information from the executive branch to Congress on defense policy" has increased significantly with "more testimony at hearings, more briefings of individual Congressmen and their staffs, and the like" (Laurence, 1976:23). Congress during the post-Watergate decade created two new organizations (Congressional Budget Office, 1974 and Office of Technology Assessment, 1972) and strengthened two others (General Accounting Office and the Congressional Research Service) to further its access to information and make it more competitive with the presidency.[19]

Congress, with its increased interest and participation in defense matters in new and more fundamental ways, has also made itself more receptive to lobbying by a broader range of public interests. Whether it is fears of productive farmland being used for missile deployment, the desecration of sacred Indian burial sites by a government project, the inflation of local prices from federal intrusion, or the annihilation of the state, the country, or the world, domestic politics are intimately intertwined with national security questions.

Thus, the traditional role of Congress as a medium for popular representation is affirmed in an area considered relatively immune from pressure group and electoral politics, except to prodefense and certain economic interests (Krasner, 1972:160-61). Too, the period since Vietnam has seen the emergence and refinement of antimilitary, and antidefense pressure groups. As these groups have become better organized, more sophisticated, better financed, and more pragmatic, they have achieved a legiti-

33

macy in Congress traditionally extended exclusively to prodefense groups. In fact, one analyst argues that interest groups have acquired so much power in defense politics that "when [they] succeed in mobilizing the interests and support of nonexecutive, governmental allies, they can effectively override the professionals in the national security bureaucracies" (Trice, 1982:506). A new defense policy system has emerged in Congress, and members are scrutinizing and modifying executive initiated weapons policies in unprecedented ways (Laurence, 1978: see also, Korb, 1979; Platt and Weiler, 1978).

Public Arena

The bureaucratic paradigm fails to take into account the changes that have occurred in the public arena. Most importantly has been the increased power and authority of the public, the states, and various interest groups in influencing the nature and direction of weapon policy.

As with Congress, the attitude of the mass public toward national security policy following World War II was diffuse at best and generally deferential to and supportive of the direction set by the executive branch (Mueller, 1971). The Vietnam experience shattered the national consensus that had existed on defense policy, and public opinion began to mobilize in different directions, rather than in a consensual one. Concomitant with the attitudinal changes, there have been institutional and structural changes in the direction of increased public involvement. The domestic consequences of defense decisions became more visible just at the time when the federal administrative process was undergoing democratization at the behest of Congress. The Freedom of Information Act (FOIA), the National Environmental Protection Act (NEPA), and most recently, the Federal Land Policy and Management Act (FLPMA), for example, were passed by Congress to broaden public participation in the federal policymaking process. By doing so, Congress, perhaps inadvertently, guaranteed a public role in defense decisions like MX that pose domestic consequences and, thus, activate these domestic laws. Laws such as these provide the public with the tools, formal authority, and direct access to the decision process heretofore unavailable. With such advantages, the public has begun to rip away the veil over national security policy, which the executive branch has previously kept hidden. With the FOIA, people can begin to tap into the superior and often secret information base relied upon by inner layer actors. As a result of NEPA and FLPMA, the public has a legitimate right to participate in all phases of policymaking on defense issues that will have significant impacts on the human environment.

The bureaucratic politics analysts have also overlooked the changing role of the states in defense policy. Most scholars subscribe to a traditional notion of limited state power in defense politics. The U.S. Constitution suggests such a peripheral role, reserving to the states some powers in military affairs and defense, but establishing the federal government's authority as clearly preeminent. The Supremacy Clause also extends to the national government preeminent status on matters within its delegated powers, both domestic and foreign. For the most part, the delineation of state powers is in the direction of restraint. The federal courts have also operated to curtail state attempts to become involved in foreign and national defense affairs.

However, the actual impact of the states and their localities in influencing defense policy has been greater than the Constitution suggests. This has been particularly true of defense issues with domestic implications such as installation projects that impinge upon state interests and activate state powers. Traditionally, the states have operated through their federal congressional delegations in the defense area. For the most part, the states were precluded from intervening directly in the defense process. But, as with the public in general, the "defensification" of Congress and democratization of the federal policymaking process, have opened up the system to state influence as well. Congress's recent interest and acquired experiences in defense coupled with its traditional representational role, suggest that a state's concerns will be aired during the consideration of a weapon system. Moreover, domestic acts such as NEPA and FLPMA, particularly the later, legislate a state role in the decision process on defense projects such as MX which will consume large amounts of public and natural resources.

Finally, the post-Vietnam/Watergate period has seen the emergence of several new groups. The first of these groups were the arms control specialists from think tanks, universities, and foundations, who had important impact on weapon decisions like the ABM and the improvement of warhead accuracy (Platt, 1978). The antimilitary-prosocial programs groups stimulated by the events of the Vietnam War formed the second segment (Korb, 1979). Both became significant lobby groups and argued against certain new weapon systems and supported arms control initiatives with the Soviet Union in the 1970s. The third group was made up of regionally based groups that developed in opposition to the deployment of a particular weapon system in their communities and states.

As indicated previously, regional or local groups such as defense industries and labor unions interested in procurement contracts and jobs were virtually the only constituent pressures on Congress and the executive branch in the 1950s and 1960s. The defense industries, labor unions, and regional chambers of commerce interests lobbied primarily at the committee level in Congress. Regional groups opposed to the deployment of specific weapons in their communities became effective adversaries of

35

supportive local interests in the late 1960s and the 1970s. Hence, these regional groups emerged as important factors in procurement decisions in the late 1960s and early 1970s for weapon programs such as Sanguine.

The regional opposition initially concentrated on influencing policy by protestations to the executive branch about the adverse effects of pending weapon deployment decisions (Klessing and Strite, 1980:17). This approach was diffuse and ineffective. These regional groups soon turned their actions to the congressional arena and to influencing local and regional officials through lobbying and elections.

Examples of Changing of Procurement Behavior

Three examples of weapon system decisions in the late 1960s and 1970s illustrate the changing character of procurement decisions: the case of the anti-ballistic missile (ABM); the issue of the refinement of U.S. counterforce capability in the first part of the 1970s through improved warhead design and guidance improvement; and the issue of Sanguine.

The ABM decision brought together several new groups of participants in procurement decisions virtually for the first time. As Congressman Les Aspin (1975:323) suggests:

> The arms control community claimed the ABM would not work and was ready to come to Washington to explain to congressmen why it would not; the peace groups said it was destabilizing, and they were frightened enough to lobby intensely; constituent pressure against the ABM (almost unheard of on a weapons system issue) was provided by people living near the proposed ABM sites. And, finally, stopping the ABM involved eliminating very few jobs. Up to that point, no part of the weapon was in production, and most of the research and development was in "software."

The debate on the ABM issue produced several coalitions that transcended traditional boundaries between the executive branch, the national legislature, and the visual and printed media profession. The proponents were composed of the military, defense analysts, scientists, industries specializing in military weapons, and some legislators and journalists. The opponents consisted of arms control and defense specialists, interests in ACDA, regional groups opposed to having an ABM system in their neighborhoods, antimilitary interests seeking reallocations of money from military programs to social ones, and other journalists and legislators. These two coalitions lobbied the executive branch when the Nixon administration was considering whether to revalidate the Lyndon Johnson decision to construct the ABM, alter the character of the ABM system to be deployed, or forego the decision for deployment. These groups then switched their attention to Congress, which had become actively involved

36

in the decision on whether to authorize the construction of the ABM system chosen by the Nixon administration. Although the system was approved, the narrow margin of victory in Congress strongly influenced the Nixon administration to negotiate away ABM during the Strategic Arms Limitation Talks (SALT I) with the Soviet Union (Newhouse, 1973:151-52).

In the modification of U.S. counterforce, the opposition of Senators Edward Brooke (R-Mass.), Clifford Case (R-N.J.), Hubert Humphrey (D-Minn.), Edward Kennedy (D-Mass.), Charles Mathias (R-Md.), John McIntyre (D-N.H.), Walter Mondale (D-Minn.), and Edmund Muskie (D-Maine) along with allies both in the executive branch, the arms control community, and the Washington media slowed the pace of improved accuracy for U.S. missiles in the early and mid-1970s. The arena was once again Congress. Through influence on authorizations and appropriations measures, this coalition was able to slow the development of an improved hard-target warhead and guidance system for a counterforce strategy advocated by Secretary of Defense James Schlesinger during the Nixon and Ford administrations. Although the decision was eventually implemented, it was done at a slower pace than that desired by Schlesinger and his successors, thus significantly affecting the strategic value of that decision (Platt, 1978:71-96).

The third example is the decision-making process for the navy's extremely low-frequency radio wave communication system (ELF), called Sanguine. The communication system was to provide command and control capability that would link U.S. decision-makers to the SLBM force. The system was to consist of transmitters and a vast antenna grid installed beneath the surface of the earth, the installation of power networks, and the construction of a military base for each site (Klessing and Strite, 1980:13-14). The antenna system became a thorn in the side of the navy.

The environmental and social effects of ELF created a storm of controversy in Michigan and Wisconsin. It was to be initially installed in northern Wisconsin. "The Navy proposed a 150 mile grid that would cover 26 counties and 20,000 square miles. It would contain 240 transmitter sites and 6000 miles of antenna cable" (Klessing and Strite, 1980:17). Political opposition at the local level and in the congressional arena from residents of Michigan, Wisconsin, and later Texas, led to the abandonment of the larger goals of the project by the late 1970s. The navy has tried to continue research about and development of ELF in hopes of deploying a smaller version in the future. The opposition, however, remains formidable.

Two unconventional types of groups were instrumental in defeating the decision to deploy the extensive ELF system in those states. First, residents of Wisconsin and Michigan organized against deployment on the grounds of the extensive environmental and social effects the expansive ELF system would create invoking the threat of lawsuits filed under NEPA (Klessing and Strite, 1980:17). Second, state officials such as governors and legislators, as well as local officials such as mayors and town councilmen, fearful of the political consequences of supporting ELF, lobbied the navy, the Department of Defense, and their delegates in Congress to oppose the deployment of ELF in their communities (Klessing and Strite, 1980:17). Although state and local officials have often been supportive of defense decisions that provide payrolls and jobs for their states and local communities, they have rarely responded to problems such as the secondary environmental and societal effects of defense decisions. The active and effective lobbying by groups concerned with these issues influenced local and state officials to see ELF in a very different light. The ELF experience of the 1970s was virtually unprecedented in the post-World War II period.

Additional Propositions For Testing

On the basis of the discussion of the criticism of the bureaucratic politics paradigm, we have generated several additional propositions for consideration.

15. Strategic policy considerations will be significant factors in procurement decisions in cases where the weapon system's strategic advantages are uncertain.
16. Foreign policy considerations will be significant factors in procurement decisions in cases where the weapon system's foreign policy advantages are uncertain.
17. Environmental considerations will be significant factors in procurement decisions in cases where the weapon system will be environmentally costly.
18. Socioeconomic considerations will be significant factors in procurement decisions in cases where the weapon system will consume large amounts of resources (material and financial) and be socially costly.
19. The president will be a decisive participant in cases where the strategic, foreign policy, and/or domestic considerations of the weapon system are in conflict with administrative policies.
20. Congress will be an important arena in cases where the strategic, foreign policy, and/or domestic considerations of the weapon system are in conflict with constituent and/or personal policy preferences.
21. The public arena will be an important one in cases where the costs and/or benefits of deploying the weapon system pose a clear and present threat to the interests of individuals.

Observations

The character of procurement activities has changed. Yet many analysts of procurement politics still view the process as readily understood by the assumptions and propositions of the bureaucratic politics approach. The ABM, missile accuracy, and ELF issues are viewed as aberrations; unusual events that are unlikely to be repeated. The MX system conforms to the new pattern of decision making. Is the MX project also an aberration? Or is it the quintessential example of the changes in the decision process for large weapon systems affected in the 1970s? These questions frame the study that follows.

Endnotes

[1] The more important contributions to the general bureaucratic perspective literature are Huntington (1961), Allison (1970), Allison (1971), Allison and Halperin (1972), Halperin and Kanter (1973), and Halperin (1974). For a review of this literature as well as a criticism of the bureaucratic perspective literature, see Caldwell (1977).

[2] The exceptions to this generalization would be Kurth (1971) and the conclusions of Greenwood (1975).

[3] Allison (1971) elaborated on his essay in the *American Political Science Review* (1970) with his book on the Cuban Missile Crisis which appeared a year later.

[4] This type of analysis is what Allison labels the rational actor model. He suggests that "this approach depends primarily on the assumption that events in international politics consist of the more or less purposive acts of unified national governments and that governmental behavior can be understood by analogy with the intelligent, coordinated acts of individual human beings. Following this approach, analysts focus on the interests and goals of a nation, the alternative courses of actions available, and the costs and benefits of each alternative.'' Allison and Halperin (1972:41).

[5] Allison in his essay with Halperin (1972) implicitly combines the two models in the articulation of the bureaucratic politics model. In that essay, they suggest that they "focus on the further development of 'Model III,' [the governmental politics framework] recognizing that organizations can be included as players in the game of bureaucratic politics, treating the factors emphasized by an organizational process approach as constraints. . .'' (p. 40).

[6] "The Bureaucratic Politics Model sees no unitary actor but rather many actors as players — players who focus not on a single strategic issue but on many diverse intra-national problems as well. Players choose in terms of no consistent set of strategic objectives, but rather according to various conceptions of national security, organizational, domestic, and personal interests. Players make governmental decisions not by a single rational choice, but by pulling and hauling. (This by no

means implies that individual players are not acting rationally, given their interests)" (Allison and Halperin, 1972:43).

[7]For a discussion of the concentric circle concept, see Hilsman (1967:541-43). See also, Spanier and Uslaner (1978:49-103).

[8]One critic of the bureaucratic perspective approach, Robert Art (1973) suggests that the "first generation" of bureaucratic perspective analysts' appreciation for the significance of public opinion, pressure groups and Congress in national security affairs was lost by the "second generation" of analysts such as Halperin and Allison.

[9]The bureaucratic perspective analysts differ on this point. Allison and Halperin tend to view the influence on procurement by members of Congress, or others outside the executive branch, as rather limited even in the case of lobbying. However, Huntington and the majority of earlier case studies on procurement and military affairs see the role of senators and representatives as potentially influential lobbyists. This point will be discussed further below.

[10]For a discussion of how the character of the U.S. Constitution affects U.S. foreign affairs and military policy, see Henkin (1972).

[11]Strategic theory concerning weapon procurement would imply that weapons were chosen by the U.S. government in light of strategic objectives and rational analysis of how best to support those objectives. This would be quite similar to what Allison labels the rational actor model. See Note 4 above.

[12]Technocratic theory assumes that policy outcome is the result of a technological imperative, i.e., the implications of the technology are so overwhelming that no alternative is possible beside that to which the technology points. For examples of such studies, see York (1973) and Lapp (1970). These studies argue that once the implications of a weapon's technology become evident, the bureaucratic momentum becomes irresistible.

[13]Democratic theory sees government responding in a direct or indirect way to public pressure. Barry Hughes (1978:4-5) suggests that democratic theory assumes, "The public elects officials with the assistance of public-based interest groups and parties; through the mechanism of election and, as importantly, of postelection influence with elected officials through groups and parties, the public controls the making of foreign policy." However, the model does not describe accurately how procurement decisions are made, at least according to the literature of the bureaucratic perspective, nor does the pluralist model associated with democratic theory in the twentieth century or with analysts such as Robert Dahl (1956). Hughes (1978:14) suggests: "The proponents of the pluralist model argue that in every issue area there are specialists and to that extent elites but that in the policymaking process there are many different sets of such elites and the elites are in nearly constant conflict. While there may be a military elite with allies in the corporate world and civilian government and while that elite may push for higher defense expenditures, there also are, say the pluralists, other elites who oppose higher defense budgets, if only because they realize that there is a budget pie to be split and that increased military expenditures may decrease their own share or force

40

an unwanted increase in the pie. . . .The pluralists do not assume that the military will win every battle.'' Bureaucratic perspective analysts reject the pluralist model as being too broad a view of the participants. Rather the participants are limited primarily to the executive branch.

[14]For a discussion of the presidential "rules of the game" during the Nixon administration and their effect on the decision-making process for national security policy, see Morris (1976) and Leacacos (1971-72). For a discussion of how the secretary of defense's "rules of the game" affect the decision process of the Department of Defense, see Roherty (1974).

[15]ACDA was ineffectual in influencing the procurement process even though an arms control impact statement was required for each proposed weapon system. For a discussion of the arms control impact statement, see Goetz Lall (1976).

[16]This is an important theme in Beard's (1976) essay on the air force and the ICBM. The air force continued to emphasize the bomber during the early 1950s as opposed to the development of the ICBM not because of general opposition to the missile but rather because of the inertia of positive decisions for the bomber.

[17]An example of a weapon far along in the process of consideration for acquisition and then rejected by presidential decision was the Skybolt. See Brandon (1963) and Neustadt (1970).

[18]See note 15 above.

[19]Another type of institutional change created by Congress was the arms control impact statement. In the fall of 1975, Congress passed legislation that required the Department of Defense along with other governmental agencies to assess the impact of weapon procurement on the Soviet-American arms race and possible U.S. arms control initiatives. The compliance never reached the level sought by Congress and has not been a factor in procurement decision making.

PART 2
ISSUES AND ACTORS

Although the bureaucratic politics perspective literature maintains that the strategic, foreign, and domestic policy implications of weapon systems are not primary considerations in procurement decisions, it is our contention that these factors were significant in influencing the decision making for MX virtually from its inception. In fact, these issues were so significant that they precipitated the formation of coalitions of individuals and groups that actively sought to influence procurement decisions about the new missile system. Moreover, these coalitions, some active for and some active against the weapon project, were operating in several arenas, ie., the executive branch, Congress, and the public arena, sometimes simultaneously. To appreciate how strategic, foreign, and domestic/policy issues affected decision making for MX, it is important to understand what the arguments about these issues were and who advocated what inside and outside the federal government between the late 1960s and the summer of 1983. The strategic questions, and the individuals and groups associated with those issues, will be discussed in chapters 2 and 3. The other two issue areas, foreign and domestic policy considerations, will be discussed in chapters 4 and 5.

CHAPTER 2

A PEEK THROUGH THE WINDOW OF VULNERABILITY: SHALL WE HAVE A NEW ICBM?

The strategic questions surrounding MX[1] were part of a much larger debate in the United States during the 1970s concerning the evolution of U.S. strategic policy from its formal assured destruction/operational limited war-fighting moorings in the 1960s,[2] to the formal and operational limited war-fighting capability[3] of the Nixon, Ford, and Carter administrations, to the total nuclear war-fighting objectives of the Reagan administration in the early 1980s, all in the name of deterrence. If one is to understand the inner and outer layers of decision-making activities for MX, one must understand the evolution and debate over strategic policy.

There were two dimensions of the strategic issues concerning MX. The first was the question of whether or not the new missile should have war-fighting capability, i.e., the capacity to destroy Soviet missiles in hardened silos (hard-target capability); and, if it was to have such a capability, how extensive should that force be? Three general alternatives have dominated the debate: (1) a total nuclear war-fighting capability; (2) a limited nuclear war-fighting capability; and (3) an assured destruction capability. The second dimension of the debate focused on how the missile was to be based. That question will be discussed in the next chapter.

The Three General Strategic Alternatives

Proponents of the first strategic option argue that we must have total nuclear war-fighting capability. This alternative has been traditionally promoted by the U.S. Air Force, specifically the Strategic Air Command (SAC). The goal of SAC since its formation in the late 1940s has been to deliver a massive strike capable of obliterating Soviet society. SAC doctrine anticipated war between the Soviet Union and the United States that would terminate after a few days of massive sets of nuclear strikes. SAC also assumed that the United States would strike before the Soviet Union — a preemptive use of nuclear weapons.[4] Moreover, the Pentagon's war plan was reputed to entail an attack on "all enemy targets in Russia, China, and Eastern Europe as quickly as possible, with the chances of restraining or redirecting the attack remote at best" (Kaplan, 1983: 277). This was the

45

thrust of General Curtis Le May's first targeting plans for SAC in 1948, and it remained the heart of SAC's doctrine two decades later (Ball, 1982).

During the Kennedy years, the civilian managers of the Pentagon, under the leadership of Secretary of Defense Robert McNamara, altered SAC's massive strike objective and replaced it with a plan that integrated the use of ICBMs, SLBMs, and bombers in a coordinated strike on the Soviet Union. The plan, known as the Single Integrated Operation Plan (SIOP), emphasized that the response of the United States to a Soviet military action should be controlled nuclear retaliation and negotiating pauses to coerce the Soviet Union to cease its actions and accept U.S. terms for an end to the confrontation. This was to be done by focusing nuclear strikes in limited attacks on Soviet military targets while avoiding the destruction of heavy urban populations. A significant portion of the nuclear force was to be held in reserve to threaten Soviet cities. This was the Kennedy administration's attempt to force "reason" on consideration of the potential use of nuclear weapons in the event that deterrence failed. It was a very different policy orientation from SAC's preemptive massive strike option, which had characterized U.S. strategic policy during the 1950s. The assumption was that nuclear weapons could be successfully used to accomplish political goals while limiting the damage to U.S. and Soviet society.

There were five target attack options in SIOP-63 (i.e., the SIOP for 1963), which reflected the new thinking of the Kennedy administration. Desmond Ball (1982-83:36-37) suggests that the order of priority was as follows:

1. Soviet nuclear forces
2. Conventional military forces
3. Military and political leadership
4. Economic and industrial targets
5. An all-out strike on Soviet cities

The SIOP involved slow escalation by "successively combining these categories" (Kaplan, 1983:279).

Nevertheless, within two years of taking office, McNamara backed away from formal emphasis on limited nuclear war-fighting. The damage limitation policy he had endorsed for SIOP-63 opened the doors for almost unlimited demands by the air force for strategic weapons to satisfy the almost unending requirements of damage limitation. The secretary reasoned that as the Soviet Union expanded its own strategic forces during the mid-1960s more U.S. offensive weapons were needed to threaten the expanded Soviet forces (Greenwood, 1975:57-65). In addition, as the Soviets placed increasing reliance on ICBMs, and deployed that force in hardened silos, SIOP's objective of destroying the Soviet ICBM force

46

necessitated increasing U.S. countersilo capability, something that was not available to U.S. strategic forces in the late 1960s. Also, as the Soviet Union diversified their strategic forces through the deployment of SLBMs, McNamara's doubts about the potential success of damage limitation intensified (Kaplan, 1983:313-27).

Regardless of these concerns about damage limitation as well as McNamara's formal rejection of it as U.S. strategic policy, SIOP-63 remained the essence of operational strategic policy for the remainder of the decade. This operational policy was the incentive for SAC to seek a new and more capable hard-target ICBM to offset the expanding Soviet ICBM capability by the end of the 1960s.

Moreover, the limited nuclear war-fighting strategic orientation regained formal credibility within the executive branch during the Nixon, Ford, and Carter administrations. A group of strategic analysts such as Albert Wohlstetter and his colleagues at RAND Corporation and former Defense Secretary James Schlesinger, and eventually his successor Harold Brown, argued that a wider set of strategic options than just nuclear retaliation were necessary since no country had the technological capacity to fight and win an extended nuclear war.[5] Brown described a nuclear war-fighting strategy as akin to a "cosmic roll of the dice" (Warnke, 1982:4).

A limited counterforce capability was seen as having important political and strategic advantages during a period when the Soviets were themselves improving their capacity to fight a nuclear war in the advent of a deterrence failure. Thus, the threat of a massive strike against the Soviet Union in retaliation for military action against the West lost credence as Soviet nuclear capacity grew in the 1960s. However, the ability to inflict limited nuclear strikes could be used to convince Moscow of the U.S. commitment to support its interests in the context of an escalating political crisis, while avoiding the unacceptable alternatives of either capitulation or a massive nuclear war.

During the past decade, a second group of strategic analysts and major conservative political figures have argued for the creation of a capability to fight, endure, and win a lengthy nuclear war with the Soviet Union to both reinforce deterrence and the political utility of nuclear weapons if deterrence should fail. This argument is presently being introduced as the strategic policy for the Reagan administration. Colin Gray, a major figure in this movement, appointed to the General Advisory Committee on Arms Control and Disarmament by Reagan, has argued that the United States should prepare for nuclear war just as countries have prepared to fight all wars in the past, i.e., prepare to wage war against the other side's military in such a way as to destroy its capacity for fighting war (Gray and Payne,

1980). To Gray and others of this school, the nuclear age should not influence how countries prepare for war. In effect, these analysts have extended the arguments of the limited war-fighters to their logical end — the preparation for total nuclear war-fighting.

The major difference between the limited war-fighting doctrine of the Kennedy, Nixon, Ford, and Carter administrations, and the total war-fighting doctrine of the Reagan administration concerns the scope of violence that the use of nuclear forces would entail. Since total war-fighting analysts see limited nuclear strikes lasting a much longer time than do the limited nuclear war analysts, endurance would be the key to winning such a conflict. SAC, which has come to support a total nuclear war-fighting concept, believes that this is the most likely way to deter the Soviet Union from initiating a nuclear war.

A third strategic option supported by another set of strategic analysts and political interests is that of assured destruction, i.e., the idea that the United States in order to maintain deterrence should possess a strategic capability to ride out a nuclear attack and respond by destroying the capacity of the Soviet Union to survive as a modern society. This was the formal policy of the Kennedy-Johnson administrations after McNamara moved away from the limited nuclear war-fighting doctrine in 1963. Nevertheless, if the United States had actually used its nuclear weapons during that period, SIOP-63 with its damage limitation characteristics would have shaped U.S. targeting strategy. In an operational sense, then, war-fighting remained the strategic policy throughout the 1960s.

Many strategic analysts remain leery of damage limitation strategies for the reasons that ultimately led McNamara to abandon that policy orientation. One can design weapon systems around anticipated levels of destruction necessary to deter Soviet use of nuclear weapons. However, a damage limitation policy erodes logical restraint on strategic weapon programs that might be introduced if assured destruction is the objective. But it may also be cheaper for the Soviets to expand their forces to offset our damage limitation capability than it is for the United States to expand that capability to offset new Soviet strategic deployments. Thus, such a strategy stimulates an intensification of the arms race to the economic and strategic disadvantage of the United States. In addition, analysts are concerned that a conscious effort to establish a war-fighting capability will develop significant preemptive pressures on both the Soviet Union and the United States and thus ultimately produce a much more dangerous world than one in which both sides accept a mutual nuclear weapons vulnerability.

To all three schools of strategic thought, MX was the critical weapon decision of the 1970s and, as it turned out, of the early 1980s as well. MX was the key to either the limited strategic options sought by Nixon, Ford, and Carter, to the total nuclear war-fighting capability endorsed by the Reagan administration, and to proponents of the assured destruction school. Each of the three schools of strategic thought sought to influence MX decision making. Consequently, decision making for the new ICBM was not immune from these specific issues and the activities of these groups. This interaction between MX decision making and the larger strategic debate is somewhat different than proposition 1 of the bureaucratic politics perspective would lead one to expect.

Strategic War-Fighting Interests

President Nixon, in his annual foreign policy address of 1973, initiated the formal change of emphasis in U.S. strategic policy from one with reliance on assured destruction to one characterized by limited war-fighting capability. An important element of this change was the need for greater military flexibility. As Nixon stated, "To extend deterrence over a wider spectrum of possible contingencies we should ensure that our forces are capable of executing a range of options" (Nixon, 1973:184). In an operational sense, however, little was changed by the Nixon initiatives, as damage limitation continued to influence day-to-day strategy. It was left to Defense Secretary James Schlesinger to smooth out the wrinkles.

The policy changes effected by Schlesinger became known as the Schlesinger Doctrine: a strategy to enhance deterrence and, theoretically, avoid a larger nuclear exchange. Schlesinger's successor, Donald Rumsfeld, continued to emphasize a greater strategic flexibility in doctrine and weapons as Ford's advisor (Ball, 1979).

During the Carter administration, the evolution of U.S. strategic policy from assured destruction to a war-fighting doctrine was advanced. An important component of the damage limitation war-fighting strategy was the civil defense program of both the United States and the Soviet Union (Weinstein, 1982:1-6). Early in 1977, Carter and Brown supported a major revitalization of civil defense programs, although those efforts came to naught. Carter and Brown also integrated the various standard operating rules for decision making during crises and upgraded and secured communications for command and control of strategic forces. After the Soviet renewal of antisatellite tests, the president and the secretary supported rapid development of a similar U.S. capability. In addition, weapon systems such as Trident and MX were promoted to provide the necessary improved yield and accuracy for an effective, yet limited war-fighting capability (Ball, 1980). Nevertheless, Carter's acceptance of MX was as much or more a gambit to attain conservative and moderate support for the SALT II Treaty in the Senate as a commitment to support counterforce (see chapter 4).

The evolution of these events along with the election year politics of 1980 culminated in Presidential Directive 59 concerning targeting priorities for a U.S. strategic strike. It formally emphasized Soviet military targets such as missiles, bombers, and command and control centers as opposed to the softer target selection in the McNamara era. However, this was an evolutionary development, not a "bolt from the blue" as often has been portrayed (Ball, 1981).

The strategic watchwords for the Reagan presidential campaign in 1980 and his strategic plans announced in October 1981 were "the window of vulnerability." This theme, also known in U.S. intelligence circles after 1979 as the strategic bathtub, is based on the assumption that the Soviets can deploy a sufficiently large number of warheads with their new MIRV technology to threaten our current land-based missiles. The combination of the accuracy improvement in the RVs and the vast expansion of the warheads inventory means that the Soviet missile force poses a distinct threat to the continued invulnerability of U.S. land-based ICBMs (Tamman, 1981).

The possible impact of this presumed erosion of invulnerability of U.S. ICBMs was most dramatically illustrated in a Soviet first-strike scenario, which became popular with those (the conservative critics of the assured destruction strategy — the war-fighters) interested in greater war-fighting capability for U.S. strategic forces. The major components of this scenario were the enormous expansion of Soviet warheads with high yields, increasingly accurate RVs, and the priority Moscow placed on civil defense measures to reduce physical and human damage. In their hypothetical account, the Soviets would launch a strategic strike with a portion of their SS-18 and SS-19 deployment. Even launching half of their more than five hundred SS-18 and SS-19 missiles[6] would mean targeting two RVs with warhead yields in the one-half megaton range at each U.S. ICBM (International Institute of Strategic Studies, 1982:104-105). Assuming the United States would not launch while either under attack or on warning, and given estimates of improved Soviet missile accuracy,[7] the critics argued that the United States could expect to lose its entire Minuteman force.[8]

Although the collateral damage and casualties resulting from such an attack would be considerable (estimated to be between 3.5 and 22 million people[9]), the authors of the scenario argued that the U.S. president would be forced to refrain from retaliation against Soviet targets for several reasons. First, with the destruction of U.S. ICBMs, Washington would no longer possess strategic missiles with hard-target capability. Bombers, with gravity bombs and short-range attack missiles (SRAMs), and SLBMs do not possess either the necessary time-on-target (most U.S. bombers would require over a dozen hours before they could reach targets within the

50

Soviet Union) or the requisite hard-target capability to be effective against Soviet hardened silos. Second, since a president would be unable to ask for strikes against the large remaining Soviet missile force, perhaps 800 or 900 ICBMs (some MIRVed), and the entire Soviet SLBM capability, the U.S. leader's alternative would focus on target lists emphasizing Soviet military and industrial targets that were not hardened and/or the population centers of the Soviet Union.

It was argued that the attractiveness of the latter option would be eroded if Soviet civil defense initiatives had begun and were deemed effective by U.S. leaders (Goure, 1976). It was also assumed that the Soviets would be willing to accept a loss of as much as 20 million people, comparable to their loss in World War II, to win a nuclear war with the United States. This scenario assumed a threshold of Soviet pain, which when combined with knowledge that the Soviets still possessed the bulk of their ICBMs and all of their SLBMs, would cause a U.S. president to capitulate rather than accept the annihilation of the United States (Pipes, 1977).

Although most conservative critics doubted such a scenario would ever materialize, they believed that the perception of this potential Soviet strategic advantage would lead U.S. decision-makers to bow to Soviet pressure in both crises situations as well as in everyday activities. To these critics the development of Soviet war-fighting potential by the early to mid-1980s reestablished the political utility of nuclear weapons in international affairs, something that had supposedly been relegated to deterrent functions since the expansion of Soviet strategic forces in the late 1960s and the development of parity in the Soviet-U.S. strategic relationship (Hoover, 1982).

Conservative critics suggested that the implications of the political-strategic prospect in that scenario, capitulation or suicide, could be partially averted. First, the United States required an updated war-fighting capability. MX answered this need, although it required developing a basing mode that would be invulnerable to the Soviet improvements in target coverage and missile accuracy.[10] In addition, civil defense programs were to be rejuvenated and expanded. Also, other elements of the U.S. triad, (SLBMs and bombers) required modernization. For example, the SLBM force was to receive hard-target capability. Command, control, communication, and intelligence (C^3I) needed significant upgrading if war-fighting capability was to be achieved. Modernization of the triad and C^3I were two of the major elements of President Reagan's strategic package announced in October 1981. This package symbolized the transition in U.S. strategic policy from formal assured destruction in the 1960s, to limited war-fighting emphasis in the 1970s, to nuclear war-winning interest in the early 1980s (Tamman, 1981). Again the importance of this is that the

51

strategic issue was of greater significance for MX decision making than proposition 1 of the bureaucratic politics literature suggests.

Changing Technical Character of Strategic Weapons

The United States possessed a short-term counterforce advantage over the Soviet Union in the 1960s.[11] However, as the Russians significantly expanded the number of their strategic forces, went to sea with strategic missiles, and placed their ICBMs, the major element of their strategic force, in hardened silos, in the late 1960s and early 1970s, the U.S. ability to destroy Soviet missiles was eroded (Kahan, 1975:109-17). Most importantly, U.S. ICBMs and SLBMs did not possess the requisite combination of accuracy, yield, and number of warheads on a target (the ability to target one missile silo with two warheads, which increases chances of destruction) to seriously threaten Soviet ICBMs after they were fitted into hardened silos. The Soviet SLBMs were even more invulnerable. As a result of these Soviet initiatives, our operational strategic policy embodied in the SIOPs of the 1960s (which had changed little from SIOP-63) faced significant difficulties (Kahan, 1975:94-97).

Several technical trends in strategic weapons, which held the promise of offsetting the expansion of the Soviet strategic arsenal, and thus restoring limited operational counterforce capability, attracted the interest of the air force, the navy, and others in the Pentagon in the late 1960s and early 1970s (Greenwood, 1975:27-50). The most important was the development of the multiple independent reentry vehicle (MIRV), which allows a missile to carry multiple reentry vehicles, each with a warhead that is independently targeted. MIRV allowed for a considerable expansion of the strike targets for the U.S. Air Force in the Soviet Union. The Minuteman III missile, the first U.S., MIRVed ICBM, was designed to carry three RVs, each carrying a warhead of 170 kilotons (kt). Each RV is designed to strike three independent targets, within limits, in the Soviet Union. The Poseidon SLBM, deployed in the early 1970s, carries ten to fourteen 50-kt warheads on its reentry vehicles (International Institute for Strategic Studies, 1982: 104-5). The United States has deployed 550 Minuteman IIIs and 400 Poseidon missiles (International Institute for Strategic Studies, 1982:104-5), thus enabling it to target 1,650 sites with Minuteman IIIs and between 4,000 to 5,600 sites with Poseidon missiles.[12]

From the perspective of strategic planners, the ICBMs are the more versatile weapon for two reasons. The SLBM is limited both by the size of the warheads it can carry and by the difficulty of communicating with submarines without compromising their position. In contrast, ICBMs have both countersilo potential, because they can carry larger warheads than the Polaris, Poseidon, and Trident I SLBMs, and a better command and control

52

potential. However, because of recent improvements in SLBM warhead size and accuracy, the Trident II (D-5) SLBM may eventually be considered for countersilo war-fighting scenarios.

The expansion of ICBM warheads by the deployment of MIRV also allows for greater hard-target potential against Soviet missile silos and other hardened targets such as command and control centers of the Soviet government and military, other military targets (e.g., Soviet air defenses and submarine bases), and certain vital industries. The chances of destroying a Soviet missile in a hardened silo increase if one is able to aim two warheads at that target. For example, all other things being equal, the chances of destroying a Soviet missile in a silo hardened to survive up to 2,000 pounds per square inch (psi) over pressure increase from 81 to 96 percent with two warheads aimed at the target as opposed to one. This assumes an accuracy (circular error probable — CEP) of 0.08 of a nautical mile (nm) or 486 feet with warheads of 340 kt.[13]

Second, improvements in the yield (kilotonage) to weight ratio of warheads along with more efficient fuels for the missiles, realized during the 1970s, created the opportunity for the old missile shell to carry a set of higher yield multiple warheads than previously. The improvement of yield also increases the hard-target kill potential of the missile. For example, the kill potential of an RV with an accuracy of 0.08 nm aimed at a target hardened to 2,000 psi rises from 65 to 81 percent as the warhead yield increases from 170 to 340 kt.[14]

Third, improvements in the accuracy of the reentry vehicles had an even more effective increase in the kill potential of a missile than did the improvement in yield.[15] The payoff in kill potential in accuracy is twice that of improvements in yield. For example, the probability of a RV kill with a 170-kt warhead with a 0.08 CEP aimed at a target hardened to survive 2,000 psi over pressure, all other things being equal, is 65 percent. If the accuracy is improved to 0.04 nm CEP (243 ft), the kill probability is improved to 97 percent — twice the improvement attainable by doubling the yield.[16] Thus, ICBMs with more secure and effective communications along with greater counterforce capability were far more important to a war-fighting doctrine than the navy's SLBMs.

The impact of these technological developments on MX decision making was similar then to that indicated by proposition 1 of the bureaucratic politics literature. MX was made possible by the refinement of the ICBM. Certainly the drive to pursue these refinements was in part the result of the interaction of design labs and the U.S. Air Force. Nevertheless, the strategic issues as suggested below provided the rationale in which the interaction between these groups took place.

MX–The Ultimate War-Fighter

The MX missile is the ultimate war-fighter for those interested in the strategy of flexibility with limited counterforce capability; a strategy embraced by three presidents, three secretaries of defense, and the senior officials of the air force in the 1970s. It is the key to the total nuclear war-fighting doctrine of the Reagan administration. The MX missile is 50 feet long, 7 feet 8 inches wide, and weighs 192,000 lbs; it is nearly twice the size of the Minuteman generation of missiles (U.S. Office of Technology Assessment, 1981:3-4 — hereafter referred to as OTA, 1981). It is designed to carry ten or more RVs with either the new Mark 12A warhead with a 350-kt yield (it recently replaced the Mark 12 warhead on the Minuteman III missiles) or a new 500-kt yield warhead, and has an initial RV accuracy 0.08 nm. That CEP is expected to improve to 0.05 nm by the time of the deployment of the missile in the mid- to late 1980s.[17] Such an accuracy combined with that yield would give two MX RVs a virtual hard-target capability (98 percent) against Soviet missiles even in superhardened silos (hardened up to 4,000 psi).[18]

This capability assumes complete reliability of the MX missile, an unrealistic assumption. The air force estimates 90 percent reliability. The kill probability would be improved by targeting two warheads on each Soviet missile silo to assure destruction of the hardened target.

The decision of the Carter administration in June 1979 to deploy 200 MX missiles translated into 2,000 warheads with hard-target potential. Some of the computer-based simulations of a preemptive U.S. attack with such a force on Soviet ICBM silos in the late 1980s indicated a probable 99 percent destruction of those silos, with the assumption that the Soviets had not launched their own ICBMs while under attack.[19] These scenarios assume an attack composed of the MX force launched from fixed sites augmented by part of the Minuteman III force with Mark 12A warheads. Over half of the U.S. ICBM missiles would be held in reserve (Baugh, 1980).

MX garnered allies from a second group of strategic analysts and other members of the executive branch and the Congress. They supported the new generation of ICBMs as a vehicle for forcing the Soviets to abandon their dependence on their new, very large and capable land-based missiles — the SS-17, SS-18, and SS-19. These Soviet MIRVed ICBMs carry more warheads with larger yields. For example, the SS-17 employs four RVs, the SS-18, ten, and the SS-19, six. All utilize warheads in the 500-kt range, the SS-17 with slightly larger warheads. The CEP of the SS-19 and SS-18 was estimated to be 0.14 nm. The SS-17 was about 0.24 nm. The accuracy of the SS-18 and SS-19 is said to be steadily improving. The combination of accuracy and the size of the warheads give these two missiles theoretical hard-target capability against U.S. ICBMs (Tsipis, 1981).

This second group interested in deployment of MX surmised that the hard-target potential of MX would be enough to threaten Soviet land-based MIRVed missiles, which because of their great size and weight, would be difficult to switch to a mobile-basing system to avoid vulnerability. If the United States placed MX in an invulnerable basing mode, the Soviets would be encouraged to abandon their reliance on their provocative heavy missiles, and move to the development of smaller, mobile ICBMs that carry fewer warheads and/or move to sea with their strategic force (i.e., deploy the bulk of their strategic forces on SLBMs). In either case, Soviet strategic forces would have fewer warheads with less accuracy, and thus present less of a threat to U.S. strategic forces. The result would be less preemptive incentive for the two forces, and thus greater strategic stability.[20]

Others in the Pentagon and the U.S. government have seen MX as providing the counterforce capability necessary to reestablish a limited nuclear war-fighting capability for U.S. strategic policy. Without the MX such a strategic targeting policy would be impossible. Thus, to these individuals MX was the key to both deterrence and a damage limiting capability if deterrence should fail in the future.

The Advocates of MX

Thus, many of the active supporters of MX split over the purpose for which the missile should be deployed. There were the conservative critics of the assured destruction concept who argued for a total nuclear war-fighting capability.[21] The Reagan administration supported the development of such an emphasis in U.S. strategic doctrine and the deployment of MX to facilitate such a strategy (Ikle, 1982). Secretary Weinberger has been the administration's most visible proponent of this strategy and the MX. Before the Reagan administration's ascendancy to power, the air force, especially the Strategic Air Command, and the engineering groups within DOD were the major advocates of such a doctrine and role for the MX. Defense contractors who would provide technology and equipment for the MX have been vigorous supporters of this idea, as well as Senators Henry Jackson (late, D-Wash.), John Tower (R-Tex.), Jake Garn (R-Utah), and Representative Jack Kemp (R-N.Y.). Groups such as the Committee on the Present Danger, the United States Strategic Institute, the Air Force Association, and the Heritage Foundation as well as publications such as *Aviation Week and Space Technology*, have also been active and effective allies. Finally, such prominent strategic analysts and political figures as Paul Nitze, Colin Gray, Lt. Gen. (Ret.) Daniel Graham, William Van Cleve, and Edgar Ulsamer have actively campaigned for MX.

On the other hand, there have been the critics of the assured destruction concept who have advocated the development of a *limited countersilo capability* for U.S. strategic forces. These critics of assured destruction see the total war-fighting strategy of Jackson, Tower and others as dangerously foolhardy. The chances of a successful countersilo strike against the Soviets that would avoid significant damage are virtually impossible. Nevertheless, the possession of a limited war-fighting capability represented by the deployment of MX may indeed be productive. It would probably drive the Soviets away from reliance on their huge land-based ICBMs.

This group, composed of individuals such as Brown and Schlesinger, several senators and representatives,[22] and many strategic analysts, have seen a limited counterforce capability for MX as providing two advantages. First, MX would provide the limited countersilo capability for the strategic flexibility outlined in Nixon's 1973 foreign policy statement. This limited nuclear war-fighting capability would supposedly bolster deterrence. Second, as noted earlier, they have seen the limited counterforce capability of MX when coupled with a survivable basing mode as a way to drive the Soviets away from their reliance on heavier missiles such as the SS-18 and SS-19 to smaller missiles with fewer RVs and smaller warheads in some type of survivable modes, hopefully verifiable, or to sea in submarines. This would also require placing limits on the number of MX missiles deployed to signal the Soviet Union that the United States did not desire to threaten the entire Soviet ICBM force (even if that were possible), but rather to force the Soviets to abandon reliance on the larger missiles.

One of the most striking features of the MX debate is that many of the opponents of MX did not perceive that the supporters of MX were a diverse group with different strategic goals, i.e., the differences between the total war-fighters and the more limited objectives for MX supported by such diverse personalities as Secretary of Defense James Schlesinger and Senator Thomas McIntyre (D-N.H.). Nevertheless, the distinction is an important one. There were actually two different coalitions of interests who supported MX and significant differences among individuals in the second group such as Schlesinger and McIntyre. Moreover, it was the diversity of interests that generated the dissension within the executive branch which in turn facilitated the broadening of the arena of conflict in which MX was discussed. Had there been greater unanimity among supporters of MX itself, proponents would have had an easier time deflecting the missile's opponents.

Critics of the War-Fighting Doctrine

There is a third group of analysts and others interested in strategic policy who have viewed MX's hard-target potential as a sinister development in

U.S. nuclear policy. For example, the former director of the Arms Control and Disarmament Agency (ACDA) and chief U.S. SALT I negotiator, Gerard C. Smith (1981:3), recently argued in testimony before the Senate Committee on Foreign Relations that

> recognizing that some part of U.S. strategic forces will become vulnerable to a Soviet first strike is a different thing from accepting the idea that either the United States or the Soviet Union could carry out with confidence an effective first strike against the other's strategic forces. It requires a leap of faith to believe that computer calculations about missile capabilities could form the basis for a reliable disarming attack which would face enormous operational obstacles.

In sum, the critics of the U.S. war-fighting strategy have argued that regardless of whether or not U.S. ICBMs are becoming vulnerable, the United States should not adopt either a total or a limited nuclear war-fighting strategy. The acceptance of that doctrine would likely lead to the use of such a strategy in crisis situation. The result would be catastrophic.

These critics of nuclear war-fighting also doubt the plausibility of the scenario of a Soviet first strike on U.S. ICBMs for two reasons. First, they argue that the assumptions and contingencies of these plans are sterile. Given the operational obstacles that a finetuned nuclear first strike would present, and the consequent probability of failure to disarm the nuclear forces of the other side, they can conceive of virtually no instance in which a Soviet or U.S. decision-maker would risk such an action given the enormity of the implications of failure in such a strike. Even if a Soviet strike could theoretically disarm the U.S. ICBM force in its silos, the critics of the war-fighting strategy do not accept the argument that a U.S. president would capitulate to the Soviets after a preemptive strike or that any president would be influenced by a presumed Soviet strategic preemptive advantage. Rather, the United States, until it adopts and deploys a less vulnerable basing mode for its ICBM force in the 1980s, will likely assume a modified launch-under-attack program. Thus, a limited first strike by the Soviets against U.S. ICBMs would be unsuccessful in that many U.S. missiles would have left their silos by the time of the attack and the Soviets would have provoked a nuclear war (Hoover, 1982:27-49).

Many critics of the war-fighting doctrine find the launch-under-attack solution to the impending U.S. ICBM vulnerability as another distressing development in the strategic relationship between the United States and the Soviet Union (Scoville, 1981b). The solution establishes a nuclear hair trigger to political crises. Nevertheless, they concede that the development of such a capability by the United States is surely unavoidable at least until a basing mode less vulnerable than the stationary silos for either the

57

Minuteman III or MX is adopted. It follows that the political utility that the Soviet Union might extract from such a supposed preemptive advantage disappears as well.

Second, even if the United States did not adopt a launch-under-attack policy, and assuming that a Soviet attack was relatively successful against U.S. missiles, the collateral destruction in the United States would be so devastating to life and property that it would be inconceivable that a president's actions would be restrained. Congress commissioned a study by the Office of Technology Assessment to evaluate Secretary Schlesinger's claim that a Soviet strike would produce significant but not cataclysmic casualties in the United States — 800,000 individuals. Instead, the Office of Technology Assessment's rigorous study estimated casualties from such an attack reaching levels of *2 to 16 million* depending on conditions, with the likely range far higher than Schlesinger's figures (OTA, 1979). The feasibility of even limited exchange scenarios pales in the light of these casualty projections. Only the most optimistic analysts are unwilling to accept that such devastation would likely result in uncontrollable and massive nuclear exchanges. For these reasons the critics of the war-fighting doctrine question that the Soviets would ever initiate such an attack on U.S. ICBMs. The Soviets must assume a probable U.S. response.

Proponents of the war-fighting doctrine respond that the combination of Soviet civil defense programs[23] and a Soviet first-strike capable of crippling U.S. ICBMs would reduce Soviet casualties from an U.S. second strike to "acceptable" levels. The figure used to describe acceptable is 10 to 20 percent of the Soviet population. This range as a percentage is slightly more than the absolute level of death incurred by the Soviet Union in World War II — 20 to 30 million. Of course, as the proponents of the war-fighting doctrine often overlook, the Soviets did almost everything conceivable to avoid war with Germany. The Soviet deaths suffered were over a four-year period rather than the period of hours in a nuclear war. The psychological, political, physical, and almost any other imaginable implications of such horror in a compressed timeframe dwarf the World War II experience.

It must be remembered that the Soviet leadership has traditionally been quite cautious in exposing their country to destruction. After all, the present Soviet leaders are the descendants of the Bolsheviks. The Communists came to power at the expense of an oppressive regime that had failed in its security responsibilities in an earlier destructive war in this century, World War I. The death and destruction of that war cannot begin to match the almost instantaneous and colossal extent of death that would be produced by a nuclear war in our era. What political stakes would lead

58

the Soviets to decide for nuclear attack with such vast risks to their society, a society which is the proud product of the Soviet Communist Party?

The critics of the war-fighting scenarios suggest that such a doctrine is sterile for a second reason as well. As Kosta Tsipis (1981:3), a critic of the war-fighting camp indicates, there are at least seven factors that may cause the theoretical accuracy of a missile to decrease during wartime conditions.

> Errors caused by imprecisions in the inertial sensing and guidance system, errors in the calculations performed on board the missile during the flight, errors in rocket shutoff, errors in determining initial conditions, errors due to imperfect knowledge of the effects of gravity on the motion of the missile and the reentry vehicles [bias], errors in determining the precise position of the target with respect to the launch point, unforeseen effects on the weather over the target on the reentering warhead.

Without terminal guidance capacity, errors produced by one or multiple factors of the above list may compound the error as the missile progresses to the target. Thus, a portion of the critics of the MX's war-fighting potential believe that Soviet ICBMs, as well as U.S. ICBMs, may not have the necessary accuracy under battlefield conditions for a successful countersilo strike.

Perhaps the most troubling element of the above accuracy problems is factor number five. It focuses on the problem of "bias" in missile accuracy.[24] Accuracy is measured by the concept of circular error probable (CEP). This is "the radius of a circle around a target in which 50% of the missile warheads aimed at that target will land" (Scoville, 1981: 220). Improvements in accuracy or the reduction in the scatter of missiles from the target were effected by tinkering with the various above factors in repeated firings from Vandenberg Air Force Base in California to the Kwajalein Islands in the Pacific (east to west). This repeated testing along with the introduction of new and better inertial guidance equipment allows U.S. technicians to better understand the gravitational effects of the standard east to west flight and the probable wind condition effects on the ICBM RV as it reenters the earth's atmosphere and descends to the target. This has led to significant improvements in the CEP for U.S. ICBMs. The Soviets in tests which fire their missiles from east to west across the Soviet Union have improved the CEP performance through similar techniques.

Despite improvements in accuracy, the problem of bias remains. As one analyst (Kaplan, 1981:7) indicates, CEP is a partially misleading factor when attempting to understand accuracy.

> The numbers typically given for CEP actually indicate only how closely scattered are the weapon's "impact points" — it does not take into account the bias factor that pushes, pulls, and blows the missile away

from the actual target. It's like determining a marksman's skill by measuring how tightly grouped his bullet holes are on the target board, without measuring their distance from the bull's eye. In other words, that a guidance system might be so finely honed as to place half the weapons inside a circle with a diameter of 450 feet is technically impressive, but that matters little if gravitational quirks and wind turbulence along the way to the real target throw the missile off an additional quarter mile.

In actual battlefield conditions, both the Soviet Union and the United States would be firing missiles on polar trajectories. Science has discovered that the greatest variance in gravitational pull in the earth's surface is at the earth's polar regions. If the bias argument is correct, without an opportunity to perfect accuracy through repeated missile firings, the RVs targeted on the adversary's silos will destroy those targets only by accident. Thus, the variance caused by uncharted gravitational pulls could negate any attempt by the Soviet Union or the United States for accurate countersilo strikes and in effect the whole idea of war-fighting strategy.

Because of bias some analysts also argue that neither Soviet or U.S. ICBMs are actually vulnerable. Former Secretary of Defense Schlesinger (quoted in Kincade, 1981:5) indicated in congressional testimony in 1974 that

it is impossible for either side to acquire the degree of accuracy that would give them a high confidence first strike because we will not know what the actual accuracy will be like in a real-world context. As you know, we have acquired from the western test range (Vandenberg Air Force Base to Kwajalein) a fairly precise accuracy, but in the real world we would have to fly from operational bases to targets in the Soviet Union. The parameters of the flight from the western test range are not really very helpful in determining those accuracies to the Soviet Union.

From this perspective, MX would be an ineffective war-fighter at least until terminal guidance techniques can be introduced. Until such time, the Minuteman missile will satisfy U.S. interests in that it will continue to be invulnerable and accurate enough to threaten Soviet soft military targets and industrial potential.

A different type of problem for war-fighting strategies employing large numbers of warheads is that of fratricide. Warheads that arrive over a field of missile silos may provide problems for others arriving moments later at the same field. The explosions and nuclear fallout of the first warheads will likely degrade the capability of the following warheads. As one analyst notes, "No one can predict precisely how this fratricide effect will impair an attack and uncertainty erodes confidence in achieving a perfectly executed attack" (Kincade, 1981: 5).

Herbert Scoville, Jr. (1981:2), one of the chief critics of the war-fighting doctrine, has best summarized the critics' argument against war-fighting and the MX as the ultimate war-fighting missile.

> It is itself a first-strike weapon, which can threaten a major portion of the Soviet strategic deterrent force but which will be militarily ineffective if not used to start a strategic nuclear war. It will be an incentive for Soviet initiation of a nuclear conflict either by accident or preemption in time of crisis. The MX is an invitation to an accelerated and endless strategic arms race with no winners, one in which we will never know whether we are ahead or behind. It will make verifiable arms limitations a fading dream. With weapons to start and fight a large-scale nuclear war, for the first time man has in his grasp the seeds of his destruction. The MX missile is the prime example of a nuclear war fighting weapon that can lead us closer to the catastrophe of an atomic holocaust.

Finally, there is the operational problem of Soviet coordination of a preemptive strike on U.S. ICBMs, B-52 bombers, and SLBMs. Critics of the conservative analyst's Soviet attack scenario have argued that no prudent Soviet military planner would consider a strike on U.S. ICBMs without a corresponding attack on U.S. B-52 bombers and SLBMs. The risk of a counterattack by those latter forces on the Soviet homeland and the damage that would result even if U.S. ICBMs had been destroyed are too great. The requirements of coordinating Soviet SLBMs to strike U.S. bombers and submarines in port with that of Soviet ICBMs on U.S. ICBM silos is argued to be beyond achievement. The Scowcroft Commission established by President Reagan in January 1983 to review the MX question eventually concluded that MX even in a Minuteman silo was not as vulnerable as previously suggested because of these operational difficulties that confronted the Soviet Union.

The individuals and groups that opposed MX on strategic grounds, such as the Center for Defense Information, the Federation of American Scientists, the Arms Control Association, and the Council for a Livable World, have been active and vigorous opponents of MX. Strategic analysts such as Herbert Scoville, Jr., Wolfgang Panofsky, William Kincade, Kosta Tsipis, Jeremy Stone, and Desmond Ball, former key executive decision-makers with experience in arms control such as Paul Warnke and Gerard Smith, a host of senators and representatives led by Democratic liberals such as Edward Kennedy, George McGovern, and Morris Udall, actively opposed the development of a ten-warhead missile on strategic grounds.

Observations

The drive to develop a war-fighting capability was important in mobilizing coalitions of groups and important individuals both inside and outside of government to support the design, research, development, and deployment of a new generation of missiles — the MX. Many of these people's interests were strategic in nature, and thus broader than the narrow interests in the air force and industry design labs where weapon ideas originate and evolve. Certainly these latter groups were important. But the strategic value of MX as a war-fighting weapon was pivotal to the debate. Moreover, the uncertainties associated with advanced MIRVed nuclear weapons, and the destabilizing implications of MX's war-fighting potential stimulated an opposition to MX. Thus, the strategic complexity of MX caused the new weapon even at its inception to be more controversial than most previous ones. The pivotal question became whether enhanced war-fighting capability would advance or retard strategic stability. Would it really make the world safer? The questions surrounding MX were quite different than proposition 1 would lead one to expect.

The crucial issue of MX as a war-fighting weapon was by no means the only issue. The basing mode questions were and remain highly contentious. For example, the potential environmental, social, and economic side effects of the MX in the multiple protective shelter basing mode received more attention that the war-fighting issue. In addition, the relationship of MX to foreign policy interests such as the Strategic Arms Limitation Talks and the theater nuclear weapons discussions in Western Europe were hotly debated items.

Nevertheless, the strategic debate over MX did affect the treatment of MX in the inner layer of the procurement process, was a factor in the 1980 election, did influence congressional debate over appropriations measures, and eventually stirred popular interest in the nuclear freeze. The lack of success in stalling or defeating MX on the strategic dimension led antagonists to attack MX on other grounds such as environmental, where greater opportunity existed for the successful use of dilatory tactics. One such ground that proved fruitful was the second dimension of the strategic question — the vulnerability of the basing mode for MX.

Endnotes

[1] For a discussion of the concept of deterrence, the heart of U.S. strategic policy since the early post-World War II days, see Brodie (1959), George (1974), Schelling (1960), Snyder (1961), and Wohlstetter (1959). For discussion of deterrence prior to World War II, see Quester (1966), Quester (1971), and Freedman (1982).

[2] Shortly after the detonation of the atomic bombs on Hiroshima and Nagasaki, Bernard Brodie argued in his seminal essay on the nuclear age and international politics that the concept of deterrence was altered dramatically by the advent of the bomb (Brodie, 1946:21-110). War-fighting with nuclear weapons was beyond the

pale. Henceforth, deterrence would rest on the threat to inflict unimaginable damage with nuclear weapons on the adversary. The refinement of Brodie's concept of deterrence by strategic analysts in the 1950s and 1960s became known as assured destruction. The concept had several components. First, there was the need for second-strike capacity. This was the capability of the United States to experience a nuclear first strike by the Soviet Union or by any other adversary and still retaliate with sufficient force to destroy the enemy. Second, assured destruction meant the development and maintenance of a force sufficient to cause an unacceptable level of destruction in a second strike on the attacker. For a thorough discussion of these two components of deterrence, see Brodie (1959:264-304). For a discussion of the intellectual history of this period and how Brodie's ideas developed (see Kaplan, 1982:75-84).

[3]The most often considered alternative to assured destruction is the war-fighting concept. The argument proceeds as follows: deterrence is most effectively established even in the nuclear age if one side possesses the nuclear forces that could destroy the war-fighting capability of the adversary. Second, the adversary must be unable through a preemptive attack to alter the balance of forces significantly. If such a capability is perceived to exist by the adversary, there is no incentive for the adversary to initiate a nuclear attack. Even more importantly, if deterrence fails for reasons of misperception, miscalculation, or irrationality, the United States must have the ability to limit the damage to its society by destroying the strategic forces of the adversary. For a discussion of the components necessary for an effective war-fighting strategy, see Brodie (1959: 173-264). See also, Gray (1979) and Gray (1980).

[4]For a discussion of the character of U.S. strategic policy during the 1950s with special attention to the role of SAC and General LeMay, see Rosenberg (1983).

[5]For an argument representative of this position, see Slocombe (1981).

[6]The SS-18s and SS-19s will be fully deployed by the mid-1980s.

[7]"Soviet's Nuclear Arsenal Continues to Proliferate" (1980) suggests that "when the accuracy of the Soviet ICBM force approaches 0.15 nautical miles, 90% of the U.S. Minuteman silos are vulnerable to an attack with two RVs targeted against each silo. A two-on-one attack would require less than half of the Soviet reentry vehicles (RVs) expected to be available by 1985. When Soviet ICBM accuracy exceeds 0.08 nautical miles, silos become vulnerable to attack by a single reentry vehicle."

[8]For a discussion of the relationship between accuracy and warhead size as it relates to the destructive capacity of missiles against hardened targets, see Schilling (1973). Also see Legault (1974) for a general discussion of the technical character of nuclear weapons, delivery systems, and defensive concepts.

[9]For an analysis of this problem, see Office of Technology Assessment, 1975.

[10]For a discussion of the ICBM vulnerability problem from this perspective, see Gray (1977).

[11]For an excellent discussion of the strategic policy of the 1960s, see Kahan (1975).

[12]Most strategists assume two warheads per site if target is hardened to prevent destruction as would be missile silos and command centers.

[13]Computed on a Boeing Vulnerability Assessment Calculator.

[14]*Ibid*.

[15]*Ibid*.

[16]*Ibid*.

[17]For a discussion of the technical aspects of MX, see Robinson (1980) and Walker (1979).

[18]Computed on a Boeing Vulnerability Assessment Calculator.

[19]Launch-on-warning, i.e., after initial determination of attack is being launched against one's forces but before attack reaches missile silos, has the drawback of potentially launching missiles because of an error in the detection technology. The missiles launched because of an error cannot be recalled or destroyed. Thus, they would probably produce an accidental nuclear war. For a more extensive discussion of the problem, see Hoover (1982:6-7).

[20]For a critique of this optimistic view of Soviet alternatives, see Hoover (1982:39-41).

[21]For representative examples of this perspective, see Gray (1979), Gray (1980), Gray (1981), Ulsamer (1978), Ulsamer (1979a), and Ulsamer (1979b). For a critical analysis of this position, see Tamman (1981) and Smith (1981).

[22]See Hoover (forthcoming).

[23]For a critical discussion of Soviet civil defense preparations, see Weinstein (1982).

[24]For the most important discussion of bias and other operational problems in the open literature, see Anderson (1981) and Anderson (1982). See also, Steinbruner and Garwin (1976), Marshall (1981), and Marsh (1982).

CHAPTER 3
A PEEK THROUGH THE WINDOW OF
VULNERABILITY:
WHAT SHALL BE THE BASING MODE?

The second dimension of the strategic questions concerning MX is what basing modes should be chosen for the new missile. There are two related aspects of this dimension: (1) the invulnerability of a basing mode; and (2) the potential of that basing mode to provide hard-target capability, i.e., protect MX so it could be used to retaliate against Soviet missile sites. Thus, the basing mode question is inextricably linked to the question of hard-target capability.

An essential requirement of deterrence is the possession of a second-strike capability. A mutual second-strike capacity is the single important ingredient in a stable strategic relationship between nuclear powers. If no incentive exists for a preemptive strike on the part of country A against country B, or vice versa, then the relationship is said to be stable.

A second-strike capacity is dependent upon the existence of what is known as prelaunch and postlaunch invulnerability. Prelaunch invulnerability is the ability of country A's nuclear force to survive a preemptive attack by an adversary and to launch an attack on the adversary. Postlaunch invulnerability is the capacity of the retaliatory force of a country to penetrate the defenses of the adversary and destroy the intended targets. The heart of the ICBM vulnerability problem in the recent past (also known as the "window of vulnerability") has been the perceived erosion of the prelaunch invulnerability of the U.S. ICBM force.

During the 1960s, many strategic analysts feared that certain technological developments in the arms race would undermine or erode the strategic stability between the nuclear powers. Of particular concern was the problem of whether the U.S. strategic deterrent force, especially the ICBM dimension, would continue to be viable given projected improvements in Soviet rocket forces and missile defenses. These concerns prompted the exploration of various basing schemes and technical alternatives to protect the triad (ICBMs, SLBMS, and bombers) in the face of contemplated Soviet initiatives. In the 1970s, Soviet rocket developments moved the discourse from speculation to specific concern. Soviet MIRVing of its newest generation of heavy missiles with large warheads (SS-17, SS-18, and SS-19) and the estimated improvements in the accuracy of the RVs of those missiles caused consternation within the air force and strategic circles about the prelaunch invulnerability of Minuteman.

The problem of bias in missile accuracy and its implications for ICBM vulnerability came to the forefront very late in the MX debate. Clear analysis of the operational problem for a Soviet attack on U.S. ICBMs and the remainder of the triad only surfaced during the Reagan administration as an issue. It was in 1981 and 1982 that analysts really began to debate the MX vulnerability question in this light. Consequently, throughout much of the history of MX, it was generally assumed that the standard criteria of missile accuracy, reliability, time-on-target, multiple warheads, and yield were the important factors in determining vulnerability.[1] Given the inevitable improvements in the performance of these criteria by both Soviet and U.S. weapons, a trend of ICBM vulnerability was taken for granted by most analysts within and outside the Pentagon.

Neither the nuclear war-fighters nor proponents of mutual assured destruction could tolerate the erosion of U.S. prelaunch invulnerability. The war-fighters, limited or total, required secure ICBMs to be able to carry out their strategic plans and thus, hopefully deter Soviet preemptive interests. Those interested in mutual assured destruction wanted a strategic force, not just or necessarily ICBMs, to be invulnerable in order to provide incentives for the Soviets to refrain from considering a first strike. All three groups were vitally interested in the question of whether or not improvements in Soviet missile technology were eroding U.S. strategic forces.

Nor were many of these analysts willing to support the idea of launch-on-warning (LOW) or launch-under-attack (LUA).[2] Either of these two approaches to prelaunch invulnerability attached a hair trigger to nuclear war. Such a mechanism might produce a U.S. launch in response to a false set of signals about a Soviet attack. This could cause an accidental nuclear war. Consequently, virtually all these analysts were interested in alternatives to LOW or LUA for meeting the potential ICBM vulnerability problem.[3]

In the STRAT-X study[4] completed in the late 1960s, the Pentagon exhaustively examined "future ballistic basing concepts and missile performance characteristics required to counter potential Soviet strategic forces and antiballistic missile proliferation" (Hodgden, 1981:31). The ABM Treaty of the SALT I agreement between the United States and the Soviet Union, which limited ABM deployment, reduced the immediate concern of strategic analysts with the Soviet antimissile ballistic missile (ABM) developments and U.S. postlaunch invulnerability. However, the other side of the STRAT-X study (missiles and basing modes) became the basis for much of the basing mode discussion that transpired in the 1970s. Virtually all of the over three dozen basing schemes considered for MX by

66

Ⓧ Wrong. Some leading arms controllers, of the MAD variety, always viewed the issue of ICBM vulnerability as a farce. E.g. Paul Warnke, Leslie Gelb...

the Pentagon, congressional committees, and strategic analysts were first NB considered in that study.[5] It set the agenda for the decision-making process on the issue of the MX basing mode. Once again an issue larger than just the interests of the air force and the design labs for industry, in this case MX basing mode considerations, would significantly influence MX decision ⊛ making. Thus, proposition 1 of the bureaucratic politics literature is inadequate to explain this procurement case.

Basing Mode Concepts

Although still classified, enough is known of the STRAT-X study to indicate that five basic concepts characterized the variety of alternative basing modes considered in the executive and legislative branches for ICBMs. These conceptual alternatives concerned hardening of the launch site, mobile launchers, concealment, deception, and active defense. Many of the basing modes considered by the U.S. government were based on combinations of these ideas.[6]

The hardening of a missile site is the concept that underlies the U.S. Minuteman I (1,000 ICBMs) deployed by the United States in the 1960s and the Minuteman IIs (450) and Minuteman IIIs (550) that replaced that force in the mid-1960s and the early 1970s. Hardening entails placing the ICBM in some type of shelter or underground silo that is reinforced by concrete or by the natural features of the topography to withstand the powerful overpressures resulting from a nuclear detonation in the immediate vicinity of the shelter or silo.

The U.S. Minuteman silos were hardened to supposedly withstand as much as 2,000 psi overpressure and still be able to fire a missile in the aftermath of a detonation. This was based on the assumption that an RV with a CEP of 0.14 nm and a warhead of 500 kt (criteria of SS-18 and SS-19 RVs and their warheads) would have only a 50 percent kill probability against a silo hardened to 2,000 psi. Although two such warheads would increase the kill probability to 75 percent, analysts speculated that neither of these kill probabilities was high enough to warrant enough of a guarantee of success to potential attackers to consider a preemptive strike against the U.S. ICBM missile field. Factoring in the problem of bias raises even higher the chances of failure involved in a preemptive strike.

On the other hand, if the problem of bias is discounted, improvements in accuracy could certainly alter this scenario. An improvement in the CEP by 0.06 nm (i.e., to 0.08 nm CEP) would increase the the kill probabilities to 90 percent for one warhead and nearly 99 percent for two warheads. Using these criteria, strategic analysts viewed the continuing refinements in the accuracy of the SS-18 and SS-19 as a significant threat to the U.S. ICBM force, even one hardened in the Minuteman silos.[7]

To meet this projected threat, analysts considered superhardening Minuteman. This would entail refortification of silos to withstand up to as much as 4,000 psi. The one major difficulty presented by this refinement would be the cratering capability of SS-18s and SS-19s. The ground burst effects of very accurate warheads of the size of 500 kt would likely destroy the silo by cratering them. In such a situation, it does not make much difference whether or not the silo can withstand 1,000 or 4,000 psi over-pressure; it cannot survive the cratering by the warhead if it is in the cratering area of the detonation. Consequently, superhardening was momentarily abandoned in the late 1960s and early 1970s as an effective alternative to the ICBM vulnerability problem even before the appearance of the SS-18 and SS-19.

However, both the Ford and Reagan administrations proposed deploying MX in regular or superhardened Minuteman silos as interim solutions until an invulnerable basing mode was discovered. During the Ford administration, the air force and Pentagon promoted the idea as a vehicle for the rapid deployment of MX, a step deemed important for three reasons. First, they argued that MX would enhance our bargaining position in the SALT negotiations by giving us a tangible new weapon system to offset the recent modernization of Soviet ICBMs. The increased counterforce capability of the new U.S. ICBM would also place pressure on the Soviet ICBM force and encourage Moscow to move toward smaller, more mobile, yet less accurate and destructive missiles. Finally, the interim deployment of the MX in Minuteman silos could enhance the limited war-fighting strategy being sought by the administration. The arguments for deployment of the MX in Minuteman silos as an interim measure in 1981 and 1983 by the Reagan administration were justified on the same grounds as the earlier Ford attempt.

Critics of the interim basing of MX in Minuteman silos argued that such a deployment would actually increase the incentives for the Soviet Union to initiate a preemptive nuclear strike. The MX with its ten warheads was far more threatening to the Soviet ICBMs than even Minuteman III deployment with only three warheads. Moreover, it was to be deployed in a Minuteman silo. If the Minuteman missiles were becoming vulnerable to Soviet ICBM developments, certainly MX missiles in Minuteman silos were also vulnerable and an even more inviting target given the greater number of MX warheads. Thus, such a deployment would strengthen the incentive for the Soviets to initiate a nuclear strike during a crisis.

Placing missiles in mobile launchers rather than in fixed silos was another conceptual alternative for the problem of ICBM vulnerability. The idea was to move the missile from place to place so that the adversary did not know where the missile was at any one moment making it difficult to destroy the weapon in a preemptive strike. On the other hand, a mobile launcher itself would never know, in precise enough terms, where *it* was, or at least with enough precision to maintain the type of accuracy required for countersilo capability. This latter problem might be overcome through technological developments that would make possible terminal guidance capability for an RV. Such a capability would allow for corrections in the trajectory during the terminal phase of the missile flight. This capacity could correct errors that developed in the course of a flight caused by confusion as to where the missile was when fired or the seven bias factors discussed in the previous section.

A third approach to overcoming the problem of ICBM vulnerability is concealment—hide the missiles from Soviet detection; if the adversary cannot find them, it cannot target them. An example of a missile system that combines concealment with mobility is the nuclear submarine carrying SLBMs. The submarine moving quickly and deeply below the surface of the ocean is concealed from Soviet surveillance. Submarine-based missiles have been the most invulnerable component of the triad, and remain so today. However, the nuclear submarine and its SLBMs do not possess the same versatility in reliability for command and control as afforded by the ICBMs. In addition, communication with submarines is difficult and problematic.

Deception is the fourth type of solution considered to address the ICBM vulnerability problem. The objective was to create ambiguity or confusion in the minds of the adversary as to the location of U.S. missiles. There were a variety of different ways this might be done. Electronic countermeasures could be used in such a way as to confuse the adversary's detection devices; or the missiles or facsimiles could be moved while partially concealed so as to create ambiguity or confusion for the detectors as to where the real missile was.

Defense of missiles is the final alternative. This conceptual solution has two dimensions—active and passive defense. Active defense envisions the deployment of an ABM system, conventional (a rapid acceleration missile or set of missiles) or unconventional (beam technology employed to destroy an attacking missile), to defend the missile site or even perhaps a mobile missile. Passive defense is produced by placing fixed impediments in the flight path of the attacking missile in such a way to cause premature detonation or the destruction of a missile before its timed explosion. This would reduce the blast overpressure and assure the survival of the weapon system.

During the 1960s, the Minuteman missile force, with its hardened silos, secure command and control communications system, and larger warhead yields, was the most versatile, reliable, survivable, and inexpensive component of the U.S. triad. However, the MIRVing of Soviet ICBMs in conjunction with their ever-increasing accuracy and large warheads caused many U.S. strategic analysts in the 1970s to view the hardened Minuteman silo as a dinosaur—a relic of the past whose demise was brought about in this case by changing technological developments. The task for those responsible for strategic policy was to find an alternative basing scheme for the growing vulnerability of Minuteman, but particularly for the air force's follow-on system, the MX. This new basing mode would have to provide the same versatility, reliability, and survivability for MX as had the fixed silo for the Minuteman missile in the 1960s. Thus, contrary to the implications of proposition 1 of the bureaucratic politics literature, MX was being shaped by strategic issues.

Approximately three dozen basing alternatives were suggested for MX that were hybrids of the five conceptual solutions discussed above. We review only the ones that were prominent in the deliberations by the government and the strategic community. They are reviewed from the perspective of the triad, i.e., air-based, sea-based, and land-based alternatives.

Air-Based Alternatives

One mode considered by the Pentagon in STRAT-X and explored with considerable interest in the mid-1970s was the air-based prototype.[8] In this mode, ICBMs would be launched from airborne bombers in North America; the feat was demonstrated by an air force test-launching of Minuteman from an airplane in the 1970s.

Despite its feasibility, the airborne launch raised several concerns (USAF Analysis of Attack Air-mobile Concept, 1981). The first was cost. The system as conceived required the purchase of large airplanes to carry the ICBMs as well as a fleet of tankers to support the launch aircraft while in flight. It also required additional maintenance and flight personnel in an era when costs for such personnel have risen significantly. Second, the system was vulnerable, at least while on the ground where missile carrying bombers are even more vulnerable to a preemptive attack than Minuteman silos. Even if airplanes and crews were sheltered in hardened hangers, the runways of the airfields could be easily targeted and thus rendered unusable by surprise attack.

A refinement of this idea, proposed by Reagan's Secretary of Defense Weinberger in 1981, was the extended flight ICBM launcher or the "Big Bird" (Barlow, 1981). The idea was to have an aircraft capable of staying aloft forty-eight hours without refueling and up to five days with refueling. However, the drawbacks remained—cost and vulnerability. As conceived, it was the most expensive alternative considered by the air force. Weinberger's scheme would have cost over $76 billion in constant 1980 dollars. In addition, Big Bird still had to land sometime, at which point it would be vulnerable, although how, where, and what part of the fleet descended was a question that could provoke considerable difficulties for a Soviet strategic planner attempting to coordinate a preemptive strike. Finally, the ICBM in this mode did not provide the necessary conditions for accuracy sought by those interested in limited or total war-fighting capability. For these reasons, it was unattractive to many groups and individuals considering ICBM basing modes.

Sea-Based Alternatives

Several sea-based modes were proposed as alternatives to land-based deployment of a new ICBM. One such system was the shallow underwater SUM missile system (SUM),[9] a basing mode advocated by civilian strategic analysts such as Richard Garwin, Sidney Drell, and many at Harvard and MIT. The SUM system called for the development and deployment of slow, small submarines, with a carrying capacity of four ICBMS, that could operate in the shallow waters off the North American coast. Although it was readily acknowledged that the movement of the small submarines would degrade the accuracy of the ICBM and thus reduce its hard-target capability, advocates surmised that this would reduce the preemptive incentives within the United States for a first strike as well as reduce the counterpressures for such in the Soviet Union. In short, the movement to sea by the United States was seen as a way to enhance strategic stability.

This approach encountered opposition and never became a viable alternative within the executive branch for several reasons. First, the war-fighters saw the erosion of accuracy in this mode as contrary to their original interests in MX. Communication, too, with these submarines would be insufficient to facilitate effective command and control for perhaps limited, but certainly an extended nuclear exchange as imagined by the war-fighters. Second, this system had no bureaucratic home within the Pentagon. Neither the air force nor the navy were likely to support this system. The air force did not want, nor was the navy likely to have ceded responsibility over, a missile deployed at sea. The missile did not fit the essence of the air force's role and tradition. The navy already had a strategic program and SLBMs already competed with the nonstrategic missions of the fleet for the limited monies available to the navy. Another missile and submarine attached to the navy might only dilute the money for Trident and the nonstrategic roles of the navy. Third, the system was an unknown quantity from an engineering standpoint. It would have required the design, construction, and testing of a new submarine. The meager submarine construction facilities available in the United States and the lagging Trident program were evidence that a second strategic submarine program could not meet the time requirements set by the Pentagon for deployment of a new missile in the mid- to late 1980s.

Finally, there was the argument that SUM submarines would be quite vulnerable to "pin-down" strikes by the Soviet Union; that is, the small subs could be prevented from launching nuclear counterattacks on the Soviet Union if the Soviets placed nuclear detonations in the waters off North America. These could cause operational difficulties for small underwater craft and prevent consistent, let alone accurate, firing.

HYDRA Another sea-based mode was the *Hydra*. An ex-naval officer proposed this idea, which for a time was vigorously advocated by former Secretary of Defense Melvin Laird (Draim, 1980). Missiles waterproofed and with flotation collars were to be dropped overboard into the water, and launched by electronic command from the ship. Since the missiles could be transported on an almost endless variety of ships, deception would be enhanced. It was also estimated to be the cheapest of any system explored by the Pentagon. However, it, too, was not popular with either the air force or those interested in war-fighting potential for MX for reasons similar to those invalidating SUM.

SLBM The final sea-based mode was the traditional SLBM, but with a new, higher yield warhead and with greater RV accuracy achieved through the introduction of terminal guidance capability. Such a SLBM might ultimately give the strategic forces of the navy a limited war-fighting capacity in a nuclear war exchange against hardened Soviet targets, although an extended nuclear war capability would be marginal given command and control communications difficulties. The cost of such an approach would be far less than that ultimately proposed for the air force's MX land-based scheme, the multiple protective shelter system. Too, the system could be online about the time the Pentagon projected completion of MX (the mid- to late 1980s), and had the advantage of being familiar technology making the system more attractive than most of the other sea-based alternatives. Finally, this approach promised to provide the best chance of prelaunch invulnerability of any alternative for the foreseeable future (Hoover, 1982:48).

The idea of moving the MX to sea in SLBMs had some support within the Pentagon, but more outside (Smith, 1982). At various times, the Carter and Reagan administrations held open the possibility of a dual design for MX; that is a missile which could fit into both a land-based mode (shelter or silo) and a submarine SLBM tube. Others supported the move to sea to attain their goals of greater reliance upon submarines and SLBMs.

The singular movement to sea was viewed as a threat to the integrity of the Pentagon's Triad, certainly to the continuation of the air force's role as

72

the major strategic branch of the U.S. services and to those interested in extended war-fighting capability. Of particular concern was any strategic decision that jeopardized the Triad by knocking out one of the three forces, the land-based ICBMs. The reduction of U.S. strategic forces by one element would allow the Soviets to concentrate their resources more effectively to counter the remaining two. Second, opponents of the diad concept (the bomber and the SLBM), such as Colin Gray (1977:9-11), were concerned about the limited war-fighting capability given the command and control problems for bombers and submarines. Diad simply did not provide the necessary capabilities for their more extensive strategic objectives. Finally, because it would alter major missions assignments in the military services, the solution was seen as facing obstacles in both the bureaucracy and Congress that could not be easily surmounted.

Land-Based Alternatives

Most supporters of MX within the Pentagon sought a deployment mode that would provide the same advantages and versatility for the missile that the hardened silo had done for the Minuteman missiles in the 1960s. This meant that the mode had to offer the proper combination of conditions for time-on-target, accuracy, responsiveness (quick firing on command), retargeting capability through effective command and control, countersilo potential (versatility in target selection plus large warheads), invulnerability, and be relatively inexpensive. Throughout the 1970s, the thrust of the search focused on these criteria for an MX basing mode. By the beginning of the next decade, however, many observers began to conclude that changing technological conditions precluded finding a single basing mode capable of providing that combination of versatility, security, reliability, and inexpensiveness found for Minuteman.

Of the several land-based alternatives considered by the Pentagon, a mobile launching system[10] was particularly popular. There were two variations investigated by the Pentagon: transporting the missiles on trucks or trains around the country; or confining their movement to a military reservation.

In the first case, the use of the interstate highway system or the railroads posed immediate problems. As one of the authors (Hoover, 1982:17) has written elsewhere:

> The use of public highways or railroads presented security problems as the government feared sabotage or theft by radical rightwing, and later leftwing, domestic groups. In addition, both the highway and railroad system entailed significant safety problems. The notorious deterioration of American railroad beds presented the probability of accidents involv-

The sheer size and weight of the missile, conditioned by its war-fighting mission, posed an additional problem since the missile would be too large and cumbersome to be safely transported by highway or rail.

When the second mobile-basing scheme, transporting the missile by rail or truck around a large military reservation, was first considered in the 1960s, the construction costs were prohibitive, at least when compared to the Minuteman alternative encased in concrete. Moreover, a rapidly moving mobile system on a military reservation created out of public lands in the West by its nature placed rather severe limitations on the size of the missiles and thus reduced their potential war-fighting capability. Also, a mobile missile would not have as much accuracy as a stationary one, unless some technological development materialized that would allow for terminal guidance capability. However, there was a feature of the system that was very attractive—transportation on a military reservation carved out of public lands would reduce the visibility problems mobile systems on interstate highways or U.S. railroads faced and the security problem of protecting the ICBM. We will return to a derivation of this mobile alternative below.

One version of the mobile prototype would transport a small, single warhead ICBM, dubbed "Midgetman," around a military reservation or on rail or wheels throughout the United States. Those who supported Midgetman sought to reestablish invulnerable ICBM status for both Soviet and U.S. missiles and in turn reduce preemptive incentives. The Midgetman's size would make it more mobile and, thus, less vulnerable than the MX; and the reduction in warheads would reduce the threat of this force to the Soviet ICBM system. It was hoped that the Reagan administration would use the system in negotiations with the Soviets as a model for change in Soviet missile deployments.

A second land-based alternative would be to actively defend the hardened missile silos with conventional ABM systems.[11] The army, old proponents of the ABM system in the 1960s such as Senator Jackson, and some new advocates such as Senator Garn lent their support to this approach.

There were several difficulties with this approach,[12] foremost the question of system effectiveness. The technical problems that ABM raised concerned the ability of unprotected radars to collect data about attacking missiles in an environment of radioactive fallout. In the past, data processing equipment had not been shown to be reliable or speedy enough to handle the problem in the limited time available for destruction of rapidly moving incoming targets. Some technical data processing questions were solved by the end of the 1970s. However, the interference to the radar caused by exploding nuclear warheads destroying incoming missiles remains.

Perhaps even more importantly, the Carter administration viewed a massive active defense of land-based MX to be in direct conflict with the limitations imposed by the ABM Treaty of the SALT I agreement, signed in 1972. The treaty limits the size of the ABM force which either the Soviet Union or the United States can possess to 100 missiles each, a number technically unable to deflect the literally thousands of warheads that make up the Soviet attack force. Not until the Reagan administration did it appear likely that the SALT process and therefore the ABM Treaty would be abandoned. Nevertheless, one ABM system was considered seriously. It will be discussed below in conjunction with the so-called multiple protective shelter mode.

The MAP Alternative

The basing mode that was the frontrunner in the mid-1970s was the "multiple aim point" system (MAP) (Nitze, 1979:30-34), essentially a variation of the carnival "pea in a shell game." Several *hundred* MX missiles would be placed in several *thousand* hardened silos, with the location of the missiles kept secret. Thus, in order to destroy all of the hidden missiles, the Soviets would have to target all of the missile silos, a fact that multiplies the number of necessary "enemy" warheads several-fold. In fact, the Soviets would have to use twice the warheads for the number of missile silos to insure a successful kill capacity, creating a condition whereby the United States could eradicate any Soviet advantage by digging more holes and deploying more missiles at a cost supposedly less than that incurred by the Soviets. Despite its mobile features, the system's success was contingent upon keeping the locations of the missiles secret since it would require about twenty-four hours to move an MX missile from one vertical silo to another. If for any reason the Soviets determined the precise location of the silos with the missiles, then a decision to attack by the Soviet Union meant that the missiles in these silos were quite vulnerable for twenty-four hours.

The possibility of the Soviets adding to their warhead inventory to offset the proliferation of targets by the U.S. MAP system was called the expanded threat problem. The Pentagon considered proliferation of silos and missiles by the United States as more cost-effective given the number relationship than the Soviet addition of launchers or the fractionation of those launchers. Thus, it was assumed that the Soviets would be reluctant to become involved in a silo-fractionation race that they would be unlikely to win, and which would be quite costly. In addition, Pentagon analysts

75

saw the MAP format as more suitable for ABM defense since there would be fewer sites (those with the missiles) in need of protection than in the Minuteman system. An active low-altitude ABM defense (LoAD) would add to the problem for the Soviets in overcoming a MAP system.[13] According to proponents, then, MX deployed in the MAP mode would eliminate Soviet preemptive incentives and reestablish a stable deterrent relationship.

Moreover, the operational requirements of MAP were attractive; they would not constrict command and control, limit the size of MX, and thus the number of multiple warheads, nor constrain the greater yield sought in these warheads as other alternative modes would have. MAP provided the prelaunch invulnerability features for deterrence without constricting the countersilo potential of MX and was cheaper than other viable basing modes.

For sometime, MAP was the favored basing mode of groups, organizations, and individuals interested in either limited or total nuclear warfighting capability. Support came from within the air force and from former civilian officials such as Paul Nitze and Eugene Rostow and strategic analysts such as Colin Gray.

However, MAP was not without its drawbacks. Preservation of location uncertainty (PLU) was a major concern (Hoover, 1982:18), especially since new technology had to be developed to accomplish deception. The objective was to conceal all "physical signatures and the associated missile equipment" (OTA, 1981:35). Given that this was a new, untested technology, and that it might not work as designed, there existed the possibility that the Soviet Union could identify in which silos those missiles were placed. Such a development would nullify the U.S. strategic advantage and reestablish preemptive incentives for the Soviet Union, especially since those missiles if compromised could not be moved easily to other silos in this basing mode. In addition, it would be difficult to ascertain when the location of a missile had been compromised. This was particularly disturbing to many analysts in light of MAP's limited mobility.

The SALT I Treaty, ratified in 1972, also raised problems for advocates of MAP, particularly verification requirements. Under SALT, each country had to be able to independently verify through "national technical means" (an official euphemism for satellite reconnaissance and electronical monitoring) that the other country was keeping within the proscribed numbers for each agreed upon category of weapon limitations. The deception features of MAP would be compromised by Soviet verification since the silos would have to be opened, and the missiles exposed, to Soviet view. The limited mobility of MX, then, would afford the Soviets at least twenty-four hours to destroy the missiles, the time required to move them to another silo. Such a vulnerability would nullify the purpose of the MAP basing mode and therefore be intolerable to the United States. Finally, the MAP approach threatened a major current of U.S. foreign policy in the 1970s since it was technically incompatible with the SALT I Treaty and the efforts in the SALT II negotiations to limit further offensive weapons. Rather than buck that wave of policy, the air force and many civilian analysts eventually turned to a variation on the MAP theme—the multiple protective shelter alternative (MPS).

MX MPS

A MPS mode, known as the racetrack (see Figure 3.1), was formally adopted by the Carter administration as the basing concept for MX in

Figure 3.1

Race Track and Grid System

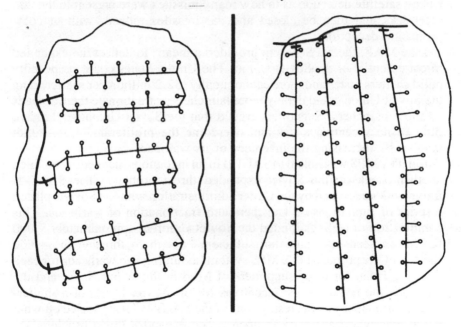

*On the left is the original design for the deployment of MX, the racetrack mode. On the right is the new mode, the grid system which uses a set of linear roads. Source: "Congress Challenges MX Basing Plan," *Sciences*, (May 30, 1980), 1007.

August 1979.[14] As originally conceived, MX MPS would consist of 200 missiles deployed individually in 200 separate oval tracks. Each track would have had twenty-three shelters hardened between 600 to 1,000 psi. A transporter in each track would shuttle the missile or a dummy missile among the shelters and simulate the movement of the missile from shelter to shelter. In some cases no missiles were actually being moved. It was another form of the shell game, only now with the possibility of constant readjustment. The transporter was designed to have a "dash capability" that would allow real missiles to move rapidly to an open predetermined space and launch in the event that an incoming Soviet missile had targeted the silo in which the MX was housed. This was the advantage absent in the MAP system. However, the air force discovered during 1980 that dash capability was not possible with the ninety-three-inch missile it desired. *large missile* Such a capability was possible only in the eighty-two-inch alternative. MPS also had a feature that provided the opportunity for independent Soviet verification. Several times a year, the silos could be opened to permit satellite detection as to how many missiles were present in the 200 racetracks and then be closed and the missiles moved, without compromising deception.

Like MAP, the MPS system provided a means to deflect the expanded threat potential of the Soviet Union. The United States could supposedly build shelters faster and more economically ($2.2 million per shelter) than the Soviet Union could deploy more launchers or fractionate the warheads on those launchers. Supporters argued that the Soviet Union would have little or no incentive to try and overcome the proliferated U.S. target number by increasing the inventory of its warheads.

Finally, MPS was linked to SALT II in an ingenuous manner. It provided another check on the Soviet expanded threat problem. The SALT II framework negotiated by the Carter administration with the Soviets placed a series of limitations on launchers and fractionation of warheads. This combination of ceilings limited the Soviet Union to approximately 8,000 ICBM warheads, a figure not sufficient enough to threaten the 4,600 shelters of the proposed MX MPS system (assuming two warheads for each shelter). Thus, for those supporters of MPS in the White House and the Pentagon the negative cost incentives for the Soviet Union of a shelter-fractionation race and the restrictions of the SALT II Treaty sealed off what might otherwise have been an open-ended expanded threat problem.

A variation of the horizontal shelter system of the MAP mode was the mobile vertical silo alternative. It found considerable support within the Defense Department as well as within the Senate (authors' interviews). In this system, the missiles were stored vertically in silos hardened to a greater degree than the shelters of the horizontal system, providing for greater

78

survivability in one sense. However, the loading of the missile or dummy missile from the vertical shelter onto the transporter was slower, reducing the dash capability of the system. The vertical mode was ultimately the loser in the competition.

LoAD was also explored as another way to seal-off the open-ended character of the Soviet expanded threat problem associated with MAP and MPS. Many suggested that even without SALT, LoAD would reduce the incentives for the Soviets to continue the expansion of their warheads by further deployment of launchers or more fractionation. LoAD would be an effective ABM system in that it would only have to defend a very limited number of the shelters—those in which the MX missiles were deployed. This was a far easier task than the defense of 1,000 missile silos.

The MPS scheme as it emerged in the late summer of 1979 had virtually all the combination of advantages that the air force was seeking. The mode facilitated the conditions for accuracy, endurance, responsiveness, time-on-target, command and control for retargeting capability, and invulnerability. MX MPS seemed to its supporters to virtually duplicate the outstanding features of the Minuteman technology in every way except cost and environmental factors. Consequently it was strongly supported by both groups interested in war-fighting capability for U.S. strategic policy. The air force formally committed itself to it in the summer of 1978, the Carter administration in late summer the following year. Most members of the Armed Services Committees in the Senate and the House were supporters. It appeared as if the deployment of MX was inevitable.

The critics of MPS raised several important questions, however. First, as with MAP there was concern as to whether or not the PLU technology would provide the concealment necessary for the Soviets to remain indecisive as to where the missile was located. The task of the PLU technology for MPS was far more difficult than that for MAP, and if not successful, the chance of defeating the MPS was easier. The dash capability would only allow the firing of the missile while the racetrack was under attack. If it survived, the missile's accuracy was likely to be seriously reduced. Critics argued that much depended on an untried technology that could prove to be enormously costly in both security and financial ways.

The critics also pointed out that MPS was unlikely to be deployed quickly enough to offset the vulnerability problem of the U.S. ICBM force until the late 1980s when it would become viable with 90 percent of the shelters and missiles in operation. Until such time the Soviets would still have a preemptive advantage, although one which was eroding. However, virtually all land-based alternatives faced this problem, one not shared by sea-launched systems, which are invulnerable from the time of deployment.

79

Most importantly, opponents took issue with the claim that the extended threat problem to MX MPS could be sealed-off. When the SALT II Treaty was withdrawn by Carter from further consideration by the Senate in January 1980, a critical check on the shelter-fractionation race was removed. Without limitations on launchers, MIRVed ICBM launchers, and the fractionation of those launchers, the launchers or fractionation versus shelters race would likely materialize. While it might be cheaper to build shelters, the Soviets nonetheless might continue to fractionate their RVs with more warheads. The Office of Technology Assessment (1981:5-29) study of MX basing modes projected that by the completion date, the United States would probably need nearly twice the number of shelters as the baseline figure of 4,600 to make MPS work without SALT II. Even more shelters might be needed later given the open-ended problem. The cost in constant dollars would double as well, with inflation pushing the figure above $100 billion in a decade. And there would have been no assurance that the added expenditures, additional construction of shelters, and the deployment of more missiles would have sealed-off the problem.

Finally, critics argued that the cost of the basing mode in financial terms, the socioeconomic disruption it would bring to the region in which it was deployed, and the environmental degradation it would cause, were too steep a price to pay for this basing mode. It was especially onerous to these critics in light of the probable expansion of the system to meet the extended Soviet threat which the critics saw as open-ended. The nonstrategic problems will be discussed in the next two chapters.

Closely Spaced Basing   DENSE PACK

The final alternative basing mode of significance was the Reagan administration's short-lived closely spaced basing (CSB) concept also called "dense pack." One hundred MX missiles would be deployed in 100 silos and spaced less than 2,000 feet apart, to increase the likelihood of fratricide in the attacking missiles: i.e., "the tendency of one warhead to destroy or deflect another when it detonates, through the release of radiation, the production of intense pressures, or the elevation of dust and debris" (Smith, 1982:1). Thus, the incoming Soviet missiles would destroy each other as their missile warheads detonated.

Critics pointed to several ways that the dense pack system might be overcome. For one, the Soviets might develop and deploy by the early 1990s, shortly after the dense pack system was operational, low-yield maneuvering warheads with consequent pinpoint accuracy; or the Soviets could "use maneuvering warheads that penetrate the earth or land softly on the surface" (Smith, 1983:1), thus avoiding the possibility of fratricide; or the Soviets could launch a series of detonations that would create a "storm of radiation'' and throw up a mountain of dust and debris to effectively prevent the launch of an MX, and thus pin down the U.S. missile system.

Observations

For those opposed and supportive of the various MX basing modes considered, technical and bureaucratic factors loomed large, as the conventional wisdom suggests. However, foreign policy considerations, particularly the two SALT agreements, and strategic factors, notably the war-fighting implications of MX and the vulnerability "problem," were prominent parts of the debate. Thus, once again, we find evidence to suggest that MX decision making was shaped, if not driven by, important strategic concerns. This the conventional wisdom and specifically proposition 1 understate.

As we will see, the saliency of strategic issues also had the effect of widening the scope of those interested in MX decision making beyond the groups and individuals suggested by the seven propositions for the inner layer of procurement activities. Two additional sets of concerns—foreign and domestic policy—provoked the involvement of nonexecutive and nongovernmental actors in ways previously unexpected. In the next chapter we explore more fully the impact of SALT and attendant foreign policy questions to the MX debate.

Endnotes

[1]How long it takes the warhead of a bomb to reach the target in the Soviet Union.

[2]For a technical discussion of LUA, see OTA (1981:147-66).

[3]There were exceptions. For example, see Westervelt (1974:701) and Henderson (1982). See also Blair (1982) and Garwin (1979-80).

[4]This was a major force requirements Pentagon study that began in 1967 and ended in January 1969. "The goal of the study was to compare the costs of alternatives in terms of numbers of warheads surviving a Soviet strike" (Edwards, 1982:59).

[5]For a short examination of thirty of the possible alternatives, see "MX the Weapon Nobody Wants" (1980).

[6]Much of the discussion that follows is based on technical information found in OTA (1981).

[7]Computed on a Boeing Vulnerability Assessment Calculator.

[8]For technical discussion of air based modes, see OTA (1981:217-234).

[9]For a discussion of SUM see Sidney Drell's testimony in U.S. Senate: Committee on the Armed Services (1980). See also "SUM" (1979). For a

discussion of the technical aspects of the various alternative sea-based modes, see OTA (1981:167-216), 235-57).

[10]See the following for a discussion of the evolution of the mobile-land based ICBM concept: Gray (1977:2-32); U.S.Senate (1977:6839-6934), U.S. Senate (1979:3476-3583); and U.S. Senate (1980:3681-3756).

[11]For a discussion of the advantages of ABM to defend American ICBMs as opposed to other alternatives, see Jacquelyn K. Davis (1978:36-44); Davis (1980); and Robinson (1981:8386). For Weinberger's interest in ABMs, see Wilson (1981).

[12]See Medalia (1981), Davis (1980), Porro (1981) and Nacht (1982).

[13]For a discussion of LoAD and how it was to complement the MX MAP or MX MPS system see, U.S. Office of Technology Assessment (1981:111-143).

[14]The best discussion of the technical aspects of MX MPS is found in UTA (1981:33-111).

CHAPTER 4

FOREIGN POLICY AND THE MX DECISION

Foreign policy considerations heavily influenced decisions about MX during the Ford and Carter administrations and were important factors during the Reagan years. Although foreign policy considerations were neither as crucial nor as pervasive as the strategic issues discussed in the previous two chapters, their effects were nevertheless pivotal at several points in the evolution of the MX saga. Furthermore, decisions about MX often cogently affected how these foreign policy issues were defined and handled. Most importantly, since foreign policy questions were significant in the decision making for MX, once again we find the conventional wisdom, the propositions for the inner layer and outer layer of the bureaucratic politics literature, misleading when applied to this particular procurement case.

There were three foreign policy issues associated with MX: (1) the symbolic value of MX in demonstrating U.S. military resolve and strength; (2) the SALT agreements; and (3) the deployment of modern nuclear weapons in the West European theater. As the MX program neared an acquisition decision in the late 1970s and early 1980s, advocates increasingly promoted the missile as a vehicle for reaffirming the first-class stance of the United States in the international community; and for demonstrating the willingness of the United States to respond to and match the expansion of Soviet military power. The SALT agreements and negotiations colored all decisions about strategic policy in the United States to one degree or another during the 1970s, and even those made by the Reagan administration in the early 1980s. Although Reagan opposed the SALT II Treaty during the presidential campaign of 1980, as president he endorsed in mid-1981 the commitment of the Carter administration to abide by the terms of SALT II at least until such time as a new treaty was negotiated and ratified or until the United States and/or the Soviet Union no longer saw enough benefits flowing from the treaty to warrant its continuation. The deployment of modern theater nuclear weapons in Western Europe became especially important in 1979, and was a critical factor in each of the three Reagan decisions for MX acquisition between 1981 and April 1983. The deployment of ground-launched cruise and Pershing II missiles, and the resolve of West European leaders to go ahead with that deployment in the face of significant public opposition within their countries, were linked in the minds of many Europeans, and raised similar concerns in both Europe and the United States about domestic opposition to MX in the United States.

Foreign Policy Issues and MX

In the spring of 1978, in a document entitled the *Declaration on National Security and Foreign Policy*, the Senate Republicans issued a broadside attack upon the detente policies of the Carter administration and of the general conduct of Soviet-U.S. relations during the 1970s. The document was reflective of the profound and growing ideological split in the United States over foreign policy, which would characterize conservative views of both presidential candidate Reagan during the 1980 election and his new national security program initiated in 1981. As the Republican senators (*Congressional Record*, 1978:12646) declared in their document:

> The Soviet Union continues to be the major threat to peace and stability in the world. Despite talk of detente, we believe the Carter administration incorrectly interprets the intentions of the Soviet Union and its commitment to achieve conventional military and nuclear superiority to secure wide-ranging geo-political goals. Statements by top administration officials indicate that they believe the Soviets merely seek strategic parity with the United States and that the Soviets regard the possibility of nuclear war as unthinkable. We believe the Carter administration has failed to understand adequately and communicate to the U.S. people the nature of the Soviet threat. . . . In 15 short months of incoherence, inconsistency and ineptitude, our foreign policy and national security objectives are [now] confused and we are being challenged around the globe by Soviet arrogance.

Conservatives firmly believed that the Soviets would confront Western civilization with an unbending, unending competition until one side was eliminated. They accused Kissinger as well as the Carter administration of overlooking the political implications of growing Soviet strategic capability and Moscow's continued conventional advantages in Central Europe.[1]

From their perspective, new and superior U.S. strategic programs, what was to become known during the Reagan administration as strategic modernization, were the only realistic ways to readdress the deteriorating position of the United States vis-a-vis the Soviet Union. Detente and SALT II stood in the way of the deployment of modern, new ICBMs, SLBMs, and long-range-bombers that would reestablish the strategic superiority of the United States. The acquisition and deployment of MX was a necessary act of national will that would restore U.S. foreign policy superiority in the continuing conflict with the Soviet Union.

Conservative opposition to detente and SALT II was not confined to the Republican party. Senator Jackson vigorously opposed detente and SALT II during the 1970s and called for MX deployment at the earliest possible date. The nonpartisan conservative Committee on the Present Danger, composed of many former national security decision-makers from previous Democratic administrations, vigorously criticized detente and SALT II, and promoted MX.

On the other hand, liberal opinion in the United States saw MX as symbolic of business as usual in U.S. foreign policy. The United States was continuing to manage Soviet power in world affairs through a reliance on bigger, ever more destructive nuclear weapons. The liberals saw the United States and the Soviet Union paralyzed in a state of constant conflict because of the threatening *U.S.* military presence that emphasized nuclear weapons. MX, and the probable increase in Soviet nuclear weapons that MX would occasion, were dangerous not only to Soviet-U.S. relations, but to the future of the human species in general. Someone had to take the first step in breaking the endless spiral in nuclear armaments. The abandonment of a dangerously provocative weapon such as MX with its preemptive characteristics would be such a first step.[2]

Thus, the general foreign policy implications of MX were significant factors in the conflict over the new missile that developed in the 1970s and continued during the Reagan administration in the early 1980s. The importance of this debate and the symbolic role of MX in the conflict drew large numbers of previously inactive individuals and groups into the procurement decision-making process, even during the inner layer of activity. The foreign policy debate was intimately linked to strategic arguments about MX and the more specific foreign policy considerations such as SALT negotiations and the deployment of a modern generation of theater nuclear weapons in Western Europe.

The SALT Regime and MX

From the late 1960s through 1983, the SALT regime affected, and was in turn influenced by, two issues surrounding MX. During the negotiations between 1969 and May 1972, which culminated in the Anti-Ballistic Missile (ABM) Treaty of SALT I, the basing mode research for MX was shaped by the assumption that the United States would deploy an ABM to protect its ICBMs. However, the ABM Treaty terminated consideration of that approach, and the Pentagon was forced to explore other alternatives featuring mobility and/or deception,[3] until the Reagan administration.

Unfortunately, mobile-basing modes were also contrary to the spirit of SALT I and the tenor of the Nixon administration's initial interests in SALT II. Independent means of national verification were the heart of SALT I and crucial to the success of SALT II. Fixed missile silos easily photographed by adversary satellites made possible independent means of national verification; missiles moved to prevent location by the adversary would prevent verification and thus were contrary to the projected requirements of SALT II and were opposed by the United States. Eventually, the invulnerability requirements for the new ICBM led the United States to alter its opposition to mobile-basing of ICBMs with the caveat that the system be verifiable by independent national means. However, the Ford administration could not settle on a basing mode that offered that opportunity. It was left to the Carter administration to develop a basing mode that would be compatible and verifiable under SALT II. Moreover, SALT II became the constraint on Soviet arms that enhanced the survivability of the mobile-deceptive basing scheme chosen by the Carter administration.

A second problem that the Carter administration encountered as it pursued MX and SALT II focused on its commitment to deploy MX. As will be discussed in the next section, the Carter administration decided to deploy cruise and Pershing II missiles in Western Europe to offset allied fears of parity produced by SALT I and II in conjunction with Soviet deployment of its intermediate missile — the SS-20. NATO has always been dependent on the U.S. nuclear umbrella. As opposition grew in the Great Basin of the United States to deployment of MX, and allied itself with other interests opposed to MX, West European governments, especially West Germany, also facing growing opposition to the deployment of Pershing and cruise missiles, closely watched events in the United States. It was difficult for Washington to argue that its West European allies should ignore public opposition if the Carter administration succumbed to it on MX. The problem became far more severe during the Reagan administration.

The Reagan administration, at least at first, was not as concerned about the compatibility between strategic arms limitation (now named START) and MX as had been the previous three administrations. Even so, the new administration came slowly to perceive that the unratified SALT II Treaty provided advantages in limiting Soviet nuclear arms. As the antinuclear fervor grew in the United States in 1981 through 1983, the administration increasingly, if reluctantly, shaped its MX decision making with an eye towards START. The endorsement by President Reagan of the recommendations issued by the Scowcroft Commission in April 1983 symbolized the administration's commitment to strategic arms limitation, albeit shaky, and thus linked MX and START.

Nixon-Ford SALT Objectives and the MX Basing-Mode Question

Between the late 1960s and 1973, the air force, DDR&E, and the design labs of the missile contractors explored missile alternatives to replace the Minuteman series and a basing mode that would continue to provide a second-strike capability even in the face of the probable massive increase in

Soviet ICBM warheads in the near future. However, with the commitment of the Nixon administration to active defense of U.S. ICBMs in 1969, the air force, DDR&E, and the design labs took for granted that hardened ICBM silos defended by ABMs would be the MX deployment mode. As a consequence, between the late 1960s and 1971, little thought was directed toward alternatives to silos and active defense or what had become known as hard-site ABM technology (Edwards, 1982:62-67).[4]

The dependence on the army's ABM was rudely ruptured by the signing of the ABM Treaty of SALT I, limiting deployments in both the Soviet Union and the United States to two sites with 100 missiles each. A year later the United States and the Soviet Union agreed to reduce the sites to one each with 100 missiles. Since MX in hardened silos could be overwhelmed by hundreds of Soviet warheads, effective active defense of the new ICBM was no longer possible under SALT I constraints.

Two factors forced analysts to continue to search for alternative basing modes to that of ABM: the probable increase of Soviet warheads as Moscow MIRVed its ICBMs, and the increasing accuracy of the reentry vehicles of those warheads. As discussed in the previous chapter, these alternatives centered on combinations of deception and mobility to offset the expanding Soviet potential for preemptive strikes. However, while SALT I virtually eliminated ABMs as an alternative, the U.S. position in SALT I and initially in SALT II was opposed to the deployment of basing systems that relied on mobility to overcome trends toward silo vulnerability.

Henry Kissinger, national security advisor to the president, and later secretary of state, was a staunch opponent of mobile ICBM basing modes (Edwards, 1982:73). He and arms controllers inside and outside the executive branch feared that the deployment of mobile ICBMs would vitiate the U.S. capability to verify through independent national means the elements of SALT I and a future SALT II Treaty. After all, if the Soviet Union or the United States could move the missiles around discretely, the other side would be less likely to know how many missiles the adversary actually had. The result of such ambiguity would be to undermine the fundamental assumption of the SALT process, independent means of verification, and to increase the pressures on the military to produce more missiles under the assumption that the other side had cheated and deployed more missiles than allowed under the terms of the treaty.

On the other hand, hardened silos without effective active defense were believed by both arms controllers and hawks to be future sitting ducks for a preemptive, counterforce strike by the adversary. The combination of fixed silos and virtually uncontrolled improvements in accuracy, expanded target coverage, and larger warheads made prelaunch vulnerability unavoidable. Those developments were inevitable given that the SALT I agreement restrained active defense, but left modernization of missiles virtually without controls. As a consequence, many urged the United States to relax its position against mobile ICBMs. Some in the Pentagon such as Defense Secretary James Schlesinger sought a less vulnerable deterrent. Others in the Senate were concerned about the destabilizing implications of the growing vulnerability in U.S. ICBMs (Edwards, 1982:73-76).

Thus, the MX debate between 1973 and 1974 about MX was critically influenced by U.S. SALT II objectives. The Ford administration settled the dispute at Vladivostok when it accepted the deployment of ICBMs in some type of mobile-deceptive basing scheme (Stockton, 1982:230-33). The chore was to discover a mobile-basing scheme that would be compatible with SALT.

Carter's SALT II Policy and the Basing Mode Question

Since one of the primary foreign policy objectives of the Carter administration was to limit the Soviet-U.S. strategic arms race, the successful culmination of the SALT II negotiations was of enormous significance to the principal national security decision-makers such as the president, national security advisor, secretary of state, secretary of defense, director of CIA, and director of ACDA. As a result, MX also had to fit the interests of the Carter administration's arms limitation objectives.

The administration first determined to utilize MX as a bargaining chip with the Soviet Union (Stockton, 1982:233-35).[5] In March 1977 Secretary of State Cyrus Vance visited Moscow to offer the Soviets an implicit trade of deep cuts in the number of Soviet heavy missiles (from 300 to 150 SS-18s) in return for the forfeiture of the U.S. MX program. The proposal was motivated by the belief that significant restraints on the further modernization of Soviet ICBMs would eliminate the projected U.S. ICBM vulnerability problem. However, the Soviets rejected the offer.

As momentum grew in the fall of 1977 and the summer of 1978 within the executive branch, some congressional groups, and forces outside government to acquire and deploy the MX, the missile became intertwined with the SALT issue in other ways. A fundamental calculation in all the studies about MX during this period was that of the presidential stipulation to have the basing mode verifiable by independent Soviet means. The Carter administration remained committed to achieving a SALT II agreement even if it deployed a mobile MX (Edwards, 1982:137-52).

Another consideration was the utility of SALT II in closing off any open-ended problems that might confront a mobile-deceptive basing mode. As discussed in the previous chapter, the SALT II agreement ultimately negotiated by the Carter administration in June 1979 placed a series of limitations on launchers and numbers of warheads, which left the Soviets with between 7,000 and 8,000 warheads. That figure, regardless of the improved accuracy of Soviet RVs, was not a first-strike threat to the U.S. MX MPS system of 4,600 shelters. Those shelters required minimally 9,200 warheads for a successful Soviet strike. The administration, then, saw the SALT II agreement as a way to resolve the problem of deploying MX in a MPS mode.

There were important critics of Carter's decision to structure MX basing mode decisions in conformity with the strictures of the SALT II negotiations. Individuals such as Senator Jake Garn (R-Utah) argued that a vertical shelter MAP basing mode offered greater actual survivability than Carter's MX MPS alternative. To these critics the survivability of the MX in the MPS mode was compromised by conforming to the requirements of the SALT II Treaty. There was also the belief among hawks that Carter had only agreed to deploy MX to engender support in the Senate for the SALT II Treaty then under consideration. Hawks such as Garn harbored a deep suspicion about the depth of Carter's commitment to a new generation of ICBMs as well as an intense opposition to the thrust of Carter's SALT II policy (authors' interviews). The Carter decision to link MX MPS to SALT II only served to reinforce the distrust of the Carter MX decision.

Reagan's START Policy and MX Basing Mode Question

President Reagan was greatly influenced by the conservatives' concern over linking MX to SALT II. As discussed previously, Reagan and his principal advisors firmly believed that the previous Soviet-U.S. strategic arms limitation negotiations had "achieved" strategic inferiority for the United States. The slowed pace of U.S. strategic weapon procurement in the 1970s left the United States without any bargaining leverage in the SALT negotiations. Thus, the United States was always negotiating from a position of weakness (authors' interviews).

According to the Reagan administration, in order for "real" arms limitation and reduction to be achieved in these negotiations, the United States had to rapidly modernize its strategic forces. After several years of such modernization, with an especial emphasis on "quick fixes," such as "off-the-shelf" technology like the B-1 bomber, the United States would be in a better position to bargain with the Soviet Union. If the Soviets remained aloof, then the United States could outdistance the Soviets in an all-out arms race. In this context, MX was not a bargaining option as it had been initially during the Carter administration. MX was the key to strategic modernization, and then maybe bargaining.

Nor was MX to be constrained by an arms limitation treaty. To Reagan and his Defense Secretary Casper Weinberger, vital national security

89

decisions about procurement were not to be produced as outcomes of bilateral Soviet-U.S. negotiations, but rather were to be the product of rational calculation of U.S. national security needs. The combination of strategic doubts, partially a function of the suspicions harbored about the linkage of MPS to SALT II (i.e., the belief that MX would be negotiated away in the next round of SALT negotiations after the conservatives had given critical support in the Senate for passage of SALT II), and western political opposition to MX MPS, led Reagan in early 1981 to reject the Carter MPS acquisition decision, as yet unapproved by Congress, and seek instead a basing mode for MX unfettered by arms control interests.

However, the administration's often careless remarks about nuclear war-fighting fueled a growing nuclear freeze movement in the United States in 1982 and 1983, a movement that reestablished a link between MX and the strategic arms limitation negotiations with the Soviet Union, now known as START (strategic arms reduction talks). At one point in an exchange of comments about nuclear war and civil defense, Deputy Under Secretary of Defense for Strategic and Theater Nuclear Force T.K. Jones suggested that one should "dig a hole, cover it with a couple of doors and then throw three feet of dirt on top. . . .It's the dirt that does it. . .if there are enough shovels to go around, everybody's going to make it" (Scheer, 1982:23-24). That comment, and many others like it, revealed a cavalier attitude about nuclear weapons which, when coupled with the intensification of Soviet-U.S. enmity, frightened large numbers of Americans and strongly contributed to the vitality of the nuclear freeze movement.

The nuclear freeze movement forced the administration to take a more assertive, and less leery, posture in the START talks. Reagan pronounced a more flexible U.S. position in the START talks in 1983, implying that the United States was once again serious about arms limitation. In mid-1981 he already had agreed formally to follow the terms of the SALT II agreement until such time as a new strategic arms limitation agreement was negotiated or the United States and the Soviet Union decided to withdraw from the terms of the agreement. The commitment to START and the acceptance of the terms of SALT II reintroduced a linkage between strategic arms limitation and the MX, especially the basing mode and verification issues.

Following the failure of the administration to win definite congressional approval for its first two basing mode proposals, Reagan had appointed a special commission, chaired by retired Air Force General Brent Scowcroft, to make recommendations to him about an MX basing mode and provide a general evaluation of the strategic relationship between the United States and the Soviet Union. The linkage between START and MX was strengthened in 1983 when the Scowcroft Commission recommended to the Reagan administration that efforts to achieve arms control be continued, that the MX should be built and temporarily retrofitted in Minuteman silos as a bargaining chip to induce the Soviets to reduce their number of launchers with MIRV warheads, and that research and development of Midgetman proceed. Reagan, who formally subscribed to the Scowcroft Commission recommendations in April 1983, effectively committed to building the MX as a way to negotiate a reduction in the number of warheads in the Soviet-U.S. inventories (*Report of The President's Commission on Strategic Forces*, 1983).

However, Reagan's formal commitment to the Scowcroft Commission's linkage of MX and START raised opposition within the administration. Those committed to MX as the ultimate basis on which the war-fighting capability of the United States was to rest, characterized the linkage as a betrayal of the administration's stated strategic objectives. Without MX and its many multiple warheads, a durable war-fighting capability was impossible. Nevertheless, these critics in the administration were unable to divorce MX from strategic arms limitation considerations. Once again, SALT was a significant factor in MX decision making, something not predictable by the inner and outer layer of procurement propositions of the bureaucratic politics literature.

Theater Nuclear Weapons and MX

As indicated above, the origins of the linkage of the theater nuclear weapon issue and MX decision making began in December 1979. At that time, West European leaders were expressing concern about the implications of Soviet deployment of a new generation of MIRVed intermediate missiles, the SS-20s, targeted on Western Europe, for strategic parity and deterrence in Central Europe. As early as 1977, Chancellor Helmut Schmidt argued openly that strategic parity between the United States and the Soviet Union made Soviet deployment of the SS-20 dangerous to West European security (Schmidt, 1978:2-10). By 1979 West European countries, including West Germany, were encouraging the United States to deploy a modern set of missiles (the Pershing II and the ground-launched cruise missile — GLCM) in Western Europe to offset the Soviet SS-20s (Kelleher, 1981:152). A not so hidden agenda objective was the use of the deployment of the U.S. missiles in Western Europe to induce Moscow to enter theater nuclear negotiations and bargain a reduction in their SS-20s force in return for a reduced deployment of the Pershing II and the GLCM (authors' interviews).

Thus, MX became linked to the issue of U.S. theater nuclear missiles in Western Europe. From parliamentary debates to public rallies, opposition in Western Europe to deployment of Pershing II and cruise missiles grew

91

swiftly in 1980 and intensified in 1982 and 1983, despite the fact that it had been the West European leadership that had caused the reluctant Carter administration to make the commitment several months earlier. The development of domestic opposition to the U.S. administration's decision to deploy MX MPS in the Great Basin in 1981 was watched closely by political leaders in Western Europe. If Carter waivered on his MX decision in the face of considerable public opposition, U.S. encouragement of West European leaders to accept deployment of the increasingly politically unpopular Pershing II and GLCM would have little credibility.

Carter's difficulties over the linkage of theater nuclear weapons and MX were negligible compared to that of the Reagan administration. The new administration's rejection of the Carter MX MPS acquisition proposal for political reasons was not a sign of strength in Europe. Secretary of State Alexander Haig argued during August and September 1981 that the United States had to deploy the MX in some type of basing mode in the Great Basin if Washington was to be successful in its efforts to maintain the West European commitment to the deployment of modernized U.S. theatre nuclear weapons in Western Europe (authors' interviews). But at the end of 1981, MX was still without a permanent home.

The interim solution adopted by the Reagan administration in October 1981 only increased the credibility problems of the United States with the West European leadership, under growing public pressure to abandon the deployment of U.S. theater nuclear weapons. The administration's proposal to retrofit 50 to 100 MX missiles in superhardened Minuteman and Titan II silos while exploring options for a future permanent basing mode was once again rejected by the Congress, which already had rebuffed that approach in 1976. The administration was forced back to the drawing board to discover a basing mode that was survivable and acceptable in financial, environmental, and political terms. The dense pack alternative proposed in November 1982 did not meet those criteria and was also rejected by the Congress.

Observations

The repudiation of three executive branch proposals for MX acquisition and deployment, one by an incoming administration and two by Congress, in two years left MX in serious trouble by 1983. To many strategic analysts and political figures in the United States the MX question was becoming an issue of national will. If we could not deploy MX, then it was a definite sign to adversaries and allies alike that the United States was not capable of effective leadership. The Reagan administration cast the argument for MX in precisely those terms in 1983 and the recommendations of the Scowcroft

Commission echoed that argument — MX was necessary to demonstrate U.S. resolve in international politics. Much of this question of U.S. resolve rested on the linkage of MX to the West European acceptance of the modern U.S. theater nuclear weapons. Once more, the importance of the linkage of these issues drew executive branch officials outside the air force, and even the Pentagon, e.g., state department officials, into this procurement issue. By 1980 those opposed to MX for strategic and foreign policy reasons were joined by individuals and groups concerned about the disturbing environmental, financial, and social effects of the proposed missile system.

Endnotes

[1]For a discussion of the conservative challenge to detente, see Hoover (forthcoming).

[2]For a discussion of liberal criticism of MX in the context of foreign policy concerns, see Hoover (forthcoming).

[3]The discussion that follows is based on Edwards (1982) and Stockton (1982).

[4]The U.S Air Force made a decision to explore basing mode concepts even before the conclusion of the SALT I Treaty and its virtual abandonment of the ABM option (Stockton, 1982:229-30).

[5]In his first press conference President Carter indicated, "If the Soviets would agree, for instance, to a cessation of the use or deployment of the mobile type missile. . .that would be very important for us to join them in a mutual agreement...but if the Soviets should move toward the development of an intercontinental-type missile that can be moved from one place to another undetected and its location cannot be pinpointed, then that would put a great pressure on us to develop a mobile missile of our own" (Stockton, 1982:235).

CHAPTER 5

MXING IT UP IN THE GREAT BASIN

Domestic considerations have been critically important in the MX policy debate. In fact, to an unprecedented extent, matters unrelated to national defense have influenced key decisions about a major weapon system. Concerns expressed by both citizens and officials about the socioeconomic, cultural, and environmental consequences of MX deployment influenced the decisions to abandon the MAP and MPS basing modes. Similar concerns have influenced decision making within the Reagan administration. For example, both interim silo basing and dense pack reflect efforts by the administration to discourage the public opposition that emerged over mobile basing from again assembling; and to circumvent the more onerous and potentially obstructive provisions of key domestic legislation such as the National Environmental Policy Act of 1969 (NEPA — 42 U.S.C., secs. 4321-4347), and the Federal Land Policy and Management Act of 1976 (FLPMA — 43 U.S.C., secs. 1701-1782) which MX opponents used or proposed to use in the West. The significance of domestic variables and actors in the procurement debate further suggests that the case of MX decision making deviates from the propositions of the bureaucratic politics literature.

The question of how and where to deploy the new generation of ICBMs added a domestic dimension to the MX controversy. But method and location questions also constituted the most important strategic and technical issues requiring resolution. While individuals in the Pentagon and in Congress debated the strategic and foreign policy implications, citizens debated the environmental and cultural implications of the various basing modes and regional sites.

The MX first became politically controversial in part because the development of a basing mode that would address major foreign policy (SALT regime) and strategic (vulnerability) objectives meant a deployment scheme requiring enormous amounts of financial and natural resources and portending massive environmental and social disruption. Once the Reagan administration abandoned the belief that MX had to close the illusive window of vulnerability in 1983, the size of the basing mode required for the missiles shrunk accordingly. However, the public controversy that developed over MPS basing continued after the demise of that scheme, fueled by concerns over Reagan's cavalier attitude towards nuclear war and the escalating nuclear arms race with the Soviets.

In this chapter we explore the domestic issues raised by MX that had the effect of expanding the arenas of conflict and proliferating the number and types of actors involved in the controversy. We also examine the consequences that domestic legislation such as NEPA and FLPMA has had in extending to more people the opportunities to participate in aspects of procurement decisions. The chapter concludes by arguing that MX is distinctive in the large scope of the domestic issues and actors it touched; the large number and types of groups that became involved; the total complex of federal and state statutes brought into play; the varied concerns motivating active involvement in the issue; the number of states actively concerned with the weapon system; and the confidence with which previously apathetic people addressed the issue.[1]

In these ways the conventional wisdom is challenged. The number and variety of groups, individuals, and issues that intruded into MX decision making contradict the assumption implicit in the bureaucratic politics propositions for the inner layer of procurement activities that decision making is limited to narrowly based interests in the Pentagon. Even the propositions for the outer layer of procurement activity do not anticipate the scope and intensity of participation.

From MAP to MPS: An Emerging Coalition

The Ford and Carter administrations' decisions to deploy the MX missiles in a mobile, land-based scheme catapulted the weapons issue out of the defense policy area into domestic politics. Here the weapon system became embroiled in regional concerns over water, land, lifestyles, and porkbarrel considerations.

Ordinarily, local communities and states aggressively compete with each other for the right to house a military base or project in anticipation of the economic advantages that generally accrue. The MX project did stimulate economic enthusiasm among commercial and chamber of commerce groups, labor, and many state and local officials, but most local citizens were opposed or hostile to the system. The antagonists focused on the projected adverse socioeconomic, environmental, and cultural impacts, raised doubts about MX's survivability, noted its perceived complexity, and expressed an understandable aversion to being a potential "sponge" for a Soviet first strike.

By the time the Ford administration formally approved the concept of interim retrofitting in Minuteman silos to be followed by some type of MAP deployment, the air force was already in the process of selecting a suitable deployment area for MX MAP. The South Platte region of Kansas, Nebraska, and Colorado emerged as the preferred area during the Carter administration. However, general and intense opposition at the grassroots and congressional levels defeated that plan (Stockton, 1982:246). From

96

town meetings to the halls of Congress, conservative farmers objected to the proposed appropriation of 5,000 square miles of wheat, corn, and cattle land. The lobbying efforts of the Southwest Nebraska Council of Governments, the American Agricultural Movement, the Rocky Mountain Farmers Union, Women Involved in Farm Economics, and the Wheat Growers Association were persistent. Even attempts by the air force to personally allay the fears of residents in these states failed to deflect the vociferous political opposition that mobilized against MAP. Instead, the air force left the area with promises to key congressional and state officials that MX would not be deployed there (*Congressional Record*, 1979:3926). These promises took on formal significance when Representative Virginia Smith (R-Nebr.) succeeded in getting Congress to endorse an amendment exempting areas with prime agricultural lands from MX consideration (*Congressional Record*, 1979:3926).

Stunned by its defeat, the air force sought to forestall a similar confrontation by conducting a series of "selling trips" to proposed deployment areas in advance of Carter's public decision in June 1979 to proceed with full-scale development of the new ICBMs. The area that now emerged as the military favorite, and the target of the air force's public relations campaign, was the Great Basin region of Nevada and Utah. Of the several criteria used by the air force in selecting deployment areas, Nevada-Utah fulfilled them all (GAO, 1981:26-27). That is, the area was composed of large amounts of vacant public land, was situated more than 200 nautical miles from coastlines, international borders, and other high-value targets, and was, as the air force noted, "geotechnically" appropriate (i.e., the area had enough flat terrain, a sufficiently low water table, not too much bedrock, and a moderate climate). So ideally suited for MPS basing did the military consider the Great Basin that it began focusing MX Draft Environmental Impact Statement III on that region exclusively in advance of a presidential decision endorsing that area and basing mode in September 1979.

At the time, citizens and officials alike in the Great Basin were essentially supportive of MX deployment, although still concerned about its impacts. However, as information about the enormity of the weapon system's impact on the fragile desert region was released, as the air force conducted its studies for DEIS III, the initial popular enthusiasm quickly turned to vitriolic opposition (Holland, 1984).[2] The air force sought to deflect opponents by proposals mitigating the system's repercussions, by promising massive federal assistance, and by appealing to residents' patriotic duties to advance national security.

However, these traditionally conservative residents were skeptical of the federal government and its promises. There was, in fact, evidence about other activities to suggest that the federal government could not be trusted. For example, atmospheric nuclear testing in Utah and Nevada, and accidents at both the Nuclear Test Site in Nevada, and the Chemical Warfare Proving Ground at Dugway, Utah, had left bitter scars among many in the Great Basin. Representatives of the Atomic Energy Commission and the Pentagon had allegedly misrepresented the dangers of the open-air nuclear testing conducted in the Great Basin desert during the 1950s. More recently the federal government had balked at compensating "victims" of that period who claimed that those tests caused widespread cancer a decade later (Hoover, 1982:26). At the time the MX debate was heating up in the Great Basin, over 200 claims by the families of deceased cancer victims had been filed against the government by residents of the area. There was a sense of *déjà vu* as residents once more saw themselves as guinea pigs in a deadly nuclear game.

For this and other reasons, Nevadans and Utahns were unwilling to accept MX MPS. Thus, an unusual coalition of western landowners, environmentalists, arms control advocates, promilitary conservatives, and religious leaders emerged to fight the plan. In fact, by 1981 the only groups to support the system were business and real estate interests in Las Vegas and southwestern Utah (Scoville, 1981:191) and the nationally based defense industry and labor unions.

Nevertheless, the air force had actively lobbied, and experienced considerable initial success in courting, local businesses and Chamber of Commerce groups, military contractors, and even some Utah and Nevada public officials. The theme was national security with the subliminal message of jobs, property, and an expanded tax base. Even after the majority of political leaders in the two states abandoned the MX bandwagon, business and labor groups remained vigorous supporters of the missile' deployment, in some cases even after the Reagan decision to reject MPS basing in 1981. But they were nonetheless a minority of the population.

MX proponents, joined by advocates of a strong defense, were disadvantaged in their struggle to broaden their constituent base by several factors. First, a national lobbying campaign never materialized with the intensity anticipated on the basis of past defense industry and labor movement behavior (authors' interview). Second, few of the high-paying, skilled jobs, which would materialized with MPS basing, were expected to go to native Nevadans and Utahns, given the lack of sufficient training among residents. Third, of the several companies with MX contracts, few were in states cited for deployment: eleven in California, four n Massachusetts, two in Utah, and one each in Maryland, Colorado, Florida, Washington, and Texas (CDI, 1980-81; Aderman, 1979). Moreover, few of these contracts were contingent upon the selection of a specific basing mode. For example, the two defense companies in Utah, Hercules (Salt Lake City) and Thiokol (Brigham City), with important MX contracts, were not affected by either the decision to deploy the MX in Minuteman silos or the dense pack scheme. Thus, few labor and business interests really stood to profit from the deployment of MX in a mobile mode in the Great Basin, accounting for the regionally circumscribed character of the pro-MX MPS movement. Finally, proponents found it difficult to counteract the pervasive fears among residents that the missile system placed their lives in jeopardy.

The overriding concern of opponents was the clear threat that the weapon system posed to a particular way of life. Ranchers were concerned about the loss of prime winter grazing land; Mormons were apprehensive about 50,000 to 100,000 nonbelievers migrating in search of jobs; environmentalists were fearful of the disruptions to the delicate ecosystem in the area; sports enthusiasts were worried about being barred from camping, hiking, and fishing in the Great Basin; and American Indians anticipated with despair the violation of their sacred lands. The very essence of these people's lives would be jeopardized by the placement of "man's largest project" in the Great Basin (Holland, 1984).

In the face of accelerating opposition in Nevada and Utah, the Carter administration once more altered the MX design in an attempt to mitigate public concerns. The administration had already abandoned two of its favored plans under regional/public pressure: deployment of MX in the MAP prototype in Nebraska, Kansas, and Colorado, and basing MX in buried trenches. Now the air force proposed modifications in MPS basing which, they contended, would reduce by 10 to 20 percent demands for land and resources (Medalia, 1980:6-8). This failed, however, to quell the roar of disapproval in the West, a position now shared by residents in New Mexico and Texas following a congressional mandate that the air force study split-basing the system in those two states (P.L. 96-342). Governors Bill Clements and Bruce King of Texas and New Mexico respectively joined the chorus of voices that sang a now-popular refrain: "We support the MX missile program but not in our state."

As will be discussed in Part 3, Reagan's decision to abandon MX MPS was in part a reaction to its unpopularity in the West. In the search for a suitable basing mode for the still homeless missile, the new administration was confronted with the task of finding a scheme that would be acceptable on strategic, foreign policy, and now domestic political grounds. Consequently, the silo basing and closely spaced basing (CSB) schemes of the administration had far more tolerable domestic consequences. Neither would require the enormous withdrawal of lands from public use required

99

by MPS basing. Both would see the missiles deployed on either private land already being used for military purposes, or on military land itself. Neither would require the vast consumption of natural and manmade resources that MPS threatened to do; both would be relatively small ventures in comparison. Neither would displace thousands of residents, disrupt lifestyles, and preempt livelihoods in the ways in which MPS basing could. And, both schemes would generate jobs and stimulate the economies of the communities in the favored areas. Thus, when Congress rejected interim silo basing the first time, and then the dense pack scheme, it did so primarily on strategic and foreign policy grounds. Absent were the regional concerns that previously thwarted the administration's plans. Nonetheless, the administration knew that in any future basing plan, it must be cognizant of the domestic repercussions lest the public be aroused once more. Thus was the administration forced to consider the socioeconomic, cultural, and environmental impacts of any MX plan — issues not normally associated with procurement decisions, according to the bureaucratic politics literature.

The Issues and the Advocates

The Land Issue

> The air force comes in here talking about "empty land." They talk about "sparse populations." Well that's me and my neighbors. This land is not empty, we live here. It's being used, and its being used well. But what really makes me mad is that the federal government, the same people who refuse us permits to make improvements on our own ranches in the name of protecting the environment, now want to rip the whole place up, suck out all the water, destroy the benchlands. . . .I'm going to fight this missile any way I can (a local resident, quoted in Hershman, 1980:10).

The domestic feature of both MAP and MPS basing that incited the greatest amount of regional ire was the tremendous quantity of land required. Under MAP basing an area the size of Connecticut would be withdrawn from public use. MX MPS would rotate 200 missiles among 4,600 shelters in an area encompassing 40,000 square miles. But, only 33 square miles (or 25 square nautical miles) would actually be fenced off from public access. Split-basing the system in Nevada-Utah and New Mexico-Texas would encompass 50,000 square miles, of which only a fraction would actually be formally withdrawn. This latter feat would be made possible by the proposed use of a security system in which only the areas on which shelters and some support facilities lay would be fenced off. This would include the 2.5 acres around each individual shelter, but not the entire 60-square-mile clusters. However, the air force retained the option of switching to an area security system, which, they argued, would be necessary to protect MX MPS if Soviet intelligence grew sophisticated enough to compromise the deception characteristics of the weapon system. The adoption of an area security system would require the withdrawal of as much as 8,000 square miles from public use (Shapiro, 1981).

The decision to use a point rather than an area security system was yet another attempt by the air force to placate western antagonists, but the attempt was futile. The enormity of the construction project alone threatened to radically transform and even permanently degrade the lands in the entire deployment region since actual construction would be dispersed over 15,000 of the 40,000-square-mile area.

As originally conceived, MX MPS would consist of 200 closed-loop roads. Within each loop one MX missile would be rotated by a transporter (TEL) among 23 buried concrete launch sites or shelters each spaced 7,000 feet apart. A rail and road system would link the loops to the missile assembly area, the operating test site and two large operating bases the size of small cities (eight square miles each). Later, the loops were straightened and became grids, but the basic design remained the same (see Figure 3.1). As a result of this design, 10,000 miles of heavy duty roads would crisscross the arid western landscape of the Great Basin, linking the clusters with the support facilities. These support facilities would include maintenance facilities for each cluster, three to six additional support centers housing 200 to 300 people who would be living and working there, and the two operating bases, mentioned above, with a permanent population of close to 20,000 workers and their families.

The consequence of this land utilization would be that thousands of acres of desert vegetation would be destroyed, disrupting a fragile ecosystem which supports plant and wildlife and which provides food for grazing stock. Potential wilderness areas and sacred Indian lands would be made more accessible to car traffic and industrial exploitation by the sophisticated road system that would be built. Air and water pollution would result from the tons of dust and debris that the project would kick up. In short, range and agricultural land would be lost, protected and endangered plant and wildlife would be threatened, and recreational, mining, and scientific activities would be preempted. "This project," asserted Nevada Governor List, "will take our land, condemn our water and confiscate our workforce" (*Salt Lake Tribune*, November 11, 1980). All of this the air force readily admitted in its environmental studies, FEIS II/Milestone II and DEIS III.

Water Issue

Water is the lifeblood of the Great Basin region. With average rainfalls of eight inches, the area is one of the most arid regions in the United States. Eight inches is necessary to support a very delicate ecosystem. But, as a Sierra Club official pointed out: "Water is one of the most critical resources in the preferred deployment area of the Great Basin. In this desert environment wildlife, livestock, agriculture, plant, and human life depend in a very fragile manner upon the limited water available."[3] The MX system would consume 190 billion gallons of water over a twenty-year period during which the project would be constructed and maintained. In DEIS III, the air force concluded that while "surface water sources are totally allocated," enough water could be found through alternative sources to supply the system (USAF, 1980:12). These would include purchasing or leasing water from existing owners, digging wells and using groundwater, tapping into the Colorado River, bringing water from other outside sources, and so on. Such alternative plans were equally vexatious to the people in the deployment areas. Among their concerns were the subsequent lowering of the water table and depletion of shallow aquifers in the areas, the repercussions of a breach of an agreement with Mexico if the Colorado River were used, the consequences from some future drought, price wars among water users, and military preemption of current water users. These were not idle fears. The air force (USAF, 1980:10) had raised some of the same concerns in DEIS III.

> Based on existing information, the annual recharge capability of most valleys in Utah and Nevada is fully appropriated. Should all approved groundwater applications actually be utilized, there would be a lowering of groundwater during construction. This would cause reduced spring-flows, interference with existing wells, reduction of regional groundwater flows and water quality, and even ground subsidence.

On the other hand, there were those who felt that the states would actually benefit from the tests and surveys the air force would conduct in search of water. "The MX will contribute to our knowledge of water availability," stated Dee Hansen, Utah State Water Engineer (*Salt Lake Tribune*, November 27, 1980). The Nevada engineer concurred (e.g., Utah, 1981, Nevada, 1981). Having the state engineers on its side was a tremendous advantage to the air force since those individuals have the authority to decide upon applications for water permits in their respective states.

The People of the Great Basin

In the past the population of the Great Basin region of Nevada and Utah has not manifested an inclination toward political activism. The people

102

there have long supported military activities in their states. However, as the implications of MPS basing emerged, the air force found itself confronted by an expanding coalition determined to fight MX MPS. Although the opposition was slow in mobilizing, once begun, the momentum was unidirectional, and pervasive — fed by concerns for physical, economic, and spiritual self-preservation.

The sheep and cattle ranchers were an important part of the coalition that emerged. The Nevada Cattlemen's Association (quoted in Scoville, 1982:181-82) echoed the sentiments of every rancher in the area when it stated that "our livestock industry cannot live with the construction and operation of the land-based MX. . . .The livestock industry will be destroyed both in the direct construction area and in a wide band of surrounding areas." The ranchers were joined by miners (Utah Mining Association) who were apprehensive about the competition for labor, materials, and equipment that MX construction would precipitate. But their greatest fears were twofold. For one, miners were afraid that for security reasons, they would be denied access to the MX deployment area, and the thirty minerals deposited there. A second concern was that miners would have to terminate operation if the pollution levels generated by the construction of MX exceeded the limits set under the federal pollution laws. In either case, if too much dust was being generated by missile construction, or if national security was threatened, mining operations would suffer accordingly.

Ironically, beryllium, which is abundant in the Great Basin, is one of the most important elements in the production of nuclear weapons. The vast increase in nuclear warheads planned by the Defense Department to meet the needs of MX deployment, as well as those of the B-1, Trident, and cruise missiles translates into an expanded demand for beryllium. The miners' concerns were not addressed by the air force in the draft environmental impact statement. This paradox did not elicit much humor among miners in the area.

The American Indians, living on the sixteen reservations within the 40,000-square-mile deployment area, were concerned about the 313 ancestral and sacred sites in the region. Of particular concern to members of the Shoshone, Pauite, Washoe, and Ute tribes was the impact of construction on the Indian relics and archeological sites that abound in the area. The tribes also feared that their access to the area would be limited because of security reasons, while sacred ancestral sites would be made more accessible to construction and military workers.

Biologists, recreationists, and conservationists joined the coalition because of their distress over the system's impact on certain wildlife and plantlife; particularly the pronghorn antelope, sage grouse, desert tortoise, big horn sheep, Golden and Bald eagles, the endangered Utah prairie dog, and twenty-one endangered plants. Such organizations as the Utah Wilderness Association, National Sierra Club, National Friends of the Earth, and Utah Audobon Society were intent upon preserving one of the last untouched natural environments in the continental United States. Rounding out the coalition were arms control, antinuclear advocates (e.g., National Committee for a Sane Nuclear Policy, Women's League for Peace and Freedom, Center for Defense Information), professional associations (e.g., Federation of American Scientists, Union of Concerned Scientists), and religious groups (e.g., Utah Clergy and Laity Against MX, National Council of Churches, Shared Ministry of Utah), who opposed the missile on moral grounds, but also saw the MX as strategically unnecessary, destabilizing, and technically unsound.

The disparate nature of the anti-MX coalition that evolved precipitated the emergence of several national and regional organizations to coordinate activities. The most active were the Great Basin MX Alliance, Citizens Alert, the MX Information Center, and "NO MX." The regional effort focused exclusively on mobilizing people in a grassroots campaign. The national effort, led by the National Campaign To Stop The MX, continues its task of monitoring and lobbying Congress.[4]

Finally, as the MX controversy has grown to include more states, first with the proposal to split-base MX MPS in New Mexico-Texas, and then with interim silo basing in Wyoming, so has the anti-MX coalition expanded accordingly. In the first case, the Texas Corngrowers Association and Plains Cotton Growers Association were particularly active. The Reagan administration's decision to deploy 100 missiles in existing Minuteman silos reactivated organizations in Wyoming (Tri-State MX Coalition and Wyoming Against MX) and Nebraska (Nebraskans Opposed to MX), originally formed to fight MAP and MPS basing there.

As noted earlier, MX MPS proponents have not been as visible or numerous as opponents. This continues to be the case. The reasons could relate to the different strategies that proponents and opponents of MX in its various basing modes have used. Traditionally, business and defense groups have been more successful when employing such conventional pressure tools as lobbying. Environmental, arms control, and consumer groups, who sometimes find the political system less penetrable, often resort to the media and grassroots organizing in order to gain visibility, and engender widespread public support. Thus, their greater conspicuousness.

Economic Issues

In addition to being the largest construction project, MX MPS was also calculated to be the most expensive weapon system in the history of the United States, a project of colossal fiscal proportions. At the time of

104

Carter's September 1979 announcement, the estimated cost of the project was $33.2 billion (Fiscal Year 1978 dollars). This figure, which continued to expand, included the costs of the development and procurement of the missiles, the deployment of 200 missiles in 4,600 shelters, and the system's operation for twenty years. Absent was the cost of the 2,000 warheads, budgeted through the Department of Energy. Also absent, according to critics, were figures calculating the additional costs of unexpected price escalations and cost overruns, inflation, impact assistance aid, monies to compensate ranchers and land-owners for income losses, and system expansion. The General Accounting Office, for example, testified in 1980 that the system could actually cost as much as $70 or even $100 billion (Scoville, 1982:162).

Currently the defense budget constitutes almost two-thirds of the federal budget subject to change on an annual basis, the rest being entitlements that cannot be altered except by legislative mandate. As fiscal managers have searched for ways to trim the deficit, the MX system has been and continues to be an attractive target, especially since a survivable mode for the system has yet to materialize, undermining the feasibility of such a costly investment. A further consideration, particularly salient during periods of high unemployment, is that MX is not as labor intensive as other nondefense projects such as public housing, mass transit, and urban renewal, which are also presently being underfunded. As one critic (Gold, 1980:3-5) has remarked:

> Every billion dollars that is spent on the MX is a billion dollars not spent on education, or housing, or consumer goods, or business investment in plant, equipment, and research. The employment generated by the MX system should be compared with the employment that could be generated if the same money were to be spent in some alternative fashion.

Many who opposed MX MPS on economic grounds predicated their arguments on a cost-benefit analysis. Although the Pentagon's $32 billion price tag for MX MPS was in itself disconcerting to many people, even more problematic was the fact that for such an investment the system's attributes were uncertain, especially in the absence of SALT II constraints. Without the ratification of that arms control agreement there would be nothing to limit the Soviet Union from acquiring more missiles and warheads capable of destroying the whole U.S. ICBM system. In other words, there was no incentive for the Soviets to not try to overwhelm MX MPS by deploying more warheads. The Pentagon's response was predictable. William J. Perry, defense undersecretary for research and engineering, estimated that without SALT II "we could get our shelters up to 10,000 by the 1989 full operational capability date" (Jacob, 1980:1402). Defense

Secretary Harold Brown told Senator John Stennis (quoted in Medalia, 1980b:7) that in the absence of an arms control agreement, "larger Soviet ICBM forces are possible to envisage. These would require a correspondingly larger MX 'force' (more shelters, and perhaps more deployment areas depending on the nature of the threat) to achieve comparable levels of survivability."

The Congressional Budget Office estimated that the price of survivability could be 23,485 shelters and 450 missiles at a cost of $100.7 billion in Fiscal Year 1980 dollars (Medalia, 1980b:8). However, the probable cost of the expansion of MX shelters and launchers to close off the expanded Soviet threat would create serious problems for MX MPS among fiscal conservatives in the Senate and House. Moreover, there was no guarantee that merely expanding shelters and missiles would be successful in forestalling a concomitant Soviet expansion in warheads. The image of a persistent shelter-warhead competition without financial limits could not be ignored. Finally, expansion of MX MPS would merely increase the costs and the already voracious appetite of the missile system for land and resources, thus making it even more controversial and unattractive.

Although the designs of the basing modes promoted by the Reagan administration have been conspicuously compact, the government has not been able to shake those who persist in opposing the MX as a bottomless pit for the U.S. taxpayer: an expensive but uncertain system. In fact much of the opposition to MX in any mode — silo basing or dense pack — continues to be based on its probable cost for the federal budget.

A related concern was the economic practicality and feasibility of MX construction in Nevada and Utah in light of competing energy and mineral projects with which the massive weapon system would vie for scarce water, resources, and land. The system's consumption of natural and manmade resources would be voracious: 2.7 million tons of cement, 121 billion gallons of water over a twenty-year period, 86.9 million tons of gravel, 22.0 million gallons of petroleum fuels annually, 1.5 million tons of reinforcing steel, and so on (Medalia, 1980b:8-23). In Utah alone construction was underway to build the Intermountain Power Project of four coal-fired electrical generating plants, and the billion dollar water and power Central Utah Project. At the time, several large synthetic fuel plants were also being considered. Moreover, thirty known minerals were found in the area including gold, silver, uranium, barium, beryllium, lead, zinc, tungsten, and potash. The construction of the bunkers for the MX MPS shelters would have required nearly twice the amount of concrete utilized in the construction of Hoover Dam, producing critical shortages at a time when both states were experiencing a construction boom. The construction industry estimated that "the project [would] consume all of the excess

106

production capacity of the entire U.S. cement industry well into the 1980s" (Hoover, 1982:3). In testimony before a House Appropriations Subcommittee, Governor Matheson spoke of the "simultaneous shock of these concurrent projects. . .[on] the tight labor market. . ." (U.S. House of Representatives, 1980a:41).

Social and Cultural Issues

The social and cultural impacts of MX MPS on the small communities of the High Plains and Great Basin were expected to be devastating. The large and rapid influx of new residents would bring a boom to otherwise marginal communities. At the peak of construction, the massive weapon system would attract 100,000 new people into the sparsely populated desert towns of the Great Basin region, doubling or tripling the current populations. It was feared by some and hoped by others that as many as 250,000 new residents could be attracted to Nevada and Utah (Scoville, 1982:183). The federal government sought to emphasize the economic benefits that would accrue from MX deployment; particularly the 130,000 new jobs which would be created. But, the economic boom could also bring the attendant social problems of such growth: crime, drug abuse, delinquency, prostitution, family conflicts, and so on. As Utah's Governor Matheson (quoted in Scoville, 1982:184) noted, "The influx of a very large number of people into a set of relatively undeveloped, sparsely populated, culturally homogeneous rural communities will destroy the chosen way of life as it is now known in those communities — forever."

The sudden influx of in-migrating laborers and dependents in need of basic services would strain the resources and service capacities of existing local and regional governments. During the boom stimulated by MX, state and local governments would be expected to help provide housing, roads, sewage, education, and police and fire protection. Nevada and Utah would be eligible to receive $2.5 million and $1.0 million respectively in community impact-assistance aid, and "608" or capital funds monies. However, the two states would be expected to absorb most of the impact costs. According to one estimate, Utah and Nevada would have faced a $73 million deficit as "the giant weapons system could trigger widespread inflation and a boom and bust economy. . ." (Utah Foundation, 1981). In the aftermath of construction, local communities would be left "bust," or as ghost towns. The end of construction would precipitate a chain reaction of businesses closing, a vast labor force unemployed, and required government services no longer fundable.

These concerns were particularly evident amongst the Mormon faithful whose membership constitutes 80 percent of the population in Nevada and Utah. Eventually the LDS Presidency made opposition to MX MPS church

107

policy when it publicly denounced the project on May 5, 1981. "Our fathers came to the western areas to establish a base from which to carry the gospel of peace to the peoples of the earth. It is ironic, and a denial of that gospel, that in this same general area there should be constructed a mammoth weapon system potentially capable of destroying much of civilization." Among the concerns, the statement pointed to the system's potential for depleting water resources, generating a boom-bust cycle, creating "grave sociological problems," and "even invit[ing] attack." The Church's position was a powerful factor in expanding the coalition of opposition to MX MPS.

A cultural group that would be similarly devastated by such an onslaught was the Indians whose plight in that area can already be measured in broken government promises. One government study concluded that the Indians would experience a double misfortune with MX. First, "Indian land claims and water rights, protected under the Native American Religious Freedom Act, would be compromised." But, second, the Indians would not benefit from the "large number of relatively high-paying jobs," which would be created, without "affirmative action programs. . ." (U.S. House of Representatives, 1981c:8-9).

Reagan's initial decision (October 1981) to deploy MX in existing Minuteman and Titan silos was in part a reaction to the active and growing opposition to MPS basing in the West. "While it is not the determining factor," a White House statement read, "it should be noted that MPS basing has strong environmental opponents who would use every available tactic, and there are many, to delay MX deployment" (*New York Times*, October 3, 1981). What the administration was referring to was the use or threatened use of the statutory provisions of domestic laws such as NEPA, FLPMA, the Endangered Species Act, the Clean Air Act, and so on, which, if used shrewdly, could delay the deployment of a weapon project long enough to jeopardize its strategic feasibility. Neither silo basing nor dense pack were thought to pose these problems. With either plan, no new land would be needed; no lengthy and cumbersome EIS would have to be done; no land management plans would require extensive modifications; no one would be displaced; the impact on the human environment would be minimal in comparison with MPS. For these reasons, the administration speculated, MX would be fairly unobtrusive. And, it has been to regional interests. Thus, the MX controversy has shifted temporarily back to the executive and legislative arenas, where the major considerations are once again foreign policy and strategic ones. But any large-scale land-based defense project could once again raise the same sorts of objections as MX MPS; and, some of the same dilatory tactics that so concerned the administration would presumably still be available.

Domestic Legislation Affecting These Issues

The construction of MX in either the MAP or MPS basing mode would have required the air force to fulfill the requirements of at least thirty-eight different federal laws, in addition to myriad state and local laws, regulations, executive orders, permit procedures, and administrative procedures. Each of these requirements contain potential legal and political obstacles to building MX. According to one Pentagon analyst, "Cutting the red tape that is certain to surround the MX program will make the Alaska pipeline project look like child's play" (*New York Times*, August 18, 1979). Some of the statutes provide for the waiving of legal requirements for defense purposes. However, the sheer number of requirements could easily have provided the grounds for delay through administrative, political, or legal channels, as we shall see. "Even without lawsuits," concludes one government study, "some air force officials fear that full compliance with the intricate network of legal requirements, from an international treaty to county procedures for applying for water rights, could delay MX for years" (Medalia, 1980b:33). This possibility is enhanced by the tight schedule that the air force has imposed on itself for completing the MX project. Further delay could result from the fact that it was and still is impossible to accurately anticipate a complete list of laws, regulations, and executive orders before construction. For example, a previously unknown endangered species or archeological site could be discovered during construction, which could then activate a federal law.

Space does not permit a detailed examination of the hundreds of pertinent provisions that have governed and continue to govern the development, construction, and deployment of MX. Thus we concentrate on those laws that provided the greatest utility in slowing or stopping the deployment of MX MPS. At the federal level those laws include the National Environmental Policy Act (NEPA) and the Federal Land Policy and Management Act (FLPMA). At the state level we examine the status of state-federal water rights. A summary section following the detailed explorations introduces some of the other pertinent laws and regulations.

NEPA

The National Environmental Policy Act requires that an environmental impact statement (EIS) be prepared by the government for any federal project that will have a significant impact on the human environment.[5] Certainly a project that consists of 200 advanced Intercontinental Ballistic Missiles, each weighing about 190,000 pounds and carrying ten MIRV warheads, rotated among 4,600 concrete shelters in a deployment area encompassing thousands of square miles of mostly public land, can be expected to have many significant impacts. The draft copy of an EIS is the official basis upon which the interested public may review and comment on a proposed government project like MX. In fact, any federal enterprise for which the government is required to conduct an EIS cannot be constructed, nor decisions be made which advance its construction, until the public comment and review process is completed. This process offers to antagonists of a government enterprise several options for modifying, delaying, blocking, and even defeating a federal project (Holland, 1984). As Douglas Heady, general counsel for the air force has said, "One of the best mechanisms that arms control groups have [against the MX] is to say the project doesn't comply with NEPA" (quoted in Ricciuti, 1979:166).

First, NEPA insures public access to government information on defense matters for which an EIS is required. The environmental statement is the major vehicle for accomplishing this objective since it must be made available for extra-agency comment and review (40 C.F.R., secs. 1502.2[g], 1502.5, 1500.1[b]). Legally, the EIS must include the following: a comprehensive analysis of the anticipated positive and negative impacts resulting from a proposed government enterprise; all reasonable alternatives to the project; feasible mitigation procedures to counteract the damaging effects of the proposed action; and anticipated state-federal conflicts arising from it (42 U.S.C., sec. 4332.2[c]).

Second, NEPA, since codified, mandates direct public and extra-agency involvement in the defense decision-making process. Several statutory requirements promote intergovernmental cooperation and consultation in the preparation of environmental studies and foster public and administrative review by the Council on Environmental Quality (CEQ) and Environmental Policy Administration of the EIS (42 U.S.C. sec. 4331; CEQ, 1979:579; 40 C.F.R., sec. 1506.2). The act requires that an environmental statement be made available for public review before an actual government decision is made. This is because an EIS is supposed to help guide an agency's decision making. For this reason two impact statements are required: a draft statement (DEIS) and a final statement (FEIS) (42 U.S.C., sec. 1500.7[a]). The government must respond to any public comments received on the draft statement in the final document (42 U.S.C., sec 1503.4).

Third, NEPA permits citizens and their governments to sue the federal agencies to insure that the environmental statements have been correctly prepared (42 U.S.C., sec. 4321; Rosenbaum, 1974; Koshland, 1978; Anderson, 1973; Notes, 1976; Anon., 1977). The several procedural requirements for public participation and intergovernmental consultation and coordination afford numerous opportunities for litigation to delay a federal project.

In short, NEPA has enlarged the number of opportunities available to the public for influencing the decision-making process on defense and MX. Furthermore, these options allow citizens to act without relying upon the advocacy of their elected representatives; and before the implementation stage of the policymaking process. Finally, NEPA facilitates political coalition building by making a larger segment of the pubic aware of project problems as a result of information disclosure.[6]

Of course, the actual utility of NEPA is limited by several factors, the most important being the judicial interpretations of NEPA rendered by the federal courts (Holland, 1984). Significantly, the federal courts have determined that an EIS is primarily an advisory document (*Andrus* v. *Sierra Club*, 442 U.S. 347, 350, 1979). This means that even if citizens are successful in winning a lawsuit, and the court mandates changes in the environmental study under dispute, the agency is not then required to alter its project decisions accordingly. Moreover, no agency can legally be compelled to make policy decisions in line with EIS recommendations (*Calvert Cliffs Coordinating Committee* v. *U.S. Atomic Energy Commission*, 449F. 2d. 1112, D.C. Cir. 1971). In short, an EIS serves only as a decisional guide to federal agencies, but is not binding in any way. The most that plaintiffs can expect is that a federal agency will be influenced to modify a government decision concerning a proposed project after collecting more technical information and advice under court order. However, it is also reasonable to expect that some agencies modify their decisions in part as a reaction to the political pressures they have become aware of as a result of a lawsuit.

A second related limitation is that the courts have decided that what NEPA essentially demands is that agencies comply with the procedural, rather than the substantive, requirements of the act. Here, too, the pattern means that successful court action is essentially confined to "alterations in the administrative procedures for making environmental decisions," rather than alterations in the substance of the decisions (Rosenbaum, 1974:261).

On the other hand the courts may, of course, entertain a legal challenge on substantive grounds where the government's decision is alleged to be arbitrary or capricious. Importantly, the courts have acknowledged that section 4331 does establish a substantive standard: "Whether the final agency decision is consistent with the environmental [protection] goals of the statute" (Notes, 1976:125). Both of these are significant checks on federal agencies.

In *Strycker's Bay Neighborhood Center* v. *Karlen* (100 S. Ct. 497, 1980), the U.S. Supreme Court reaffirmed these two judicial limitations when it noted:

We [in *Vermont Yankee Nuclear Power Corporation* v. *Natural Resources Defense Council*] stated that NEPA, while establishing "significant substantive goals for the nation," imposes on agencies duties that are "essentially procedural." As we stressed in that case, NEPA was designed to assure a full-informed and well-considered decision but not necessarily "a decision that judges of the Court of Appeals or this court would have reached had they been members of the decision making unit of the agency."

In so stating the court also reaffirmed its position of judicial self-restraint enunciated in *Vermont Yankee*.

A final limitation exists in the limited national security exemptions that CEQ regulations allow. Now, EISs on classified projects "may be safeguarded and restricted from public dissemination. . ." (40 C.F.R., sec. 1507.3[c]).

FLPMA and the Engle Act

One of the factors which made the Great Basin region attractive as an area for probable missile deployment is that the lands are almost exclusively owned and managed by the federal government through the Bureau of Land Management (BLM). Thus, the administration reasoned that by deploying MX on public lands, it could avoid additional problems associated with purchasing and/or seizing through eminent domain, private and state lands. The preference for lands in Nevada and Utah introduced jurisdictional conflicts nonetheless, as we have seen. The Federal Land Policy and Management Act of 1976 is what provides state and private interests with legal status in intergovernmental land disputes.

FLPMA becomes activated when federal projects such as MX will consume large tracts of public land, and, therefore, require a new or revised land-use plan: that is, a redefinition of the use, management, and status of the land. In the case of MX MPS, the public land also would have had to be formally withdrawn from the public domain to reserve its exclusive use by the military. This latter process for land withdrawal activates several procedural requirements in FLPMA mandating public participation and state-local-federal consultation and cooperation. But even the preliminary work in anticipation of a reclassification of the land from public to military use necessitates significant involvement by state and local governments and members of the general public.

Although the federal government exercises proprietary power over public lands (U.S. Constitution, Art. IV, sec. 3, cl. 2), there are restrictions on the use of the land which are set forth in a land-use plan officially called a Management Framework Plan (43 U.S.C., sec. 1712 [c]). A management framework plan is legally effective unless it is replaced or modified, until

112

which time the land can only be used for the purposes specified in the plan. Thus, to use the land for other purposes such as the construction and deployment of a major weapon system requires the revision or replacement of the area management framework plan. This then sets in motion the procedural requirements for public and governmental input.

In section 1712(c), Congress gives to the secretary of the interior the power to develop and revise land use plans. But in doing so the secretary must "coordinate" his or her work and consult with local and state governments, consider state and local plans and programs, and offer "meaningful" and "early" opportunities for state and local government personnel to become involved in the land planning process. Additionally, in section 1739(e) Congress directs the interior secretary, in managing or using the public lands, to "establish procedures, including public hearings where appropriate, to give Federal, state and local governments and the public adequate notice and an opportunity to comment upon the formulation of standards and criteria for, and to participate in, the preparation of plans and programs for, and the management of, the public lands."

Additional provisions in FLPMA and in CFR cover preliminary activities on public lands not covered by an existing Management Framework Plan. Activities are considered preliminary unless they actually promote the lands' conversion to a different use. Preliminary activities might include seismic, mineral resources, and environmental studies; and geotechnical, biological, and archaeological surveys, in advance of land withdrawal, and/or in preparation for an EIS. In such cases special authorization from the Department of Interior is required. For private contractors, temporary use permits are adequate to authorize such activities. Federal agencies other than the Department of Interior, however, may use public lands only under rights-of-ways, withdrawals, or cooperative agreements, all issued by the interior secretary (43 U.S.C., sec. 1714; 43 C.F.R., sec. 1761).

Before a defense project could actually be constructed, the land would have to be formally withdrawn from the public domain to "reserve" its use for that project alone and to legally restrict other activities on the land (43 U.S.C., sec. 1714). Actually two federal statutes govern land withdrawals for military purposes. The Engle Act of 1958 (43 U.S.C., sec. 155-57) covers lands for defense facilities such as missile shelters and operating and assembly bases. Under the Engle Act, an act of Congress is required for withdrawals of public land in excess of 5,000 acres. The Engle Act contains no formal requirements for state and public input outside the legislative process.

FLPMA covers the withdrawal of any additional lands indirectly required by a government project, such as those needed to accommodate the residential and commercial needs of the people involved in the construction and operation of a military system. The procedures which FLPMA contains for the withdrawal of ancillary lands further extra-agency involvement (43 U.S.C., sec. 1714). Too, the Department of Interior is required to inform Congress of its efforts to involve and coordinate with state and local governments when a withdrawal request is made. Congress has the option of a veto through enactment of a concurrent resolution by both chambers (43 U.S.C., sec. 1714). Of course, with the Supreme Court's recent decision in *Immigration and Naturalization Service* v. *Chadha* (103 S.Ct. 2764, 1983), declaring the legislative veto unconstitutional, the status of this provision remains in doubt. It should be evident also that the land withdrawal process for a project the size of MX would be so complex and time-consuming that the potential for program delay is great even without the system being politically sensitive.

The requirement that the Department of Interior, like all federal agencies, comply with the environmental mandates of NEPA redoubles the available opportunities for state and citizen involvement in the land-use and management process. The secretary of interior must authorize any activities in conjunction with an EIS conducted on public lands and not covered by the area Management Framework Plan. Again, the secretary may issue temporary use permits, cooperative agreements, and rights-of-ways.

FLPMA also contains provisions for judicial redress. First, formal administrative adjudicatory procedures are required to "assure adequate third party participation, objective administrative review of [land decisions], and expeditious decision making" (43 U.S.C., sec. 1701). The administrative adjudication process consists of a two-step system of appeals of a land decision, terminating with an opinion by the Interior Board of Land Appeals. Under the current mandate of FLPMA for third-party participation, any citizen or state has standing to make an administrative appeal to revoke someone's authorization to use, occupy, or develop the public lands (43 U.S.C., secs. 1701, 1766).

Second, judicial review is authorized for "public land adjudication decisions" (43 U.S.C., sec. 1701); and is an option after a party has exhausted all administrative remedies. However, the federal courts exercise only a quite limited role in the administrative process, since they seek to avoid substituting their judgments for that of an agency. When it occurs, judicial review of an administrative appeal under FLPMA will generally focus on the procedural rather than substantive aspects of the act. For this reason, a state or public interest initiating a suit will more often focus on the failure of a Department of Interior official to comply with any of the numerous procedural requirements in the act; and, seek to delay or even prevent a land-use plan or decision from being implemented.

114

This is not to suggest that FLPMA is devoid of substantive standards. On the contrary there are several provisions on which a court could invalidate a land decision as being arbitrary or capricious. For example, FLPMA commits the government to the retention of public lands in federal ownership unless a contrary decision would serve the national interest (43 U.S.C., sec. 1701). The act also establishes as policy the management of public lands in ways that advance and protect historical, scientific, environmental, recreational, biological, and ecological values, and the nation's domestic resources (43 U.S.C., sec. 1701).

State-Federal Water Rights

MX in MPS basing, given its enormous consumptive need for land and its predicted massive impacts on the human environment, activated two federal laws, which both contain extensive opportunities for public and private involvement in the policymaking process. The weapon's voracious need for water brought into play the status of water rights on public lands. As one author (Haslam, 1978-79:154) has suggested, the states can use "their power to control water rights on public lands as a public land management device." This power can prove decisive in any land use dispute since land is generally useless without access to water, particularly in the arid and semiarid West.

In several states, including Utah and Nevada, all unappropriated water is controlled and allocated by the state through its water engineers. To acquire a legal right to water, a party must submit an application that specifies the proposed use to which the water will be put. The state water engineer has the discretionary power to reject or dismiss an application for water rights or appropriations if the engineer decides that insufficient water is available, that the proposed use does not constitute a "beneficial" one according to state law, or that the proposed use is "contrary to public interest." Any of these criteria can be used to reject an application, even one which the federal government submits. Hearings are held to allow the public to react to and comment on requests for water. The public option enhances the dilatory potential of state water rights as a land management tool; more so because of possible litigation, which can delay the water permit process for up to two years (Holland and Benedict, 1982:39-44).

On the other hand, the reservation doctrine, set down in *Winters* v. *U.S.* (207 U.S. 564, 1980), established that the federal government has the power to reserve the rights to unappropriated water when it withdraws land from the public domain. Later the reservation doctrine was qualified to legitimize federal rights only for the original purpose for which the land was withdrawn (*U.S.* v. *New Mexico*, 438 U.S. 696, 718, 1978). Presumably, then, if the air force was successful in receiving congressional approval for public land withdrawal for MX, this would also reserve the rights to a sufficient amount of unappropriated surface and groundwater in the area to meet the needs of the construction and maintenance of that weapon system. For any additional water, say, for expansion of the system, the air force would be required to comply with state water law (*Cappaert* v. *U.S.*, 426 U.S. 128, 145, 1976), unless Congress were to direct otherwise (*California* v. *U.S.*, 438 U.S. 365, 1978). Nevertheless, Congress may also do the contrary: insert language in a bill that requires a federal agency to comply with state water laws (see National Parks Act of 1976). Moreover, ''when federal agencies acquire privately owned water through purchase or eminent domain, the use of such reserved water is not subject to state laws'' (Holland and Benedict, 1982:41). Finally, in cases involving national defense projects the federal government's privileges in avoiding state water law limitations are great. For example, in *Schamberger* v. *U.S.* (165 Fed. Supp. 603, 604 D. of Nevada, 1958), the federal courts upheld the authority of Congress to delegate to the Department of Defense the power to acquire unappropriated water without having to secure a permit from individual states, in this case Nevada. This is the case despite the fact that the Engle Act of 1958 essentially mandates compliance with state water law on military projects involving land withdrawals.

The status of federal nonreserved water rights is even more uncertain. In *U.S.* v. *New Mexico* (438 U.S. 696, 718, 1978), a majority of the judges said in dicta that a federal agency must comply with state law in acquiring nonreserved water (1978:701-3). Thus, the status of intergovernmental disputes over water rights is contingent upon the nature of the water sought — appropriated/unappropriated, reserved/nonreserved — and what statutory actions Congress takes. The air force itself concluded in Milestone II that ''while water [in the Great Basin] may be physically available, legal impediments may hamper routine acquisition in other than narrowly prescribed applications'' (USAF, FEIS II, 1978:159-60). Not only can a state invoke its right to regulate water supply, but also in the case where the supply has been fully allocated, as in parts of the Great Basin region, individual permit owners could challenge the federal government's right to preempt their use, further tying the project up in litigation.

Other Laws

Hundreds of other federal, state, and local laws and regulations probably would apply to a large-scale, land-based defense project. Table 5.1 lists only the federal laws and regulations that the air force would have been expected to comply with had the MX MPS system not been abandoned. All contain provisions that mandate compliance with certain federal standards and, thus, provide opportunities for administrative, political, or legal

116

Table 5.1

ACTS AND LAWS PERTAINING TO MX

A. *Cultural Resources Protection*
   1. Archaeological and Historical Preservation Act of 1974
   2. National Historic Preservation Act of 1966 (Sec. 106)
   3. Antiquities Act of 1906
   4. Executive Order 11593
B. *Water Quality, Water Resources, Floodplains, Wetlands, Coastal Zone*
   1. Marine Protection, Research and Sanctuaries Act of 1972
   2. Safe Drinking Water Act of 1974
   3. Flood Disaster Protection Act of 1973
   4. Coastal Zone Management Act of 1972
   5. Estuary Protection Act
   6. Executive Order 11988 (Floodplain Management)
   7. Executive Order 11990 (Wetlands)
   8. Federal Water Project Recreation Act (Sec. 6 [a])
   9. Clean Water Act (Sec. 208, 303, 401, 402, 404, 405, 511)
   10. River and Harbor Act of 1899 (Sec. 9, 10)
   11. Wild and Scenic Rivers Act of 1968 (Sec. 7)
   12. Federal Power Act
   13. Water Resources Planning Act of 1965
C. *Wildlife*
   1. Endangered Species Act (Sec. 7)
   2. Fish and Wildlife Coordination Act
   3. Fish and Wildlife Coordination at Small Watershed Projects
D. *Public Lands, Open Space, Recreation*
   Environmental Review and Consultation Requirements for granting easements, rights of way, and use permits on public lands, Indian reservation lands, parks, wilderness areas, etc. Statues involved include:
   1. Federal Land Policy and Management Act
   2. Engle Act
   3. Mineral Leasing Act Amendments of 1973
   Environmental Review and Consultation Requirements for using special purpose lands for non-related purposes. These requirements are found in a number of statutes such as:
   1. Land and Water Conservation Fund Act of 1965 (Sec. 4 [f])
   2. Open Space Lands
   3. Forest and Rangeland Renewable Resources Act

117

E. *Transportation*
1. Department of Transportation Act of 1966 (Sec. 4 f)
2. Federal-Aid Highway Act of 1958
3. Urban Mass Transportation Act of 1964
4. Airport and Airway Development Act of 1970
5. Federal Aviation Act

F. *Air Quality*
1. Clean Air Act

G. *Miscellaneous*
1. Intergovernmental Coordination Act of 1968
2. Demonstration Cities and Metropolitan Development Act of 1966
3. Resource Conservation and Recovery Act of 1976
4. Wilderness Act
5. Noise Pollution and Abatement Act of 1970
6. Noise Control Act of 1972

Source: Medalia, 1980:47.

challenges by extra-agency interests. For example, the Clean Air Act and the Clean Water Act require that the federal government comply with federal, state, and local laws and regulations respecting air and water quality and pollution control. Although both statutes empower the president to exempt from statutory restraints military projects such as weapon systems (42 U.S.C. sec. 118; 33 U.S.C. sec. 313), it is not clear whether support systems not on federally withdrawn land would be covered; nor the extent of federal control. For example, from Utah's perspective the state would have jurisdiction over the dust created by MX construction and would consider each air force base a separate polluting operation under state law.

The Endangered Species Act prohibits the federal government from committing actions that jeopardize the continued existence of threatened or endangered species. Again, while the act contains provisions for national security exemptions, the reach of federal power is unclear in a case where only thirty-three square miles are to be formally withdrawn. Under the Intergovernmental Coordination Act of 1968, a government project would be examined to insure that it was not interfering with "appropriate [federal, state, and local] land uses," the "development and conservation of natural resources [in the area by federal, state, and local governments]," and the "protection of [federal, state, and local] areas of unique beauty, historical and scientific interest" (42 U.S.C. sec. 4231).

Finally, it is not difficult to imagine individual citizens or groups executing suits against the federal government on an array of other grounds

118

not anticipated by the air force. The U.S. Constitution provided the basis for challenges of the MX system on Second and Fifth Amendment grounds (*Farley, et al.* v. *Air Force, et al.*, Civil No. C81-04075, U.S. Dist. Ct., Ut., 1981). And, some Indian tribes have long-standing claims on lands in the MX area. The Western Shoshone Te Moak Ban, for example, have a claim against the Department of Interior that is currently being litigated.

Observations

With the exception of national emergencies, it is essentially impossible for the federal government to avoid the legal, administrative, and political obstacles posed by the numerous federal, state, and local laws, regulations, executive orders, and court decisions that would affect a large-scale, land-based procurement decision. Although several of the laws contain national security exemptions, the sheer number of provisions with no or quite limited exemptions such as NEPA and FLPMA are enough to frustrate an executive agency overseeing the construction of a federal project as the case of MX illustrates. Of course, the onerousness of these provisions is contingent upon the willingness of people to invoke them. Not surprisingly the very conditions that stimulated citizen opposition to the MX MPS missile project in the Great Basin were those that would activate the tools by which antagonists could seek to block, modify, postpone, or defeat the weapon system.

In contrast to Carter's proposed MPS basing for MX, the Reagan administration's alternatives have not provoked the same intensive opposition on socioeconomic and environmental grounds. All three proposals — interim silo basing, dense pack, and Peacekeeper — would be deployed on relatively small plots of mostly private or military lands with socioeconomic, cultural, and environmental impacts deemed manageable by area residents. The exception is Midgetman which, if developed, is expected to be deployed in a mobile-basing mode. On the other hand, a completely new EIS would be required before the construction of any of the proposed MX schemes. Thus, several of the laws and regulations cited above *would* be operative.

Moreover, few of the organizations either formed or mobilized against MX MPS have disbanded. Most of the environmental organizations are supporting those residents in Wyoming and Nebraska who are fighting the deployment of Peacekeeper in their states. Consumer, professional, religious, and arms control groups are still challenging the moral, fiscal, and strategic feasibility of a new generation of ICBMs. Many of these organizations have mobilized to promote the nuclear freeze issue. Despite Reagan's decision to abandon MPS basing, the MX controversy has not disappeared. Rather, it has taken on new form. During its ten-year political life, the MX system has activated more people, groups, governmental units, and legal provisions than any other procurement decision in the history of the United States. The sheer scope of participation and intensity of involvement in the issue challenges the validity of the bureaucratic politics paradigm for at least those weapon programs that share similarities with that of MX.

Finally, the use of the public arena for access to procurement decision making is certainly contrary to the thrust of the propositions of the bureaucratic politics paradigm. The use of this arena was very significant, if not decisive, in MX decision making between 1979 and 1981. Although less visible after October 1981, the public arena's existence was certainly a factor in MX decision making as the Reagan administration sought to avoid its reactivation in future proposed basing systems.

Endnotes

[1] The authors are indebted to Dalmas Nelson for assistance in clarifying these points.

[2] These phenomena are supported by opinion polls taken during this period. For the results of polls conducted by Dan Jones & Associates for the *Deseret News*, and Bardsley & Haslacher for the *Salt Lake Tribune*, see especially, *Deseret News*, 20 March 1981, 19 November 1980, 24 November 1980, 21 April 1980; and *Salt Lake Tribune*, 1 March 1981.

[3] T. Dennis Willigan, Sierra Club, speaking at the DEIS III public hearing, Salt Lake City, 5 May 1981.

[4] The authors are grateful to Stan Holmes for clarifying some of this information. Phone interview, May 22, 1984, Salt Lake City, Utah.

[5] Some of the analysis in this section appears in Holland (1984).

[6] We are indebted to Dalmas Nelson who pointed this out to us.

PART 3
MX DECISION MAKING

This portion of the manuscript evaluates the fourteen propositions of the bureaucratic politics perspective used to explain the inner and outer layer of procurement activities with evidence drawn from the MX case. Chapter six reviews MX decision making from the late 1960s to the Carter administration's decision in August of 1979 to proceed with full-scale engineering development of a new generation of ICBMs. The focus of activities during this period was on the design, research, development and initial testing of the components of the missile. Chapter seven examines MX decisions during the last years of the Carter administration and the first years of the Reagan administration when the arena of conflict shifted to Congress. During this period the national legislature was instrumental in guiding the acquisition and deployment decisions, particularly those concerning an appropriate basing mode, through active use of the legislative authorization and appropriations powers. Chapter eight surveys the activities in the public arena, where citizens were involved in using statutory and legal tools to influence the nature and direction of decision making for the MX. Chapter nine analyzes MX decision making from Reagan's 1981 announcement to abandon Carter's MX MPS decision to the October 1983 congressional appropriations vote to support the purchase of the first MX missiles for retrofitting in Minuteman silos.

CHAPTER 6
FROM THE ORIGINS OF MX TO TWO DECISIONS FOR ACQUISITION

The decision in June 1973 to proceed with full-scale research, development, testing, and engineering of a new generation of ICBMs capped years of wrangling among individuals in the Department of Defense and defense contractors over the characteristics of a new generation of ICBMs to follow the Minuteman. Up until then, the debate over the character and capability of the new ICBM was generally confined almost entirely to this small group of interested individuals and organizations. Hence, the decision making about MX prior to 1973 concerning ideas about the new missile and initial design and research tasks conforms for the most part to the bureaucratic politics literature, i.e., decision making was confined to experts in a narrow portion of the executive arena responsible for the procurement and operation of the weapon system.

Even so, there already existed several discrepancies. The Office of the Secretary of Defense (OSD) was active in resisting counterforce accuracy and warhead yield improvements in missiles for strategic reasons. Significant members of Congress, especially in the Senate, were also opposed to such developments and their opposition contributed to the OSD decisions to kill such improvements in the early 1970s. Therefore, both senior executive branch officials as well as senators, representatives, and their staff members were involved in the very first stages of MX decision making, i.e., the initial research and design of a new missile to replace the Minuteman series.

After June 1973 the combination of the potentially large financial cost of the missile system, strategic questions about the missile's first-strike capability, vexing technical problems associated with MX survivability, and the difficult, yet significant requirement of meshing SALT II with a verifiable basing mode for MX, intensified the involvement of individuals and groups outside the narrow confines of the weapon procurement community and the halls of the Pentagon. These factors enlarged the locus of decision making to include other governmental arenas and greater public visibility.

To summarize, the character of MX decision making from late 1960s through August 1979 during the design, research, development, testing phase and first step in acquisition (i.e., an executive branch decision to request authorization and appropriation for a prototype, but not an affirmation or rejection of that request for authorization-appropriation by Congress — the inner layer and the first step of the outer layer) reflects several of the propositions of the bureaucratic perspective analysts. The origins of MX may be traced to the air force's desire to develop and to deploy a follow-on missile to the Minuteman program of the 1960s and early 1970s. Much of the initial design of the new missile and its basing mode resulted from the interaction of air force doctrines and interests, the requirements of engineering groups within the Defense Department, and the ideas of defense contractors' engineering interests. The Strategic Air Command (SAC), the responsible organization for the proposed new ICBM, had an enormous impact on the character and pace of the development of MX. In addition, decisions involving MX were virtually always incremental as research, development, testing, and engineering began, but they became much less so as this period evolved.

Nevertheless, the MX decision-making experience during this phase of activities also differs significantly in three critical ways from the pattern suggested by the bureaucratic politics propositions. First, strategic considerations as they related to MX were important factors in the decisions made about the new missile, especially the basing mode considerations. Also, the literature suggests that senior officials in the executive branch outside the Pentagon would not normally be instrumental in this phase of MX decision making. On the contrary, they were and strategic factors most often dominated their motivation. Finally, again in contrast to the bureaucratic politics literature, Congress became a crucial arena during the research, development, engineering, testing, and initial acquisition phase of MX activities. Although pork-barreling occurred, strategic questions were cogent considerations in this arena as well.

The Origins of MX

The official beginnings of the MX program came with the establishment of a U.S. Air Force MX Office at Norton Air Force Base in San Bernadino, California, in June 1973. However, the air force and defense contractors had been exploring the concept and technology of an advanced ICBM since the mid-1960s (U.S. Senate, 1974:3321). Thus, the new MX office at Norton integrated a series of existing, but disparate programs on guidance, reentry vehicles, and warheads. Six months later General John Hepfer was placed in charge of the program and the new office that would be known as the Ballistic Missile Office (BMO).[1]

Although an ICBM to replace the Minuteman program did not receive high priority within either the Department of Defense or the U.S Air Force during the 1960s, interested groups and individuals within SAC and the defense industry were quite precise in the specifications they desired in a new ICBM. As analyst Paul Stockton (1982:227) indicates:

124

The absence of a pressing need for a new ICBM [in the 1960s] did not deprive this research [on a new ICBM] of a focus. Since the laboratories working on advanced ICBM technology already had helped develop earlier missiles, they simply concentrated on surpassing the "effectiveness" of their previous designs. Effectiveness in missile guidance systems is generally equated with precision in directing a missile to its target. Therefore, laboratory engineers tried to develop systems that would make a new ICBM far more accurate than existing ones. Similar efforts were made to improve missile propulsion. A crucial measure of effectiveness in propulsion systems is the amount of missile "payload" they can launch. By working on more efficient fuels, better engine designs, and related developments, engineers tried to increase the payload-lifting potential that a new ICBM might have [and thus the number of reentry vehicles and warheads the missile could transport].

The war-fighting interests of the air force reinforced this research focus of the design laboratories of the weapon industry. Both the idea and prodding for a follow-on ICBM to the Minuteman generation fit very closely the ideas suggested in propositions 1 and 2 for the inner layer of procurement in the bureaucratic politics literature.

As indicated in chapter 2, the U. S. Air Force, especially SAC, viewed ICBMs, and thus any potential new missile such as MX, as a weapon system that would allow SAC to improve on its mission objective of destroying Soviet nuclear weapons, in advance of their full use against the United States, in the advent of war. Therefore, SAC sought in the mid-1960s to develop a much larger warhead for a proposed follow-on missile, which could be used to destroy Soviet ICBMs in their hardened silos. The larger missile would carry more warheads with greater yield than the Minuteman III's Mark 12 warhead (120 kt). That warhead development program was called WS 120.[2]

The WS 120 program encountered stiff resistance from OSD, especially Secretary of Defense Robert McNamara. He opposed the new warhead on the grounds that without increased accuracy in ICBMs the larger warhead would still not have the required combination of accuracy and warhead size (kilotonage) to destroy a Soviet missile in a hardened silo. Thus, we would be pursuing a weapon program that would be unlikely to meet its intended mission objectives; and the program would not be worth the anticipated cost of its development.

The secretary eventually persuaded the air force to MIRV its Minuteman missiles as opposed to developing and deploying a new and larger missile. This was a cheaper alternative, but one that still did not have the requisite combination of accuracy and warhead size to pose a serious threat to the Soviet missile systems. However, by the late 1960s, the air force explored the idea of a larger MIRVed missile warhead than that of the Minuteman Mark 12 warhead — the WS 120A program. The larger warhead on a MIRVed missile would, they believed, eventually provide potential countersilo capability for the U.S. ICBM force.

The WS 120A program also encountered stiff resistance elsewhere for several reasons. It was believed by many members of the executive and legislative branches that the development of a counterforce capability for the U.S. ICBM force would be counterproductive. It would cause the Soviets to adopt a launch-on-warning attack posture, i.e., to fire first during a crisis. Thus, rather than deterring a Soviet preemptive attack, the deployment of our hard-target capability would actually provoke preemptive measures by the Soviet Union. Potential opposition in the Congress over these strategic questions led OSD to eventually reject continued funding for the WS 120A program.[3] It is interesting to note that political officials outside the Pentagon and executive branch were disturbing the inner layer of this procurement decision almost from the very beginning; and the strategic issue motivated interests outside the Pentagon and executive branch to attempt to influence the procurement process. This is contrary to propositions 3 and 4 for the inner layer.

In 1971, following the OSD rejection of the WS 120A program in the face of Congress's probable opposition, the air force, persistent to the end, asked for an official Required Operational Capability (ROC) request to begin the development of a new, larger, more accurate MIRVed missile to be the follow-on to the Minuteman program. The target date for the deployment was 1977. In addition, the air force also wanted a land-based deployment mode for the missile that would be invulnerable to the growing Soviet ICBM capability.[4]

The first dimension of the ROC proposal centered on the performance characteristics of a new ICBM. The new ROC sought to integrate existing programs working on advanced ICBMs including research and development on newer, heavier missiles, increased warhead kilotonage, improved accuracy through better navigation devices, and so on (U.S. Senate, 1974:3321-22). Thus, hundreds of disparate decisions during the research and development of advanced ICBM technology were eventually merged as the basis for the MX design. This fits the pattern suggested by proposition 6 for the inner layer.

The key organizational actors affecting design decisions for an advanced ICBM system during this period were SAC and the design laboratories of major defense corporations. As the future proprietor of the new ICBM, SAC wanted and got the performance characteristics that matched its missions objectives. The design laboratories furnished the ideas for how to improve the accuracy and throw-weight characteristics of the new missile

126

in comparison to the previous Minuteman program. Of course this is what one would expect on the basis of propositions 1, 2, 3, and 7 for the inner layer.

The second dimension of the MX ROC focused on the survivability of a new, advanced ICBM given the growing effectiveness of Soviet strategic forces. U.S. Air Force basing studies for ICBM survivability have been a constant phenomenon since the late 1950s. By the mid-1960s industry scientists and engineers were discussing and exploring proposals about a basing mode for an advanced ICBM. One such proposal was a "garage mobility" concept. It was introduced in 1966 by Albert Latter,[5] and became the forerunner of the Multiple Protective Shelter (MPS) mode for MX adopted by President Carter in August 1979. Importantly, the mode combined deception and mobility (Edwards, 1982:101-2), two critical elements for survivability. Consequently, the evolution of ideas for MX basing modes also initially fits propositions 1 and 2 for the inner layer.

As discussed in chapter 3, the deceptive and/or mobile basing mode alternatives received increasingly less attention in the Pentagon during the first part of the Nixon presidency because of its apparent commitment to the deployment of an ABM system by the administration. Thus, active defense of ICBMs, ballistic missile defense (BMD), became the predominate interest of the Defense Department; and funds were authorized and appropriated in Congress, although narrowly, for its deployment.

The Anti-Ballistic Missile Treaty, part of the SALT I agreements, effectively negated the ability of a BMD to protect ICBMs if improvements in Soviet ICBM technology continued; and *vice versa*. On the U.S. side, it was unlikely that 200 interceptors (ABM missiles), the number SALT allowed, could successfully defend 1,000 or more ICBMs from an attack by over 1,000 or more Soviet warheads. As a result, interest in the Department of Defense and the air force returned to deceptive and/or mobile basing schemes (U.S. Senate, 1974:66). Thus, contrary to a key assumption of the propositions for the inner layer, foreign policy issues did have a significant impact on the design activities for MX.

At the time of the formalization of the MX program in 1973, the air force favored air-mobile and covered trench basing mode alternatives. In 1973 the air force was prepared to test the air-mobile concept with a launch from a converted B-52. The Ballistic Missile Office was also exploring the ramifications of a 4,000-mile covered trench that would extend across the Great Basin of Utah and Nevada, and perhaps Arizona and New Mexico as well. Both alternatives encountered considerable problems during the next two years. Of particular concern were questions about the survivability of either approach and in the case of the air-mobile system the significant cost of such an enterprise. In fact, the cost of a 4,000-mile trench would have

127

been far more prohibitive than even the eventual MPS system chosen by the Carter administration.

In summary, prior to the formalization of the MX program in June 1973, the decision making for the advanced U.S. ICBM program, the MX, proceeded incrementally as one would expect given the propositions of the bureaucratic perspective analysts. As the bureaucratic politics paradigm would lead one to expect, at first, the MX was simply a refinement of the Minutemen program. The initial design of the new missile was the product of the interaction of air force doctrine and interests with the ingenuity and resourcefulness of industrial engineering groups within the defense community. The rudimentary design was strongly affected by the organization within the air force most associated with air force doctrine, SAC.

Nevertheless, decisions about the need for and character of a new ICBM were critically influenced during this period by unexpected forces, unexpected at least in the context of the bureaucratic politics literature. First, various research and development programs necessary for a new ICBM were altered or curtailed by decisions of the OSD, decisions that attempted to link weapon procurement with the strategic policy interests of the OSD. In addition, strategic questions about the weapon systems raised in Congress were a deterrent to OSD's pursuit of some of the various disparate missile and warhead programs that preceded MX. Also, decisions about the new ICBM were shaped by larger strategic events such as the SALT I negotiations. Moreover, the formalization of the MX program in 1973 created increased visibility that produced even more striking and significant decision-making departures than the bureaucratic politics framework would lead one to expect.

Decision Making in the Republican Executive Branch Arena (1973-76)

Between 1973 and 1976, the air force and the Department of Defense began research, development, and testing of the MX missile and evaluating various basing schemes for its future home. By 1976 the acquisition and deployment of MX in Minuteman silos as an interim solution was being promoted. During this period, MX decision making entered the engineering phase of procurement and the executive branch made the first request from Congress for authorization and approval of funds for MX deployment. The executive branch arena for MX decision making expanded accordingly. While the OSD became an even more significant factor in the decision making about MX, more importantly, the executive branch arena expanded to include the larger national security community of the White House, the Department of State, and ACDA. Since MX was now linked directly to SALT II, this necessitated a wider review within the executive bureaucracy than previously undertaken, further enlarging the scope of participation. Finally, Congress, especially the Armed Services Committee of the Senate, became an active and important arena during the research, development, testing, and acquisition phase of activities.

The Air Force and DOD Decision Making

Four organizations within DOD, another within the executive branch, and a defense contracting company were the key forces in influencing MX decision making during this period: BMO, SAC, DDR&E, OSD, the National Security Council, and TRW Corporation (the prime contractor during the research and development activities). The BMO possessed the day-to-day responsibility for the design, research, development, and testing of MX and reported to the Air Force Systems Command. The Air Force Systems Command in turn reported to the Air Staff of the air force, which reported to DDR&E. In effect, BMO and DDR&E were the chief commands. Personal contacts between individuals in BMO and DDR&E often led to circumvention of the two intervening offices. SAC, the future proprietor of the weapon, was consulted and considered at every move. TRW, the civilian contractor, managed the actual research and development of the program. DDR&E was instrumental in the major decisions about the character of MX. Defense Secretary James Schlesinger's strategic interest in the MX gave it the needed senior official support to survive if confronted by opposition. The National Security Council was also important for MX especially as MX influenced the SALT negotiations (Edwards, 1982:95-100). This pattern is representative of propositions 1 and 2 for the inner layer.

SAC and other important air force actors, such as BMO and DDR&E, along with the civilian contractor, TRW, sought an ICBM and basing mode that combined the following features: more RVs on a MIRVed ICBM, improved yield to weight (greater kilotonage), improved accuracy, invulnerability in the basing mode, continued reliability in command and control, and continued versatility of targeting, all at the least possible cost. The greatest priority was placed on the performance criteria of the missile. The basing mode was second (Edwards, 1982:95-122).

The appearance of a new generation of Soviet missiles (the SS-16, SS-17, SS-18, and SS-19) in 1974 was used by the air force to justify to OSD, the president, and senior national security officials outside DOD, and the Congress, the need for an advanced ICBM, in particular, MX in a survivable basing mode. A mobile Minuteman III system was of little interest to SAC. Minuteman would not have the advanced missile performance characteristics sought by SAC, i.e., hard-target capability. It is significant that the air force's request for MX in 1971 occurred three years before U.S. intelligence discovered the new generation of Soviet MIRVed ICBMs. Thus, it was actually the advanced countersilo characteristics of MX that were of special interest to the air force, particularly SAC, rather than the mobile-deceptive basing scheme.[6] This behavior is representative of the propositions for the inner layer.

In seeking to develop an ICBM with the desired performance criteria, SAC and BMO concluded that the new missile should be considerably larger than the old Minuteman system. A larger missile could carry more warheads, perhaps as many as ten warheads or more. This required a missile with a diameter of ninety-two inches and a length considerably longer than the Minuteman series. It was no accident that a missile of such size would not fit into a missile firing tube on the proposed Trident submarine program or any other submarine. The missile was to belong solely to SAC. On the other hand, such a missile would just slip into a Minuteman silo partially modified to hold the MX (Edwards, 1982:132). Again, this behavior is representative of proposition 3 for the inner layer.

Increased accuracy of the RVs was essential to meet the SAC and air force interest in greater hard-target potential for MX. Although this objective would be partially achieved with the greater yield and proliferation of warheads, a product of the greater size of the MX, SAC also demanded a missile with improved accuracy. This combination of more warheads with greater accuracy in turn meant expanded target coverage with hard-target capability. This was really what the air force sought (U.S. Senate, 1974:66).

As to the basing mode for MX, although each year between 1973 and 1976 saw a different approach taken by the Department of Defense at budget hearings, BMO continued to explore several alternatives: a MAP system, a trench system, an air-mobile system, and the retrofitting of MX in Minuteman silos as an interim solution. The latter alternative was especially interesting to SAC because it could be achieved quickly. Thus, in 1975 the air force asked Congress to authorize the retrofitting of the MX in Minuteman silos as an interim solution, and OSD and the White House supported that request in the FY 1976 budget. In addition to the expanded hard-target capacity that such an alternative offered, it also guaranteed the production of the missile sought by SAC and the air force, something that became problematical as the laborious search for a secure basing mode continued. The important actors within the air force wanted this capability operational by the late 1970s. Thus, even if a basing system was not found by 1975 that solved the ICBM vulnerability problem, the air force was prepared to retrofit the missile in old Minuteman silos. The strategic

130

implications of the counterforce performance characteristics of MX was the driving force of this request from the air force (Edwards, 1982:95-122).

OSD and Executive Branch Decision Making

Strategic considerations were important to more executive branch individuals and groups than just the air force, OSD, industry groups, and DDR&E. Others outside the Pentagon emerged as supporters of MX for strategic reasons as well. This movement of support for MX was stimulated by two developments in the modernization of Soviet strategic forces that significantly bothered many U.S. strategic analysts. U.S. intelligence concluded in 1974 that the Soviets had made critical strides in reducing the vulnerability of missile targets. This had been achieved by the intensive hardening of potential Soviet target sites such as ICBM silos. A successful destruction of those Soviet targets by U.S. ICBMs necessitated increased hard-target capability. Moreover, Soviet modernization of their strategic forces threatened the survivability of U.S. ICBMs. The combination of these developments stimulated reexamination of U.S. strategic doctrine and weapon systems in light of the rapidly improving character of Soviet strategic technology and Moscow's emphasis on nuclear war-fighting strategies (U.S. Senate, 1974:3321).

At the forefront of this reexamination of U.S. strategic policy in 1973 was the new Secretary of Defense James Schlesinger. Well steeped in the arcane business of strategic analysis from his days at the RAND Corporation, Schlesinger was charged by Nixon with providing greater strategic targeting flexibility during political-military crises, with the desired goal of relinking the utility of military weapons such as nuclear ones with political strategy (Kaplan, 1983:372-84). In addition, Nixon desired other options than mutual suicide or capitulation in the face of early but partial use of strategic nuclear weapons by the Soviet Union (Nixon, 1973:183-84).

The reappraisal of the targeting doctrine was actually begun prior to the conclusion of SALT II and the appointment of Schlesinger. The Office of Systems Analysis began such an in-house study in 1971, which laid the groundwork for the higher level reevaluation begun after Schlesinger's arrival. John Foster, the director of DDR&E, was appointed chair of a special committee to evaluate contemporary targeting doctrine embodied in the SIOP of July 1972. The committee concluded its evaluation by the fall with recommendations for greater flexibility in SIOP. This flexibility required greater hard-target capability along with greater ease of retargeting (Edwards, 1982:68).

Foster's committee recommendations led to an interagency committee study mandated by National Security Study Memorandum 169 (Weapons Employment Policy). The committee felt that input from other agencies such as the Department of State was necessary if strategic policy was to adequately support political objectives. By mid-1973 the committee concluded that a more flexible targeting strategy be adopted to support U.S. national security policy interests. One of the keys to such a policy was the so-called Command Data Buffer System that would allow for retargeting of individual ICBMs by rapidly reprogramming the onboard computer. The second key was the MX. The missile's potential to expand the target list by increased MIRV capability and thus its greater destructive capacity provided a weapon system with the versatility to implement the more demanding targeting strategy. National Security Decision Memorandum 242 on nuclear weapons eventually issued by President Nixon formalized the commitment of the executive branch to the development of this capability to support such a targeting policy (Edwards, 1982:69).

Schlesinger was most instrumental in the formal adoption by the administration of this policy and its commitment to new hardware. In 1973 and 1974, he articulated both within and outside the executive branch the need to adopt a more flexible targeting strategy and construct the necessary hardware to implement the program. Thus, it was not accidental that MX was receiving significant support from the highest levels within the administration at precisely the moment the Department of Defense approved the MX R & D program. OSD's critical advocation overcame the resistance to the development of performance criteria for a new ICBM that had been rejected for the previous several years.

Two other things about Schlesinger's critical intervention in the MX decision are significant. First, Schlesinger's motivation was primarily strategic. In other words, it was not the mission of SAC that led to his intervention in the MX decision, but rather his driving concern for the readjustment of formal U.S. strategic policy and the hardware necessary to produce a capability to support that strategic policy. This is contrary to proposition 3 for the inner layer. Second, Schlesinger was a critical factor in the decision of the executive branch to pursue an MX with hard-target capability. What is surprising is not that the secretary of defense was instrumental, but that he was instrumental so early in the decision-making process. Again, the strategic stakes involved appear to have been the crucial factor in his involvement.

The role of OSD as well as other executive branch actors was also significant in decisions about the basing system between 1973 and 1976. In 1973 and early 1974 two alternative basing schemes were under review by BMO: the trench system and the air-mobile system. To support this research Schlesinger requested $37 million in 1974 to explore basing systems for MX (U.S. Senate, 1974:66). However, technical difficulties as well as soaring cost estimates for the air-mobile system led BMO and then

132

the air force to argue in 1975 within the executive branch for an interim solution of retrofitting MX in Minuteman silos. In January 1975 DOD budget proposals deemphasized the urgency of MX. The Ford administration adopted a wait-and-see attitude on MX in relationship to the apparent breakthrough in SALT II negotiations made at Vladivostok in November 1974. Nevertheless, by summer as the Vladivostok aide memoir proved limited, the air forces's argument again began receiving considerable support both within the Ford bureaucracy as well as among conservatives in the Senate. In fact, several senators asked President Ford to consider an interim deployment of MX in Minuteman silos (authors' interviews). The Ford administration responded to pressures within the executive arena and from Congress by asking Congress for $294 million in the January 1977 budget request to support continued engineering programs for the MX and further research on and development of alternative mobile-deceptive basing modes. The outgoing Secretary of Defense Donald Rumsfeld proposed $1.5 billion in authorization for MX for the FY 1978 budget (Rumsfeld, 1977:126).

Rumsfeld's request for an early IOC resulted from critical decisions with DOD during early 1976. First, the air force presented a series of alternative ICBM packages to the Defense Systems Acquisitions Review Committee (DSARC) in March 1976, alternatives designed to cope with the growing concern about Soviet strategic capability and potential U.S. ICBM vulnerability. Each option addressed two problems — improved hard-target capability and a survivable basing mode. The options ranged from the Pave Pepper Program (increasing the warheads on Minuteman III from three to seven) and the MX missile in one of two sizes (either an eighty-three-inch or a ninety-two-inch ICBM), to basing mode alternatives of superhardening Minuteman silos and various mobile-deceptive basing schemes. The DSARC recommended to the the DDR&E that the larger MX design be readied for final engineering, construction, and deployment and that three basing alternatives for MX be further explored with the possibility of interim deployment of MX in Minuteman silos.

In a recent account of the MX story, John Edwards (1982:132) suggests that the DSARC recommendations were important in two respects. He (1982:132) indicates that first, the recommendation meant that

> even in 1976, the submarine alternative and many land-mobile alternatives had already been rejected because the 92" missile was too big and too heavy to move around, except in specially built vehicles on specially built roads. It would not move quickly. Nor could it ever be deployed in the Trident submarine, since its diameter was greater than that of the Trident firing ports. Effectively, the decision to build it in that size put back work on the D5 submarine launched missile. Another very impor-

133

tant implication of the March 1976 decision was that the Ford administration had gone along with the idea of deploying the missile in fixed silos before the new bases were ready. Since the new bases might never be ready, this was a lurch in the direction of the air force's declared preference for accuracy and firepower first, and invulnerability second.

Malcolm Currie, director of DDR&E, accepted the DSARC's recommendations and forwarded them to Rumsfeld. As indicated, the secretary asked for full development of MX in the lame duck budget presented by Ford to Congress in January 1977.

Thus, Schlesinger's, and later Rumsfeld's, role in supporting MX were critical to the survival of the MX program in 1975 and 1976. They became dominant actors in the MX process for reasons of nuclear strategy. The role of these secretaries was vital in another manner as well. The official position of the U.S. government during SALT I and the first part of SALT II was opposition to mobile-basing of ICBMs. This had been codified in SALT I and remained a negotiating objective of the U.S. team during the first years of SALT II. However, as propositions 1 and 2 for the inner layer suggest the air force was pursuing every tactic to avoid the development of ICBM hardware that might allow the missile to be retrofitted into a navy submarine. The air force was facilitated in the achievement of this objective because its interests converged with the strategic interests of defense secretaries during this period. The navy alternative did not provide the necessary hard-target potential for the damage limitation strategy of interest to Schlesinger, Rumsfeld, and others within the executive branch. Although the success of the air force is predictable if its interests converge with strategic and foreign policy interests in the outer layer of procurement decision making, this convergence of interests took place during the gray area between the inner and outer layers.

SALT II and MX Decision Making

From the late 1960s through 1972, the Department of Defense, concerned about the impending ICBM vulnerability problem, focused primarily on the options of active defense of missile silos by BMD systems. The ABM Treaty with the Soviet Union effectively eliminated that approach as a feasible means to cope with ICBM vulnerability. In addition, the air force had to discover a basing mode soon to prevent the navy's SLBMs from becoming the preferred strategic weapon in the U.S. nuclear arsenal. As a result, the air force developed a renewed interest in basing systems that emphasized mobility-deception. The air force's interest in such basing alternatives clashed sharply with the formal position of the United States in the SALT negotiations with the Soviet Union — opposition to mobile-basing systems (Stockton, 1982:229-30).

The United States opposed mobile-basing systems on the grounds that such schemes would undermine the foundation on which the SALT regime had been constructed — national independent means of verification. ICBMs in silos or in submarines especially designed to carry SLBMs could be verified by satellites; mobile ICBMs presented problems for such identification. After considerable intra-governmental negotiation over this issue, Washington steadfastly refused to compromise in the SALT I deliberations. Although the Nixon administration was unable to gain Soviet agreement on banning mobile ICBMs in SALT I, the United States issued a unilateral declaration of opposition to mobile-basing modes. In the initial SALT II negotiations, begun in the fall of 1972, the United States continued to push for the exclusion of mobile-basing systems.

Nevertheless, with the demise of the possibility for active defense of missile silos by BMD, mobile-deceptive basing schemes were again keenly explored by BMO and DDR&E. Two such modes were of special interest by 1974 — the air-mobile and the trench concepts. Both would have violated the U.S. requirements for independent means of national verification for ICBMs — fixed, immobile firing sites, easily verifiable by satellite monitoring.

Schlesinger and his successor Rumsfeld played important roles in inducing the Ford administration to reverse its position on mobile missiles in the SALT II negotiations and accept the option of a mobile-basing scheme. One analyst of the MX decision suggests that Secretary of State Henry Kissinger attempted to block the approval of MX in a mobile-deceptive basing mode "because he feared the missile would complicate efforts at reaching a SALT II agreement" (Stockton, 1982:233). Schlesinger prevailed over the formidable opposition of the secretary of state. The secretary of defense urged the president to continue to explore MX in a mobile-deceptive basing mode for two reasons: as a bargaining chip and as a hedge against future impending ICBM vulnerability. His arguments proved persuasive, and the Ford administration decided in favor of Schlesinger's position prior to Vladivostok (Stockton, 1982:234).

Rumsfeld pushed even harder for the acceptance of MX in a mobile-deceptive basing mode than did Schlesinger. Rather than seeing it as a possible hedge against ICBM vulnerability or as a bargaining chip in SALT negotiations with the Soviets, he viewed it as a necessary weapon system for U.S. national security vis-a-vis the rapidly improving Soviet missile force. A decision to build and deploy MX required immediate attention. At his urging, the Ford administration announced in 1976 its intention that MX be moved to an engineering development stage with the intention to construct and deploy MX as quickly as possible (Stockton, 1982:232-33).

135

Although the story of how and why the United States changed its position on mobile-basing in 1974 is not yet fully known,[7] it is argued by one important chronicler of the SALT experience that the requirements of the Schlesinger strategic initiatives forced the administration to alter its position on mobile-basing systems in SALT II. At Vladivostok in November 1974, the United States ended its opposition to mobile-basing of ICBMs with one caveat: such a deployment scheme would still have to be verifiable (Wolfe, 1979:176-77). As David Stockton (1982:233) suggests:

> The different positions from which the Ford administration and Air Force viewed the MX did not prevent them from agreeing that the missile was necessary; although the Air Force already had shaped the basic characteristics of Missile X by the time Ford was inaugurated, his defense secretaries soon decided that the weapon met their own conceptions of what was militarily essential [countersilo capability]. Furthermore, while the MX's mobile basing originally conflicted with the U.S. arms control objective of banning mobile ICBMs, that conflict rapidly disappeared — first by developing the MX as a bargaining chip, and then by reversing our SALT negotiating stance when the chip became too valuable to cash in. No countervailing pressures existed within the Ford administration to undermine this support of the weapon.

Strategic rationale and the influence of the Office of the Secretary of Defense were decisive in altering U.S. SALT policy in favor of mobile-deceptive basing for MX. The strategic interests of OSD and the institutional drives of the air force triumphed over the arms control objectives of the Department of State in the MX debate.

The Congressional Arena and MX Decision Making

Contrary to the argument of Huntington and others, the strategic implications of MX became critically significant in the congressional arena during this period (1973-76) and had important effects on MX decision making. Interest in missile accuracy and the damage limitation implications of that accuracy, U.S. ICBM vulnerability, and MX's relationship to the ongoing SALT negotiations were cogent strategic issues in Congress, or at least in the Senate, especially the Senate Committees on Foreign Relations and Armed Services from 1973 to 1976. By 1976 congressional action and debate had slowed the evolution of increased accuracy in ICBMs and had also restricted air force consideration of MX basing mode alternatives to those that seriously grappled with the ICBM vulnerability problem. As a result of the latter directive, Congress told the air force to abandon its immediate plans to retrofit MX in Minuteman silos, something the Reagan administration would twice propose again five years later. In effect, action within the Congress forced the air force to reconsider its basing plans in

136

1976. This action in combination with the need for a MX basing mode compatible with the verification stricture of the SALT regime, led the Department of Defense on a path that eventually produced the MX in a multiple protective shelter mode (MX MPS).

Thus, missile accuracy and the strategic implications of such became important issues in the Senate following Schlesinger's public articulation of the administration's argument for a more flexible targeting strategy.[8] Senator James Buckley (R-N.Y.) was a proponent of increased ICBM accuracy and destruction in the early 1970s. Senate Armed Services Committee members John Stennis (chair, D-Miss.), Henry Jackson (D-Wash. — an active supporter of the new strategic emphasis), and John Tower (R-Tex. — the leading Republican on the committee) were powerful allies of the administration's new strategic policy emphasis. Together, they supported such programs as improved guidance systems (NS-20) and larger, multiple warheads (Mark 12A warhead), for both an improved Minuteman III program and, of course, for the development of MX.

Senate opponents of Schlesinger's new strategic policy were active on several fronts. Within the Foreign Relations Committee, Senators Edmund Muskie (D-Maine), Clifford Case (R-N.J.), and Hubert Humphrey (D-Minn.) opposed Schlesinger's strategic policy shift and the specific programs which would facilitate that policy orientation — improved guidance systems and larger multiple warheads. Senator Edmund Brooke (R-Mass.), operating through the subcommittee on defense for the Senate Appropriations Committee, was a very visible opponent of the new doctrine and especially the accuracy improvement programs. Senators Edward Kennedy (D-Mass.) and Walter Mondale (D-Minn.), although without specific committee assignments in this issue area, were important opponents of both the new doctrine and implementation programs. Muskie's subcommittee on Arms Control of the Senate Foreign Relations Committee, the defense subcommittee of the Appropriations Committee, and the floor of the Senate were the places where the opponents of Schlesinger's doctrine were very active (Platt, 1978:71-97).

The Senate Armed Services Committee was another important place where questions about Schlesinger's doctrine and improved accuracy were aired. With such stalwart proponents of the new doctrine as Stennis, Jackson, and Tower present, it was virtually inevitable that the committee would be supportive of increased hard-target capability and specifically such a capability for the MX. However, Senator Thomas McIntyre (D-N.H.), chair of the subcommittee on research and development of the Armed Services Committee, was a vigorous opponent of the idea of developing an extensive counterforce capability in the MX. He believed, as did many others, that it would lead the Soviet Union to adopt in the short

137

run a launch-under-attack mode in order to safeguard its ICBM force. Such a policy decision would add a hair trigger to the Soviet-U.S. strategic relationship (authors' interview).

The opposition in the Senate to the Pentagon's improved accuracy programs reached its zenith in 1975. McIntyre and his subcommittee staff assistant, Larry Smith, concluded that year that MX in some type of survivable basing mode was necessary for reasons associated with the potential vulnerability of Minuteman in the next several years, but that the counterforce capability of the weapon system had to be limited. They surmised that the tide of opposition against improved accuracy had peaked. Thus, the limitation on counterforce capability had to be achieved in another manner (authors' interview).[9]

McIntyre and Smith believed that a promising alternative for limiting counterforce capability was a constraint on the number of MX missiles deployed and the number of RVs on each MIRVed MX. If the combination of limits on those two indices produced a total number of warheads (the MX warheads plus those of the Minuteman force) that was less or virtually the same as the total number of Soviet ICBMs, it was believed that there would be virtually no incentive to launch a preemptive strike. This in turn would calm Soviet nerves and lead them to avoid adopting a launch-under-attack mode for their strategic system. McIntyre and Smith's intention was to limit MX numbers to 200 with ten warheads each with a corresponding reduction in Minuteman IIIs. Those numbers would mean that MX itself would not threaten the Soviets, i.e., even if the entire U.S. ICBM force were used (MX plus Minuteman) for a preemptive strike, it would probably not destroy the entire Soviet system. It is interesting to note that the numbers eventually adopted for MX during the Carter administration were the 200 missiles and ten warheads recommended by McIntyre and Smith. The Reagan proposals reduced the missile numbers to 100. That number was obviously less of a threat to the Soviet force than the larger one (authors' interview).

Although leery of Schlesinger's new strategic emphasis and the war-fighting potential of MX, McIntyre, Smith and other important senators and staffers also saw the deployment of MX as a means to overcome the impending ICBM vulnerability problem. If a deployment mode for MX could be found which would secure an invulnerability status for U.S. ICBMs in the 1980s and beyond, it would continue the viability of the ICBM, the most versatile, reliable, and controllable dimension of U.S. strategic weapons. Consequently, the air force's proposal in 1976 to retrofit MX in Minuteman silos until a more permanent solution was determined encountered stiff resistance in the Senate. After considerable consensus building within the Armed Services Committee, the Senate, and the House

138

of Representatives, the authorization conference committee decided in favor of the McIntyre position when it stipulated that the air force could not spend money to support research on and development of silo basing for the MX program. The report (U.S. Senate, 1976a:40) concluded that

> the development of an alternate basing mode as opposed to a fixed or silo based mode is the key element in insuring this survivable force. The conferences are in agreement that providing a survivable system should be the only purpose for this effort, that the design of this system should not be constrained for silo basing; that none of this program's funds shall be expended in fixed or silo basing for MX; and that none of the program reduction shall reduce the Department's proposed investigations of mobile deployment.

The actions of the conference committee demonstrated that strategic matters in the congressional arena affected weapon decisions; pork-barreling need not be the only factor. Thus, given able and knowledgeable actors, Congress can affect procurement policy because of strategic concerns — something clearly contrary to both Halperin and Huntington's arguments about the role of Congress in defense policy.

The Carter Executive Arena (1977-79)

The air force's success in securing approval by the Ford administration of the ninety-three-inch MX missile and interim basing in Minuteman silos was not only sidetracked by the Congress, but reversed by the incoming Carter administration. Decisions were made quickly within the new administration which in effect left the future of MX in limbo in 1977 and 1978. The year of decision was 1979. By June of that year, the administration had decided to deploy the experimental missile. By August the administration had chosen the horizontal MPS basing mode. Deployment was to begin in 1983 with completion of the project in 1989. From the air force's perspective, the Carter administration's delay had retarded the MX IOC by nearly three years.

Important members of the Carter administration (beginning with the president) were wary of the Ford administration's 1976 MX decision. Candidate Jimmy Carter expressed early doubts about the new missile during the 1976 presidential campaign and apparently had not changed his mind by the time he assumed office in 1977 (Talbott, 1979:38-41). At best, he saw MX as little more than a bargaining chip in the SALT negotiations, a chip that could be played hopefully before decisions about the procurement of MX would be made (Stockton, 1982:235). In addition to the president, White House officials such as Vice President Walter Mondale, Presidential Science Advisor Frank Press, and Deputy National Security Affairs Assistant David Aaron were skeptical of the air force's plans for MX. However, the possible tradeoff in the SALT II negotiations of the U.S. MX for Soviet heavy missiles was an attractive alternative for all of these individuals.[10]

At the Department of Defense, Secretary Brown, and new director of DDR&E William Perry, were also quite suspicious of both the Ford administration's rationale for the need for MX and the air force's interest in hard-target capability of the new missile. Brown was initially concerned that the construction and deployment of MX would actually encourage the Soviets to preemptively launch their missiles in a crisis situation. The hard-target capability of MX would provide an incentive for the Soviets to either "use'em or lose'em" (Stockton, 1982:234). Perry was reluctant to believe that the air force really needed either the increased hard-target capability of MX or one of the mobile-deceptive basing schemes being considered. He apparently felt that the ICBM vulnerability problem would not become a reality until late in the 1980s (Edwards, 1982:136-38). Thus, it was too early to adopt a basing scheme in light of the unknown technological environment that would characterize that period of time. Despite these fears, both Brown and Perry also were attracted initially to the idea of using MX as a bargaining chip in the SALT II negotiations.

Although many in the Carter administration had serious reservations, there were important senior officials who from the beginning were sympathetic to the rapid construction and deployment of MX. They were Zbigniew Brzezinski, national security advisor, and Seymour Zieberg, Perry's deputy at DDR&E with responsibility for missile systems (Stockton, 1982:237; Edwards, 1982:138-39). They would be important supporters of MX during the thirty months in which the administration slowly changed course and finally decided to construct and deploy MX.

SALT II and MX from 1977 to 1978

Within two months of taking office in 1977, the administration decided to use MX as an inducement to the Soviets to reduce their heavy missiles (SS-9 and SS-18) by half (from 300 to 150). This was a major component of the proposed sweeping reductions embodied in the deep cuts March 1977 proposal presented by the Carter administration to the Soviets in Moscow. This deep cuts package was decided upon by Carter and his senior advisors virtually without the participation of the JCS, the air force, and most senior civil servants within the bureaucracy with special expertise in either arms control negotiations or Soviet politics. Importantly, the president and a small group of advisors without any consultation with interested parties in the military proposed to abandon MX in return for concessions from the Soviet Union (Talbott, 1979:39-67).

Although the Soviets rejected the U.S. deep cuts proposal in March 1977, and, in effect, the trade of a potential U.S. MX program for part of the Soviet heavy missile inventory, senior leaders in the Carter administration still held out the hope that MX could be traded for Soviet concessions somewhere down the line. Until that time, work would have to proceed on MX in order to convince the Soviets that the bargaining chip was credible. In mid-1978 the Soviets promised not to deploy their own mobile missile (the SS-16) if the United States abandoned MX.

The offer was too little and too late. There were several reasons for this. First, the administration had considerable sunk costs in the MX system by 1978. These sunk costs gave the MX weapon system considerable momentum in the bureaucratic process. More importantly, however, were the strategic factors that drove the administration as they had the previous one. It was apparent by the summer of 1978 to Brown and others that the ICBM vulnerability problem was quite real. It could not be solved by reductions in Soviet SS-18 missiles. Rather than being a function of Soviet heavy missiles, the U.S. ICBM vulnerability problem was the result of the combination of Soviet MIRVed launchers and their improved accuracy. To combat that problem, the United States needed a basing scheme which through deception and mobility would provide more than twice the targets than the Soviets had ICBM warheads. In addition, Harold Brown and others in the administration accepted the idea that the new missile, in order to drive the Soviets away from their dependence on large MIRVed ICBMS, needed performance characteristics similar to those suggested by SAC. Thus, key individuals in the Carter administration were for strategic reasons now committed to MX (Stockton, 1982:235).

The Carter Administration's Reevaluation of the MX

The first order of business for the new administration was the evaluation of the Ford administration's previous work on MX. Several studies were begun within the administration to determine the value of the RDT&E undertaken to that date. In the White House, presidential science advisor Frank Press was assigned to direct a study by the Office of Science and Technology. At OSD, Brown assigned a Defense Science Board panel of defense specialists the task of evaluating the air force's plans for MX. The Air Force Systems Command also began its own reevaluation. While the commitment varied among these three different groups, each committee stressed the necessity for a new missile such as MX to replace the aging Minuteman program. All three groups pointed out the critical weaknesses of the trench concept and thus rejected the thrust of the air force's research and development for that basing scheme. The reservations raised by these three different committees reinforced the skepticism of senior Carter offi/

cials and the president himself about the trench concept (Stockton, 1982:237; Edwards, 1982:137-52).

In this climate, old alternatives reemerged and were accompanied by new options raised by the new players. In addition, interest in a smaller missile resurfaced, one which would provide greater maneuverability than that afforded by the ninety-three-inch MX missile design, in a mobile-deceptive basing scheme. In November 1977 the air force and the Department of Defense abandoned the trench concept, but intensified efforts to select a basing system. The basing scheme which received the most interest within the administration after the eclipse of the trench was one recommended by the special Defense Science Board panel — the vertical silo variant of the MAP concept (U.S. Senate, 1979:3478-80 and U.S. House of Representatives, 1978:892-907).

In the fall of 1977, U.S. intelligence identified significant improvements in Soviet missile accuracy, especially that of the SS-19 (Talbott, 1979:99-102). This information offered cogent evidence for the proponents of MX. They argued persuasively in the administration that the improved Soviet accuracy accelerated the ICBM vulnerability problem for the United States. Even for skeptics like Perry, the evidence suggested that the vulnerability problem was a very real threat at that time and not a decade away; and, that MX provided the potential means to cope with the growing Soviet strategic capability and the menacing war-fighting doctrine ascribed to the Soviets by many U.S. analysts. With the growing acceptance of the need for the missile, the emphasis was now on finding an invulnerable basing mode (Edwards, 1980:143-44).

The Missile Ballistic Office now turned its attention to the vertical shelter MAP mode. After several months of review at Norton Air Force Base, the air force presented the vertical shelter MAP mode to an April DSARC meeting (Edwards, 1982:153). However, two problems plagued the basing alternative. First, it would take twenty-four hours to move the missile in the event its position in one of the missile silos was compromised. With this length of time, the MXs, if compromised, would be sitting ducks for a Soviet preemptive missile attack. Second, silos had been categorized as launchers in the SALT negotiations and agreements. According to the counting rules of SALT, every MAP silo would have to be counted as a launcher, whether a missile was stationed in that launcher or not. The vast number of vertical silos considered in this basing mode (4,500) simply would be unacceptable if the counting rules of SALT were continued. Thus, this approach could undermine the entire SALT regime. As a result of these problems, the administration continued to explore basing mode alternatives throughout 1978, although the vertical silo MAP mode was still the front-runner.

These decisions about MX were not made in a vacuum. As indicated in chapter 2, the strategic policy of the Carter administration was evolving during this period. Carter, pushed and prodded by Brown's changing views about strategic policy and the hawkish Brzezinski, adopted in summer 1980 Presidential Directive 59: a strategic orientation that expanded on Schlesinger's emphasis. As Desmond Ball (1981:229) suggests:

On August 24, 1977, President Carter issued PD-18, entitled U.S. National Strategy, which explicitly reaffirmed the continued use of NSDM 242 and NUWEP [the National Security Council directive and the Defense Department Nuclear Weapons Employment Policy of the Nixon-Ford administrations] in "the absence of further guidance for structuring the U.S. strategic posture." This further guidance was provided by a Nuclear Targeting Policy Review (NTPR), an interagency study directed by Leon Sloss in the Pentagon. Various supporting studies were undertaken throughout the Defense establishment during 1978, on such subjects as Soviet views on nuclear fears of China, and problems of termination of nuclear war. Phase One of the NTPR was completed in December 1978, and formed the basis of a new Presidential directive drafted in early 1979. Although the NSC staff pressed for the formal acceptance of this draft, there was opposition from the State department and from some elements within the Pentagon, and it was shelved for more than fifteen months — until it was revived just prior to the Democratic Convention, revised and updated, and formally signed by the President on July 25 as PD-59.

During 1978 and 1979, then, when the Carter administration was moving toward further refinement of the strategic initiatives begun by Schlesinger, MX was clearly an integral element of the capability required to support a refined strategic policy orientation (Ball, 1981:227).

A critical event in the evolution of the decision on MX by the Carter administration was an August 1978 meeting at Camp David between Carter and his key advisors concerning MX.[11] According to John Edwards, Secretary Brown argued persuasively at that meeting for MX because of the unexpectedly rapid improvement in Soviet MIRVed ICBM missile accuracy. In addition, other senior officials and President Carter had apparently concluded that the new missile was a critical inducement necessary to build a consensus within the Senate for support of the SALT II Treaty. The treaty negotiations were nearing culmination and an agreement would likely be submitted to Congress in 1979.

At the Camp David meeting Brown supported the deployment of the vertical silo MAP alternative then being explored by BMO. However, two objections were raised concerning that mode. The first focused on the verifiability of the mode; the second centered on the preservation of location uncertainty (PLU). Given the doubts raised about the survivability of this basing mode, and Carter's commitment to a mode that complied with the verification stricture of the SALT regime, the vertical silo MAP scheme was abandoned as unacceptable. Nevertheless, the commitment by the Carter administration to the deployment of MX in a survivable and verifiable basing mode was established at Camp David. A number of senior officials such as Brown and Brzezinski, along with others in the executive and legislative branches, had formed an informal coalition in support of MX. Together, they persuaded President Carter of the wisdom of their views. The remaining questions after the Camp David meeting were the size of the missile, and what mode would offer survivability.

The coalition supporting MX was divided over those questions. On the one hand, there were officials such as Perry, Aaron, and others in the Department of State and the Arms Control and Disarmament Agency who supported the eighty-two-inch MX design. In the Senate, senators such as McIntyre and later John Culver (D-Iowa) and Gary Hart (D-Colo.) were vigorous advocates of this missile (authors' interview). Its smaller size would have allowed it to be effectively utilized for the dash function of the racetrack MPS system (Talbott, 1979:167-76). On the other hand, Brzezinski, Zieberg, Hepfer, and SAC were proponents of the large heavy MX missile. Its ninety-three-inch diameter allowed greater MIRV expansion (beyond 10 RVs) than the eighty-two-inch alternative. If the administration was unsuccessful for one reason or another in negotiating limits on MIRVs through the SALT process, the increased MIRVed potential of the ninety-three-inch option would prove to be a greater threat to the Soviet ICBM field. This, it was hoped would reinforce the incentive for the Soviets to alter their dependence on heavy missiles, and move instead to some type of mobile missile system. This latter group was also fearful that the vulnerability problems confronting the ICBM would ultimately lead to the eighty-two inch-missile being based in the Trident submarines. They knew that the ninty-three-inch MX design was too big to be fitted into the Trident launch tubes.

In December 1978 the air force submitted its evaluation of the alternatives for MX basing to another DSARC meeting. Edwards indicates that the air force "reiterated" its commitment to a ninety-three-inch missile in the vertical silo MAP alternative (Edwards, 1982:169). The proposal was accompanied by the air force's first Environmental Impact Statement for MX, Milestone II (U.S., Air Force, 1978). The five-volume study evaluated three dimensions of the MX system: the flight test program, the technical activities incorporated in the new missile design, and the possible environmental implications of alternative basing modes. The Carter administration committed to the engineering development, construction, and deployment of MX in response to the recommendations of the DSARC, but left for further decision questions about the size of the missile and the deployment mode. The air force was directed to reevaluate an air-mobile basing mode (Ball, 1980:235). A supplemental Milestone II on air-mobile basing was completed and filed by March (U.S. Air Force, 1979). Thus, while the administration remained divided over the size of the missile and the basing mode, it requested supplemental authorization for the full-scale engineering development of MX following the December DSARC meeting (Edwards, 1982:169-70).

In a presidential review committee meeting (the Carter administration's intra-governmental committee established to review national security policy) in May 1979, the Department of Defense submitted five program options for coping with the impending ICBM "crisis."[12] The options were: (1) to go to sea with a new, more accurate SLBM known as the Trident II, or the D-5 SLBM program (this was to be supplemented by deployment of a large number of cruise missiles on B-52s); (2) the MX MPS missile option; (3) the MX land-mobile system of truck launchers on the nation's interstate highway system; (4) an air-mobile system; and (5) an option that accepted the present strategic situation. Edwards (1982:186) indicates that the latter three

> were no longer serious options. They were included partly to enhance the attractiveness of the remaining two options, and partly to build the federal case in the environmental law suits which would certainly be brought against the plan for thousands of shelters in the western states. Under the federal law, the administration would have to demonstrate that it had considered all reasonable alternatives.

Although Admiral Stansfield Turner advocated the SLBM alternative, the others present reached consensus on option two. Nevertheless, division still remained over the proper basing mode for the missile.

In a June NSC meeting,[13] the administration formally decided to deploy MX in a mobile-deceptive basing scheme beginning in 1983. The exact nature of the basing scheme was to be determined in the early fall. This decision was linked both in time and in concept to the administration's initialing of the SALT II Treaty later in that month. Although the decision was opposed by Turner, former opponents such as Vice President Mondale and Secretary of State Vance[14] were apparently supportive given the linkage of MX to SALT II. At this time Carter apparently accepted Brzezinski's argument for a ninety-three-inch missile. This decision to engineer and to deploy MX was linked to the need to build the support of the JCS, the air force, and later members of the Senate for the SALT II Treaty (Edwards, 1982:161-65).

The SALT II Treaty also solidified the numbers game involving silos and shelters for the deployment of MX. The conclusion of negotiations, and the limitation on MIRVed ICBM warheads incorporated in the treaty through the combined restrictions on launcher ceilings and RV warhead limits, closed off the expanded threat problem to a MAP or MPS system of 4,600 shelters or silos. Thus, to the senior officials within the Carter administration MX was necessary to cope with both the U.S. ICBM and SALT II vulnerability problems — the latter "vulnerability" problem being centered in the Senate. In addition, SALT was the necessary ingredient in freezing invulnerability into the future strategic relationship. Finally, to members such as Brown, Brzezinski, Jones, Perry, and Zieberg, MX was a vehicle to drive the Soviets away from their reliance on heavy missiles such as the SS-18s and SS-19s that would be vulnerable to MX (Talbott, 1979:178-81).

Strategic considerations clearly had been crucial factors in the decision for MX by the Carter administration in 1979 as it had been in 1976 for the Ford administration. The air force's interests and the inertia of bureaucratic decision making had been complemented by the strategic interests of both the Carter and Ford administrations. Nevertheless, the pattern of decision making in the executive branch during this period was not incremental; on the contrary it was synoptic. Senior administration officials met and launched new directions for MX policy after deliberate evaluation of political and technical alternatives, and strategic objectives. Finally, the consensus that formed within the Carter administration for MX was supported by interests within Congress, causing that arena to be a critical forum once again.

The Congressional Arena (1977-79)

The locus of interest for MX in the Senate was in the Committee on Armed Services during this period. Senators Jackson, Tower, Barry Goldwater (R-Ariz.), and Jake Garn (R-Utah) advocated the rapid deployment of a big ICBM missile, perhaps even in Minuteman silos as an interim solution. Garn was especially interested in the vertical silo MAP mode as a long-term basing solution. Since he did not believe that a ninety-three-inch missile could be dashed about with ease, Garn's preference was for a vertical silo that offered greater hardening capability than that associated with horizontal shelters (authors' interview). On the other hand, Senator McIntyre was also an advocate of the MX, but for the smaller version deployed in some type of mobile-deceptive basing scheme other than the vertical silo MAP alternative. Senator Culver, who replaced McIntyre on the committee after McIntyre's defeat in 1978, shared McIntyre's general views. Senator Stennis, the chair of the committee, also favored MX, but

146

was reluctant to tie the hands of the administration by legislative mandate for one system or another (authors' interviews).

These senators, although all supportive of MX in a general sense, were in conflict with each other over whether to formally prod the administration to begin engineering on the larger MX missile and deploy immediately, or to seek a smaller version with more potential for effective mobile-deceptive basing schemes. The committee's consideration of the defense authorization bill became the primary occasion for this debate, which occurred in closed door sessions (authors' interview).

One interesting feature of this conflict was the informal cooperation between members of the executive branch supportive of a particular position on MX, and those senators and staffers of the Senate Armed Services Committee who shared their views. Both sets of senators tried to influence debate in the executive branch over MX from their positions on the Armed Services Committee by employing two strategies. For one, they used the public hearings process, and seized upon opportunities for visibility in the Senate, to disseminate information about the MX supportive of their views. Second, like-minded allies in the administration became important sources of information, a useful commodity in legislative debates (authors' interviews).

An important element in the Carter request for authorization to begin engineering and deployment of the ninety-two-inch MX was the belief that such a decision would sway hawks such as Jackson, Tower, Goldwater, and Garn to support the SALT II Treaty. The key was the obvious linkage between the survivability of the MX basing mode and the treaty. Thus, the activities and positions of key actors in the Senate had a crucial impact on the MX decisions and SALT II as Carter and his senior advisors prepared to submit the SALT II Treaty to Congress. Again the concerns were strategic and arms control ones.

During this period, congressional interest in MX was largely confined to the Committees on Armed Services. There was little support of or opposition to MX expressed on the floor of either house prior to 1979 when the administration's decision on MX became more visible. Even then, with certain exceptions, it was another year before MX became an issue of such salience that others were provoked to join the battle and participate in the decision-making process (authors' interviews). During this period, then, the decision-making process did conform to the underlying assumption of the bureaucratic politics approach — namely that the decision process is executive branch based, but with members of Congress influencing Carter's actions at crucial junctures.

Observations

Conceptually, the origins of MX were not the result of deliberate strategic analysis, but rather the product of organizational doctrine, technological opportunities, and changing perceptions of the enemy threat. MX was a result of SAC, DDR&E, and design labs in industry interacting on these issues. It is also clear that the decisions for research, design, development, and testing of MX were the culmination of hundreds of separate yet interrelated actions by individuals in the above groups. Moreover, SAC dominated the early stages of MX development, although that dominance waned as MX's visibility increased between 1973 and 1979. In those later years, deliberate strategic decisions as well as political expediency crucially affected the character of MX and the various basing modes considered for its home. In fact, strategy was as significant as organizational doctrine in shaping the characteristics of MX during this period. The impact of strategic considerations and political expediency were far greater than one would expect given the propositions for the inner layer of the bureaucratic politics literature.

Although MX was considered for acquisition and deployment in the executive branch only after extensive design, testing, research, and development, such was not the case for the various basing modes recommended at one time or another between 1973 and 1979. The most obvious examples of this contention concerning basing modes were the Ford administration's interim decision to retrofit MX in Minuteman silos and the Carter MPS (horizontal shelter) system explored during the summer of 1979 and adopted in September. This latter decision in particular did not reflect incremental choices, but rather was synoptic, and thus contrary to proposition 6 for the inner layer.

Another dimension of MX development that deviates from what the bureaucratic politics literature suggests is the role of senior political officials. Contrary to conventional wisdom, President Carter and to a lesser extent Ford, along with their senior officials, were not only decisive actors in many of the decisions that shaped the character of the missile, but also were especially critical in affecting the basing mode. In fact, the senior officials were often so dominant in the basing mode search that at times the decision process was closer to synoptic than incremental. Because of the synoptic character of decisions about the basing mode, the longer a basing mode was considered had no necessary connection to the alternative ultimately chosen to develop. Nevertheless, there was a cumulative effect for the weapon system in general. Small decisions made about MX in the early years of development did in fact build an inertia for the system

148

especially the diameter of the missile. Consequently, in other ways the MX experience does reflect proposition 6 for the inner layer.

Finally, the congressional arena significantly influenced MX decision making during the development and testing period. The impact was driven by strategic concerns rather than by pork-barreling, something completely contrary to the thrust of the bureaucratic politics literature. The impact of the congressional arena was especially important for the decisions about a basing mode for MX, as the 1976 authorizations debate indicates, but it was also important in the issue of the size of the missile. Of fundamental significance was the role of Senate staffers such as Larry Smith in shaping the debate on MX within committee and among members of the Senate. Thus, congressional importance in the MX decision-making process departed dramatically from the proposition suggested by the bureaucratic politics literature that such decisions are primarily executive branch based. On the contrary, the congressional arena was activated and was a crucial factor in the decision making for MX, especially in 1976. It would become even more important in 1980 following the Carter administration's request for authorization and appropriation of funds for MX MPS.

In sum, the MX decision-making experience during this period provides evidence to support several of the additional propositions suggested at the end of chapter 1. The nature and scope of decision making within both the executive branch and the Congress is supportive of propositions 15, 16, 19, and 20. More specifically, strategic and foreign policy considerations were important factors in MX decision making; the president was more than just another MX decision-maker in the executive branch; and Congress was an extremely important decision-making arena. Consequently, the bureaucratic politics paradigm is not completely helpful in understanding the decision-making process for MX during that period.

Endnotes

[1]BMO's responsibility for MX was begun under a $6 million authorization and appropriation in the Fiscal 1974 Defense Budget. The authorization and appropriation included hardware development and testing of air-mobile and ground-mobile deceptive basing modes (U.S. Senate, 1973:3519).

[2]For an interesting discussion of the origins and development of MIRV and how McNamara used that weapon system to "contain" SAC's interest in more launchers with larger warheads, see Greenwood (1975:1-51).

[3]There were several sources of opposition to that program: OSD, State, ACDA, and a powerful set of legislators in the Senate arena (Edwards, 1982:95-125).

[4]For a discussion of the general evolution of the program eventually labeled MX, see U.S. Senate (1974:3321-22).

[5] Albert Latter and his brother Richard were physicists at RAND corporation during the 1960s and 1970s. He was an influential actor in the deliberations of the mid-1960s over whether or not to MIRV our ICBMs and SLBMs. In addition, he was the intellectual father of the MAP concept for the basing of MX. For a discussion of his role in the MIRV decision, see Kaplan 1983:360-62. For a discussion of his role in the MX basing mode development, see Edwards (1982:50-54, 138-39, 144-46, 152, 161, 203, 248). Finally, for a general discussion of his role in strategic policy and technology from the 1950s through the 1970s, see Parfit (1983:32-41).

[6] For a discussion of this point by Senate Armed Services Committee staff assistant Hyman Fine while questioning General Richard Cross, see U.S. Senate (1974:3335-38).

[7] For an interesting discussion of how the United States altered its position on mobile-basing, see Stockton (1982:233).

[8] For a discussion of this conflict between the Air Force/DOD and senators over increased ICBM accuracy from the perspective of Senator Muskie's legislative assistant, see Platt (1978:71-97).

[9] A similar set of motivations and strategy is ascribed to McIntyre and Smith in Edwards (1982:95-121).

[10] For a discussion of their suspicions, see Edwards, 1982:122-53. Secretary of State Vance, also skeptical of MX, suggests: "At the beginning of August it seemed to me that the outlines of a ratification (bargain) were taking shape. The president approved the MX missile deployment in June, and by August, studies of a mobile basing scheme were far advanced. If Carter would decide to deploy the MX in a mobile basing mode, agree to an increase in the defense budget, and acquiesce in several conditions acceptable to the administration in the Resolution of Ratification, he would satisfy many of the critics" (Vance, 1983:357).

[11] For a discussion of that event, see Edwards (1982:165-69).

[12] See Edwards (1982:186-87) for a discussion of those options.

[13] See Edwards (1982:189-99) for a full discussion of that important June NSC meeting.

[14] See note 10 above.

CHAPTER 7
CONGRESS AND MX

The movement of MX into the acquisition phase of procurement saw the more direct involvement of the congressional arena in the decision-making process. Here, funding decisions on the weapon system became embroiled in concerns over the strategic arms limitation agreement with the Soviet Union, environmental issues, budgetary problems, and the 1980 presidential election. By employing the available resources of the national legislature in an aggressive manner, members of Congress were able to use the institution to direct MX procurement activities in the executive arena.

According to the conventional wisdom, congressional involvement in a weapon decision has been more evident at the acquisition and deployment phase than the R&D stage of procurement. Although even acquisition and deployment have found Congress's role to be characteristically deferential, supportive, and parochial. On the one hand, the case of MX confirms the more active participation of Congress at the second stage of procurement decisions. However, contrary to propositions 4, 5, and 9 of the bureaucratic politics perspective, congressional involvement at the acquisition stage has been distinctive in the widespread participation of a variety of legislators; the varied concerns motivating active legislative involvement; the total complex of committees and subcommittees brought into play; the amount and scope of information generated within and by Congress; and the nature of legislative-executive coalition building.

The case of MX suggests that congressional involvement in procurement decisions will deviate in character and scope from the assumptions of the conventional wisdom in cases where (1) the procurement issue has emerged from a conflictual environment in the executive branch arena; (2) the proposed procurement decision is strategically uncertain or flawed; (3) the proposed weapon decision will have an impact on legislative constituencies which will then require congressional member responses; (4) the institutional resources are available for generating the information and internal chamber interest necessary for reversing the inclination of Congress to defer to the president's prerogative in defense policy; and (5) the procurement issue is capable of inciting enough opposition that coalition building is successful in overcoming the extreme decentralization within the institution. In short, we posit that Congress is more likely to become an active arena for procurement decision making in cases where the executive branch is marred by indecision, the solution the administration advocates is controversial for strategic and political reasons, and members of Congress are motivated and equipped to do battle with the White House and the Pentagon.

Furthermore, we suggest that the degree to which the above conditions are operable affects the role of Congress in both R&D and acquisition and deployment. As illustrated in the previous chapter, members of Congress were significantly involved in R&D for MX between 1975 and 1979. As the discussion in this chapter will illustrate, the congressional arena was even more instrumental in the decision-making process after the decision to enter acquisition and deployment. Although the bureaucratic politics paradigm does anticipate some congressional interest at this latter stage, it does not fully anticipate the scope and nature of legislative involvement in the MX process.

Power and the Willingness to Use It

Money is the lifeblood of government operations. And Congress controls the supply. No missiles can be designed, researched, tested, developed, acquired, and deployed without money. No basing mode — not dense pack, MPS, continuous airborne, or SUM — can become a reality without congressional funding. The potential for a significant legislative role at any stage of procurement is present because of the appropriations power. How effectively Congress uses this tool determines the strength of Congress as an institution capable of providing independent review of executive branch proposals. Four times each year on the floor of the House and Senate, and innumerable other times in committees, subcommittees, conference committees, and hearings, the MX system was debated, analyzed, scrutinized, and modified. Attempts were made to block, change, kill, or endorse the system. The occasions were congressional consideration of the annual defense authorization and appropriations bills.

Conventional wisdom suggests that members of Congress have been negligent in using their power over the purse to direct defense politics, particularly weapon procurement. Congress, it is argued, is handicapped by several institutional, structural, and behavioral factors. Among these are (1) the pervasive decentralization of power in the institution, which obviates against a consensus developing and, thus, weakens Congress's ability to stand as a unified force equivalent to the executive; (2) inferior data-gathering apparatus, which make congressional members more dependent upon the executive branch for both information and direction in making weapon procurement decisions; and (3) the constituent (reelection) orientation of most legislators. In the past, these three factors have operated to advance the disproportionate power of a small group of legislators with key positions (committee or subcommittee assignments), strong motivations (districts advantaged by military contracts, for example), and a deferential and supportive attitude toward the Pentagon ("they know more than we do").

As we saw in the previous chapter, the treatment of the MX missile program in Congress between 1975 and 1979 illustrates that the conventional wisdom of the bureaucratic politics literature (propositions 1, 2, 3, 4, 5, and 9 for the outer layer) is only partially correct. The experience between 1979 and 1981, while not totally discrediting conventional wisdom, further illustrates that the bureaucratic politics perspective is incomplete. First, while decentralization of power in Congress continues to make consensus building difficult, it also provides numerous opportunities for dilatory tactics to be employed to postpone decision making. A score of legislators including Senator Mark Hatfield (R-Ore.) and Representative Paul Simon (D-Ill.) adopted this ploy. Too, in the case of MX, other ancillary issues emerged that had the effect of mobilizing large groups of legislators in ways that fused positions on MX with other issues, providing the basis for coalition building. The intimate relationship between SALT II and MX MPS is such a case. Finally, the newly developed budgetary process provided a regular and comprehensive way of guiding weapon procurement in the midst of power diffusion.

On the other hand, Congress continues to rely upon the executive branch for information in national security affairs. As yet Congress is not equipped to match the technical expertise of personnel in the administration. However, the national legislature now has the means to begin generating a separate, although not necessarily independent, data base from which alternative proposals can be promoted. Thus, the changes which we observe on MX are less in the direction of the independence of Congress, and more in the willingness of Congress to scrutinize what information is available. For example, when Congress empowered the Office of Technology Assessment (OTA) to study alternative basing modes, members were concerned about verifying the validity of the Pentagon's analyses, not with discovering new basing options. Similarly, the General Accounting Office (GAO) was instructed to examine the validity of the studies the air force conducted in preparation for DEIS III; not to prepare a separate study that would duplicate the environmental document. Hearings and staff reports for the committees enhanced members' understanding of the controversial issue. Thus, what is interesting about MX is that members of Congress have been less likely to defer to the credibility of executive branch information. And, by being more involved in generating and scrutinizing data, senators and representatives have made themselves better informed. This, in turn, has enhanced Congress's bargaining position, particularly with the Pentagon.

153

Third, the bulk of defense decision-making power continues to reside with the Armed Services Committees in both chambers. And these committees by and large still maintain a cozy relationship with the Pentagon. But changes in the budgetary process, and in the committee-subcommittee system during the 1970s have expanded the role of other actors in the defense arena. This is evident in the MX experience. House and Senate Budget and Appropriations Committee members have become skeptical of military projects requiring massive expenditures. Members of the public lands and natural resources committees were brought into the MX conflict because of congressional involvement in the public land withdrawal and environmental impact statement processes. Legislators from the states cited for possible MX deployment, many of whom are strategically placed on key committees and subcommittees, have used their positions to monitor the critical R&D stage of weapon procurement.

As we trace the treatment of the MX system during the 96th (i.e., 1979-80) and first session of the 97th (i.e., 1981) Congress, we will observe members at once active and passive, aggressive and deferential, resistant and supportive. Nevertheless, while playing out the whole gamut of reactions, Congress as an institution ultimately was and continues to be instrumental in guiding weapon procurement, and at the same time is one of three arenas, at times the most important one, in which contending coalitions of interests have vied for influence over MX policy. The guidance that resulted from congressional deliberation has had and continues to have important strategic and defense policy implications.

Carter, Congress, and MX MPS

The air force realized MPS basing would be controversial. Several senior Carter administration and congressional members had been reluctant to support MX MPS. Even President Carter had referred to the scheme, at one time, as "the craziest idea I've heard of," but had ultimately endorsed it for foreign policy (SALT II), political, and perhaps even strategic reasons (Stockton, 1982). Thus, in advance of the formal administration request for acquisition and deployment funds, the air force sought to deter a congressional showdown with an accelerated and expanded lobbying campaign. That the military's campaign stretched into the states cited for deployment suggests that the legislator-constituent link was deemed critical by the air force. And so it was. The air force would ultimately encounter resistance from the South Platte Plains states of Nebraska, Colorado, and Kansas, the Great Basin states of Nevada and Utah, and the High Plains states of New Mexico and Texas. It was the intent of the air force to solidify congressional and public support for the weapon program before the

154

probable opposition had an opportunity to act; and to later use this support as a force to counter those in the administration and Congress reluctant to support MPS basing. (For a list of the congressional laws enacted during this period that related to MX see Table 7.1.)

The Pentagon's success in Congress in achieving both objectives was at first decisive. In advance of any formal commitment by the president to MPS basing, Congress, at the behest of its Armed Services Committees, began funding decisions that ultimately encouraged Carter to embrace a mobile, land-based scheme. The first step toward the authorization of MX MPS was taken on May 3, 1979, when the Senate approved (77 to 12) a defense supplemental authorization bill (S.429), which contained a strong presumption in favor of MPS basing. To mollify Defense Secretary Harold Brown and arms control advocates, the supplemental also authorized the $75 million requested to study the air-mobile alternative.

A pro-MX coalition in the House, with important prodding and information from members in the Pentagon, gave Carter a more direct message and erased any doubts about that chamber's position on MX deployment (authors' interviews). First, the House defeated (100 to 291) an amendment attempt by Berkeley Bedell to reverse the legislative bias toward MPS basing in S. 429. Then members deleted the funds for the air-mobile version.[1] As passed out of conference (H. Rept. 96-282), the final bill contained several fairly explicit directives to the Carter administration. All of these elements were the results of compromises forged *in advance* by the air force and a few critical members of Congress, most notably Armed Services Committee members Richard Ichord (D-Mo.) and Melvin Price (D-Ill.), and Representative Virginia Smith (R-Nebr.). The bill (P.L. 96-29) was signed on June 27, 1979, and mandated that the air force proceed "immediately" with "full-scale engineering development" of MX in the MPS mode; expressed the sense of Congress that a land-based ICBM system was "necessary" to national security; and conveyed the opinion that the system be deployed on nonagricultural land. In anticipation of a clash with the administration over vertical versus horizontal launching sites, members of Congress added the qualifier (section 202) that the study of alternative basing modes was neither prohibited nor restricted by the act.

In the administration, forces were also pushing Carter toward the MPS option. National security advisor Zbigniew Brzezinski, with support from Defense Secretary Harold Brown, encouraged the president to adopt a tougher policy orientation towards the Soviet Union, one that placed renewed emphasis on strategic modernization, and thus MX (Brzezinski, 1983:331-36). On the other hand, Secretary Cyrus Vance and others in the State Department and ACDA, were urging Carter to exercise restraint in

155

Table 7.1

responding to the cries from congressional and executive branch conservatives for a harsher stance toward the Soviet Union. To buttress his position of influence within the executive branch, Brzezinski built a contingency of support in Congress. Majority Leader Robert Byrd, Minority Leader Howard Baker, and key members of the Senate Armed Service Committee, notably Sam Nunn, became critical advocates of the need for greater defense spending for strategic modernization to support a tougher foreign policy (Brzezinski, 1983:336-37). Thus, an important coalition within the executive branch, the House, and the Senate emerged which transcended institutional lines and had as its objective influencing the president's decision on MX.

Carter's acquiescence first to MX and then MPS basing resulted from Brzezinski's successful exploitation of several key arguments and from Carter's growing political vulnerability as the 1980 presidential election neared. First, there was the problem of achieving Senate approval for the SALT agreement about to be submitted. Carter's clumsy handling of the B-1 bomber and neutron bomb issues, and his general indecisiveness towards the Soviets, had created serious credibility problems for him. Questions about the president's ability to manage Soviet-U.S. relations undermined the credibility of the SALT II Treaty as well, which his administration had negotiated. Brzezinski and allies argued that the MX was necessary bait to lure the support of conservatives and moderates with reservations about SALT. Vance and administration doves also promoted the MX as a necessary bargaining chip in the SALT debate, but warned of the dangerous implications of the MX's hard-target capabilities (authors' interviews).

Second, the push in Congress for increased defense spending and ICBM modernization, with the sanction and support of many of Carter's own officials, was decisive. This pressure, fed by growing public support, became even more intense following the Iranian hostage incident and the Soviet invasion of Afghanistan.

Third, there was pressure from the Pentagon, particularly the defense secretary and Joint Chiefs of Staff (JCS), to adopt more quickly the tenets of the damage limitation strategy, which they saw as necessary for enhancing deterrence in the Soviet-U.S. strategic relationship. Carter had been moving towards this policy since 1977, and MX, with its hard-target capability, emerged as an indispensable ingredient for such a program.

Despite his initial reservations, then, Carter ultimately embraced the MX in June 1979 and the MPS basing mode three months later. International events such as Afghanistan and Iran, public opinion, pressure from important members of Congress, and encouragement from key advisors in his administration, led the president to firmly commit to a weapon and

157

basing mode he once rejected as an outrageous "Rube Goldberg" scheme. Thus, to this point at least, the bureaucratic politics perspective correctly anticipates that legislative involvement in procurement matters will be confined to a few key actors with close ties to the Pentagon. On the other hand, that perspective does not capture the impact of strategic and foreign policy issues on legislative and executive behavior.

Pass the Salt

As fiscal year 1979 came to a close and SALT II was placed on the agenda for the Senate, Carter had to announce a funding decision for MX. Carter's paramount commitment to arms control led him to propose a weapon system about which he had doubts, but, which he hoped, would serve as the symbol of his administration's hardening attitude toward the Soviet Union. As discussed in chapter 4, MPS basing was designed with SALT II constraints in mind. It was inevitable, then, that MX would become embroiled in the wider controversy over a Soviet-U.S. strategic arms limitation agreement.

Defense Secretary Brown had learned several important lessons from the administration's past problems with Congress on defense policy. To win, the administration needed the support of the services, particularly the Joint Chiefs of Staff (JCS), and powerful members in Congress. The testimony given by service and JCS officers in particular can be pivotal in swaying congressional opinion on defense policies. Carter wanted to win on SALT II. MPS basing was fielded specifically to bring the services and hawks in Congress on board. The chairman of the JCS had publicly admitted that he would have "deep reservations" about supporting the arms limitation agreement without MX MPS (Stockton, 1982:236). Ironically, in order to win that support Carter had to endorse the largest and most lethal weapon in the nuclear arsenal. This alienated liberals both in the administration and Congress.

Liberal arms control proponents had persistently argued that mobile, land-based ICBMs would jeopardize arms control negotiations, and, in fact, increase the risk of nuclear war. Difficult to verify, and with a first-strike capability, MX MPS could upset the already precarious balance on which deterrence rested. But Carter reasoned that the aversion of liberals to MX and MPS basing would not cause them to imperil the success of an agreement whose consequences for arms control were significant. SALT was used to justify MPS basing to anti-MX groups; and MX MPS was used to woo conservatives, moderates, and anti-SALT individuals to support the arms control treaty.

For the anti-SALT senators, a new mobile, land-based missile was essential to buttress the nuclear triad and counter the increasing accuracy of

Soviet missiles. Too, only land-based ICBMs could be made accurate enough to undertake "limited" counterforce attacks in a limited war scenario. MX MPS was promoted to reassure moderates and hardliners that SALT II would not jeopardize the U.S. arsenal. A key blow to the administration's MX MPS proposal was Carter's withdrawal of the SALT II Treaty from Senate consideration in January 1980 following the Soviet invasion of Afghanistan.

Without SALT II the strategic viability of MX MPS was uncertain, since there would be no constraints on land-based missiles, and particularly the number of warheads deployed on these missiles (i.e., the open-ended problem). Thus, the Soviets might be able to overwhelm the system by deploying excessive numbers of missiles and/or warheads, a problem the United States could address only by building more shelters and/or an ABM system. The first strategy would be costly and would throw the superpowers into a dangerous shelter-warhead race. Developing any type of meaningful ABM system would violate the SALT I agreement, and encourage the Soviets to do likewise. It soon became clear that MX MPS, once endorsed to win SALT II approval, was now only viable with SALT II constraints.

This military problem was accompanied by an important political problem concerning the coalition of support for MX. Without the linkage of SALT II to MX MPS, many in the Senate and House, especially liberal Democrats, would no longer be inclined to go along with a weapon system about which they harbored deep suspicions. Also, moderates who saw SALT II as closing off the open-ended problem of MX MPS were increasingly suspicious of the Carter proposal. Conservatives who saw MX MPS as the bargaining chip to attain their support for SALT II were at best uneasy about a weapon system they perceived as designed to meet SALT II verification requirements. The strategic logic of the coalition that supported MX MPS was severely damaged by the demise of SALT. Thus, once more MX was significantly influenced by a foreign policy issue.

Regional Considerations: The Constituent Link

In the meantime, another integral part of the MX MPS coalition was eroding as the congressional delegations from the states considered for MX deployment began to tie their support to regional considerations; considerations which ultimately argued against MX MPS. As both the strategic logic and regional support for MX MPS dwindled, the Carter administration now found itself under intense pressure in the congressional and public arenas to abandon the program.

As noted earlier, the administration had anticipated some resistance from citizens and their representatives in the deployment areas. Having watched the states of Michigan and Wisconsin defeat the navy on the ELF issue a few years earlier (Klessig and Strite, 1980), the air force sought to forestall a similar encounter with direct negotiations with key congressional and state actors in advance of legislative debate (authors' interviews). These negotiations, many of which were ultimately formalized in legislation, burdened the MPS system with so many conditions that, as one congressional member predicted, "The system will fall of its own weight."

The first condition enacted by Congress significantly circumscribed the choice of the air force in selecting deployment regions by precluding the placement of MX MPS on "productive land." The limitation was imposed in response to air force consideration of the South Platte Plains as a suitable deployment area (Holland and Benedict, 1981:18-21).

Representative Virginia Smith (R-Nebr.) was disturbed in the spring of 1979 by the findings of the air force study "Milestone II/FEIS II" that identified the South Platte Plains as one of seven areas "geotechnically" suitable for MX deployment.[2] Smith, in private consultations with the air force, relayed her concerns. After being assured that the military really had no intention of placing the MX in Nebraska, Smith, in conference with Representatives Melvin Price (D-Ill.) and Richard Ichord (D-Mo.), chairs of the Armed Services Committee and its R&D subcommittee respectively, and air force personnel, drafted an amendment to the FY79 DOD supplemental authorization bill (S.429). The amendment effectively eliminated the South Platte Plains region from consideration. Smith's bill, sponsored by the entire Nebraska and Kansas delegation and the eastern Colorado representative (James P. Johnson) stated, "The sense of the Congress is that the basing mode for the MX missile should be restricted to location on the least productive land available that is suitable for such purpose" (P.L. 96-29, 93 Stat. 79).

Smith's amendment not only eliminated the highly productive agricultural lands of the Plains states from consideration, it also increased the likelihood that the MX would be placed in Nevada and Utah. The definition of "productive land" was tightened on the House floor to mean "prime agricultural land" (*Congressional Record*, 1979:13028f). Contending definitions of the term, such as "grasslands" suitable for livestock grazing or coal and mineral leasing lands, were rejected. The effect was to reduce the appeal of other alternative locations such as the High Plains region of Texas and New Mexico, with fertile farmland; while precluding any future attempts by Nevada and Utah to exempt their region, rich in mineral and livestock value.

Although Congress was making a fateful decision that would heavily influence the future of MX decision making, at the time the delegations from both Nevada and Utah were pleased with the preference for the Great Basin. Porkbarrel was certainly on their minds; and with their help, the Smith amendment passed on a voice vote, with no recorded opposition (*Congressional Record*, 1979:13030). The absence of any visible opposition from the Nevada and Utah representatives can be attributed to two related factors: the air force's success in wooing the states; and the states' enthusiasm for the economic advantages that would accrue from the weapon project (authors' interviews).

Nevadans and Utahns were highly receptive to the idea of housing the MX system, at least during 1978 when the air force was in those states holding briefings and informal talks, following the release of Milestone II. Governors Scott Matheson (D-Utah) and Robert List (R-Nev.), for example, pledged their unequivocal support in letters to Defense Secretary Brown and President Carter (appendix A). The seven members of the congressional delegation calculated that support of MX meant considerable political advantage in their reelection aspirations. Likely defense contractors such as Hercules, Litton, Sperry-Univac, and Thiokol in Utah began a soft lobbying campaign through their liaison Senator Orrin Hatch (R-Utah) (authors' interviews). Public opinion polls taken in the area during the time document pervasive citizen support for MX in the Great Basin.[3]

It was the positive financial implications (porkbarrel) of the construction and deployment of MX, and the inclination to accept the air force argument about the national security needs for the weapon system, that led to the initial commitment by citizens and officials alike. The MX system promised to give a boost to the marginal economies in the Great Basin area, and residents in both Nevada and Utah have a long tradition of support for the Pentagon. In this respect, Senators Hatch, Jake Garn (R-Utah), Howard Cannon (D-Nev.) and Paul Laxalt (R-Nev.), and Representatives Dan Marriott (R-Utah) and Gunn McKay (D-Utah), had served their constituencies well. They were strategically placed on committees that allowed them to exercise considerable influence in the MX debate. Garn and Cannon were members of the Senate Armed Services Committee, and Laxalt and McKay were ranking members of the military construction subcommittee, Appropriations Committee of the Senate and House respectively. During the 97th Congress, Garn would trade his position on the Armed Services Committee for one on the Appropriations Committee, where he served on the defense appropriations and military construction subcommittees.

The only holdout from the Great Basin states was Representative James Santini (D-Nev.), although Garn and Laxalt had been uneasy about MPS basing for strategic reasons (authors' interviews). Santini was one of only several dozen congressional members in 1979 who comprehended the enormity of the environmental, socioeconomic, and cultural devastation that MX MPS could bring to Nevada and Utah; and the consequent political implications for the congressional delegations. The air force release of a preliminary draft of its environmental study of the impacts of MX MPS in the Great Basin confirmed his fears. The findings were overwhelming: natural resources depleted, wildlife harmed, industries ruined, people displaced, and cultures destroyed. In response Santini, in whose state 70 percent of the system was expected to be based, searched for ways to mitigate these effects on his constituents. The occasion was floor consideration of the fiscal 1980 DOD authorization bill (H.R. 4040), on September 13, 1979.

Santini was caught between the proverbial "rock and a hard place." On the one hand, Congress, up to this time, had consistently and enthusiastically given its support to the air force in the service's drive to sell MX MPS. The few opponents of the program such as Representative Ron Dellums (D-Calif.) and Senator Mark Hatfield were considered ideological purists, mavericks not to be taken seriously, although the assessment of Hatfield was to change when he became chair of the Appropriations Committee in 1981. Even seasoned liberals such as Senators George McGovern (D-S.Dak.) and William Proxmire (D-Ill.) were careful to couch their positions on MX within the context of their reciprocal support for SALT II. On the other hand, Santini himself had a reputation for being prodefense, one which had served him well as the representative from conservative Nevada. His amendment, then, could not attack MX per se, but had to attempt only to mitigate the impacts of the system on Nevada. If passed, the amendment would prevent more than 25 percent of the missile shelters from being placed in any one state, thus mandating split-basing.

In defending his bill, Santini wisely reaffirmed his support for the system first, and then appealed to his colleagues' sense of equity (Holland and Benedict, 1981:21-22). No state, he argued, should be expected "to assume 70 to 80% of the blessings and the burdens of missile siting" (*Congressional Record*, 1979:24458). Armed Services Committee members Price and Ike Skelton (D-Mo.) were quick with their counterattack, as they sought to demolish the foundations of Santini's claims. Skelton pointed to the 150 Minuteman II missiles that his district had accepted to enhance national defense. Price cited both a Nevada newspaper poll showing that 65 percent of the citizens there in fact supported MX deployment in Nevada and a letter from Nevada Governor List to President Jimmy Carter welcoming MX MPS, a letter the existence of which Santini was not aware (see appendix B). Santini could not even enlist the help of Utahns. Representative Gunn McKay voted against the measure, while Representative Dan Marriott did not vote.[4] Even liberal ideologues reserved their energies for an attack on the missile itself, rather than on the devastating environmental and social implications of the basing mode. In the end, Santini could barely find eighty House members who even knew about MX MPS, and fewer who were interested (authors' interview). He had been out-thought and out-organized by proponents of MX MPS in the Congress and their allies in the executive branch. The amendment went down to defeat, 84 to 289.

The defeat of Santini's amendment effectively illustrates the nature of congressional consideration of MX by September 1979. A few key congressional members, with strong ties to the Pentagon, had been steering the fate of the missile system, just as conventional wisdom suggests. These savants and their allies in DOD were successful in swaying legislative opinion and in influencing the debate about MX MPS within the Carter administration as well. The bureaucratic politics paradigm also anticipates the relative ignorance and disinterest among the majority of members of Congress on MX MPS; and the influence of economic concerns. However, neither the paradigm nor congressional records can account for Santini's lone efforts to protect his constituents from a certain fate.

Santini would make several other concerted efforts to deflect MX MPS, at times using his strategic position on the House Interior and Insular Affairs Committee to exert leverage. For example, under Santini's impetus, the committee authorized the General Accounting Office (GAO), Office of Technology Assessment (OTA), and Congressional Research Service (CRS) to conduct studies about the adequacy of DEIS III, of alternative MX basing modes, and of the MX system, respectively. Also, oversight hearings were held by his subcommittee between October 2, 1979, and June 18, 1980, in both Washington, D.C. and the Great Basin states, to assess the possible impacts of the MX system on the public lands. But Santini's greatest immediate success was in getting the Interior Committee to repulse the fast-track legislation introduced by the air force in December of 1979.

Fast-Track Legislation

Shortly after Santini's failed attempt to legislate split-basing, the environment in Congress and the Great Basin began to change. The release of a preliminary DEIS III provoked threats of lawsuits and public obstructionism in Nevada and Utah. In Congress too, a new coalition of MX skeptics, whose paramount concern was finding a survivable basing mode, began to emerge. (This concern would become a legislative mandate in November 1979 in the form of an amendment by Senator Ted Stevens which precluded the use of appropriated funds for MX in ways "which would commit the U.S. to only one basing mode" for the project, H.R. 5359).[5]

To the air force these were clear signs that MPS basing would encounter increasingly more resistance in both the congressional and public arenas, resistance that could kill the weapon system itself. Thus they took the rather drastic step of drafting legislation to expedite the missile system. During the fall of 1979, the air force quietly circulated a draft copy of fast-track legislation among members of several key subcommittees (*Congressional Record*, 1979:35101f). Called Draft 22, the bill was made public by an astonished Senator William Proxmire (D-Ill.) in December 1979.

The bill would have had the effect of negating much of the dilatory utility of the Engle Act, FLPMA, and NEPA discussed in chapter 5 (Holland and Benedict, 1981:45-47). First, the bill would allow the air force to short-circuit the land withdrawal process mandated by the Engle Act. Instead of requiring a congressional act, withdrawal of military lands could proceed (under Draft 22) with the submission of an order so declaring by the Secretary of Interior to Congress. The order would become effective immediately unless Congress adopted a concurrent resolution disapproving it within ninety days.

Second, Draft 22 would have imposed on the states a time limit within which response could be made to permit requests by the military. Failure to respond within 270 days would have allowed the air force to proceed without state consent. A third provision would have allowed the air force to circumvent a key provision of NEPA that an environmental study consider all viable alternatives to the proposed action. Rather, an EIS would still be valid without doing so.

Finally, and most disturbing to the opposition to MX MPS, the fast-track bill would have restricted legal challenges of the missile system to review in the U.S. Court of Appeals for the District of Columbia Circuit, not in the regional district courts. Additionally, the D.C. courts would be instructed to give preference to such petitions, and would have allowed plaintiffs only fifteen days to file appeals to the Supreme Court. These provisions would severely circumscribe the time available for litigation and also would allow the air force to circumvent judicial examination of MX MPS in any area cited for deployment.

Draft 22 produced two unintended effects: it exacerbated congressional concerns about MPS basing; and it helped alienate legislators from Nevada and Utah. Many members of the House and Senate became suspicious of efforts to short cut the decision-making process. What did the air force have to hide? Furthermore, the delegates from the Great Basin states felt betrayed since Draft 22 violated some basic promises and commitments originally made to them by the air force. Santini demanded that the "pernicious notion" of Draft 22 be put to rest (U.S. House of Representatives, 1980c:160). And so it was, if only temporarily, since the threat of fast-track legislation resurfaced in April 1981 (U.S. House of Representatives, 1981a:141f).

The air force and the administration seriously misjudged the nature of the opposition in the congressional arena at this point. The opposition that was forming was not directed at MX nor a mobile, land-based mode; but rather the MPS mode endorsed by Carter. When Stevens, in defense of his amendment to H.R. 5359, stated that "we cannot accept any basing mode so expensive it will soon be abandoned, so complex and untested that it will never work, so prone to delay that it will come into service years after it is needed" (*Congressional Record*, 1979:31873), he was not threatening the air force. He was warning them about congressional concerns over the *survivability* of MX in the MPS prototype, not MX itself. The lack of any real opposition to the ten-warhead missile should have been clear on November 9, 1979 when the Senate voted overwhelmingly to defeat (77 to 11) an amendment by Hatfield to delete all R&D funding for MX (H.R. 5359).

The year ended with firm congressional commitments to the development of a land-mobile MX, but growing skepticism about the specific racetrack launching system. During 1980 this skepticism among many members of Congress would turn to outright opposition to both MPS and the MX itself. The demise of SALT II and the threat of fast-track legislation had alienated certain factions in Congress. The official release of DEIS III in January 1980 further ruptured the coalition of support. The emergence on the presidential scene of a Republican candidate publicly uneasy with MPS basing set the stage for the bumpy road that MX would travel during 1980.

1980: An Election Year

The skepticism about MX MPS that began as a ripple during 1979, developed wave like proportions during 1980, an election year. Many liberals and doves, who had refrained from attacking the MX favored by their hardline colleagues as long as SALT was a live issue, now found themselves free to oppose it as strategically destabilizing and technically uncertain. Joining the liberals were conservatives and moderates uncomfortable in the role of defense critic, but who were concerned about the enormous price tag of MX, the massive environmental, socioeconomic, and cultural impacts of the system, and citizen resistance in the Great Basin.

The first signs of this portentous development took place in the House Budget Committees. Until the new budgetary process was inaugurated in 1975, weapon development and procurement decisions were essentially made, sealed, and delivered by the substantive Armed Services Committees in both houses, and, more recently, by the Appropriations Committees

165

as well. Here was yet another set of legislative actors for the Pentagon to contend with, members of the Budget Committees. The skepticism of Budget Committee members toward MX and the racetrack mode, shared even by prodefense colleagues, was motivated primarily by strategic concerns. It was understandable that members would be concerned about the cost. But their report on the budget resolution for 1981 also expressed apprehension over the very feasibility of MX (*Congressional Quarterly Weekly*, 1980:779). Members of the committee were no longer willing to concede expertise to the Pentagon or play dumb about technical military weapon considerations. For a $30 to $100 billion investment, budgetors wanted some guarantees of a payoff.

The Pentagon acted to forestall a probable showdown on the issue during House action on the $53.1 billion fiscal 1981 DOD authorization bill (H.R. 6974), by announcing modifications in the racetrack basing scheme. In letters dated April 29 and May 6, 1980, and in testimony as well, Defense Secretary Harold Brown and Defense Under Secretary William Perry indicated changes in the racetrack method that would, they contended, reduce both the costs and impacts on deployment areas by 10 to 20 percent. The changes in vehicle type, shelters, and road configuration (oval to linear); the elimination of the automated dash system; and the addition of mass simulators were not enough, however, to quell congressional concerns about MX MPS.

Nor did the changes silence the growing and vitriolic opposition from many in Utah and Nevada to the deployment of the new ICBM system in the Great Basin. The formal release of the draft copy of an environmental study of the system's impacts on the Great Basin states (DEIS III) had fanned the fires of public concern. Federal representatives from Nevada and Utah became visibly sensitive to these concerns during 1980, an election year. The first legislative expression of regional-parochial concern during the 1980 session was a concurrent resolution introduced on May 14, 1980, by Representative Marriott and cosponsored by McKay and Santini. The crux of the resolution (H. R. 326), which failed, was to prohibit the transfer of public lands to DOD for MX use until Congress was given a written plan discussing: (1) the socioeconomic and environmental impacts of the system on Nevada and Utah; (2) the feasibility of split-basing; (3) alternative basing modes; (4) security requirements and public access restrictions; (5) the cost-effectiveness of the system; and (6) the ability of the system to actually survive a Soviet nuclear attack. Clearly, Marriott's intent was not to kill the missile system, although colleagues would accuse him of such; but rather to insure that if the missile was deployed in the Great Basin, that decision would be made with the full understanding of its consequences. In short, Marriott was demanding that the Pentagon and

166

White House share as much information as possible with members of Congress on the system so that the House and Senate could better assess the soundness of the administration's decision.

Marriott offered his resolution again, this time as an amendment to the fiscal 1981 defense authorization bill (H.R. 6974), on May 15, 1980. "The people of Nevada and Utah have no idea what's coming," he began. "It's like a freight train bearing down on you — and you're tied to the track" (*Congressional Record*, 1980:11456). It was Marriott's intention to forewarn Great Basin dwellers that the freight train was coming so that they could either get out of the way or build concession stands. "The people of Utah and Nevada have a right to know what the future holds for them."

But opponents of the amendment, such as Majority Leader Jim Wright (D-Tex.), Sam Stratton (D-N.Y.), and Armed Services Chair Melvin Price, demolished Marriott's position by imputing ulterior motives to the amendment (*Congressional Record*, 1980:11456). Moreover, they were better organized to defeat the resolution than Marriott was to support his proposal. Price first accused Marriott of wanting to "kill" MX through his challenge of the basing mode, since the "essence" of the system was the MPS scheme. "Stopping the basing mode stops the whole system." Representative Ichord accused Marriott of "set[ting] up a ripe atmosphere for lawsuits to be filed ad infinitum. . .thus killing the system through endless delay." (Ichord was referring to the use that could be made of the National Environmental Policy Act.) Finally, Sam Stratton accused Marriott of sacrificing national security for parochial-constituent interests. "I can certainly understand the desire of the gentleman from Utah to protect his own district and his own turf." But "we have an overriding obligation to do whatever is required to protect our country. . ." Following an impassioned defense of the amendment by Santini, Marriott concluded by noting with some derision: "If this project were 50 miles outside of Dallas or New York or Washington, D.C., or St. Louis, this would be the hottest amendment we are going to deal with this year, and it would pass overwhelmingly. I think that the same courtesy belongs to Utah and Nevada." Only 135 of his colleagues agreed, as the amendment went down to defeat with 268 no votes (*Congressional Record*, 1980:11483). However, that was nearly twice the votes that Santini's amendment had achieved the previous fall.

Although the weapon procurement bill (H.R. 6974) that the House passed on May 21, 1980 (*Congressional Record*, 1980:11980) was a victory for defense hardliners and Armed Services Committee members, MX MPS advocates encountered resistance from some unexpected foes in the Senate: defense stalwarts John Stennis (D-Miss.), Orrin Hatch, Jake Garn, Paul Laxalt, and Howard Cannon. While House members were busy accusing each other of jeopardizing the safety of the United States, Laxalt and Garn were quietly building a coalition of opposition to MPS basing in the Senate. The Carter administration was forewarned of the emerging disquiet: "The racetrack is clearly a product of an era of presumed U.S.-Soviet cooperation which, if it ever existed, is clearly no longer with us," wrote the Nevada and Utah senators to Carter. "As we see it, the time has now come to recognize that the changed security environment also provides us with a chance to build a new generation ICBM and base it in a mode which would be cheaper, more effective, and come in line quicker than would be possible with racetrack" (Edwards, 1982:213).

The changes in MPS basing that DOD approved in April and May failed to adequately address the objections which Utahns and Nevadans were raising. In May Laxalt and Garn held joint hearings before the defense and military construction subcommittees of the Appropriations Committee to force the basing mode issue onto the legislative agenda and "to construct a strategic and environmental objection to the shell game" (Edwards, 1982:210). From those hearings emerged a controversial split-basing amendment authored in part by Garn and Hatch, and introduced at the committee level by Cannon. Under the direction of Chair John Stennis, the Armed Services Committee and then the Senate, adopted the Cannon amendment limiting the initial phase of MX construction in Nevada and Utah to 50 percent until the feasibility of housing the remaining shelters in alternative areas was studied (H.R. 6974).

House-Senate conferees retained the Cannon provision but added an important qualifier: the entire system could be placed entirely in the Great Basin region if defense officials determined that split-basing was precluded by economic or military considerations. According to one observer, "Conferees reworded the language to in effect allow the air force to put all the missiles in Nevada and Utah, but still permit affected senators to claim victory at home by guaranteeing a Pentagon study of split-basing" (*Congressional Quarterly Weekly*, 1980:2284). The bill was signed into law on September 8, 1980 (P.L. 96-342).

What might have prompted this rather harsh assessment of the motives of the senators from the Great Basin states was an article in the *New York Times* (April 20, 1980) that told how Cannon, at least, stood to profit financially from MX deployment in Nevada. The construction of MX MPS would swell the value of an airport land development, hotel and casino in Tonopah (Nev.) in which Cannon has financial interests. As if to verify these suspicions, Cannon was also successful in getting the Senate to adopt an amendment to the fiscal 1981 military construction bill (H.R. 7301) that would make any community affected by the MX system eligible for substantial federal economic impact aid. (The $5 million federal impact

168

assistance provision was also added to the military construction appropriations bill.)

Perhaps a lack of complete sincerity could also be attributed to Hatch who was perceived even by his colleague Garn to be the spokesperson for the probusiness interests in Utah. But Laxalt's and Garn's concerns were genuine, although neither was willing to jeopardize the weapon system with too stringent an opposition to MPS basing. And this is what separated Garn and Laxalt and their conservative allies ideologically from liberals like Senator Hatfield and Representatives Paul Simon (D-Ill.) and Thomas Downey (D-N.Y.), whose opposition was geared to be immobilizing to the system. In the end though, their mutual discomfort with the shell game brought liberals and conservatives together in an odd coalition that would be fully realized in 1981.

Until that time, however, Congress would exhibit considerable ambivalence toward the missile system; an ambivalence which would ultimately operate to the advantage of anti-MPS forces. On the one hand, a majority of congressional members would remain committed to a major defense buildup, and the development of a new generation of ICBMs to facilitate that buildup. Thus, the weapon authorization bill (H.R. 6974) that Congress passed out was $5.9 billion fatter than what Carter had requested. Moreover, the defense appropriations bill for fiscal 1981 (H.R. 8105) survived two significant liberal attempts by Representative Paul Simon and Senator Thomas Eagleton[6] to slow the MX program by postponing a congressional commitment to funding MX MPS, or cutting money altogether. The bill, as adopted, appropriated $1.4 billion for MX research, development, and engineering, a figure $60 million less than Carter had requested.

On the other hand a sizeable number of moderate and conservative legislators were becoming more reluctant to give their unqualified support to the MPS basing mode. Congress had been persistent in insisting upon a feasible replacement for the aging and soon to be vulnerable Minuteman fleet. It was becoming increasingly more evident that MX in the MPS mode would not solve either the vulnerability problem nor insure a counterforce capacity. Instead of voting to delete MPS funding, however, a move which would align moderates with liberal arms control advocates, efforts were made to delay a funding commitment to the construction of the basing mode. The military construction bill of 1981 (H.R. 7301), as approved, contained a critical mandate: "No part of the funds appropriated in this act may be obligated for design of any site specific facilities for the MX missile system until the terms, conditions, and requirements of the National Environmental Policy Act (42 U.S.C. 4332) are met, which will include a

169

complete analysis of a split-basing alternative" (P.L. 96-436, H.R. 6592, signed into law October 13, 1980).[7]

The use of dilatory tactics to postpone the construction of the MX MPS system suggests the influence of several factors operable at the time. For one, the election of Ronald Reagan was important, as several congressional members cited his opposition to MPS as reason to be cautious in committing funds prematurely to a system that might never be built (authors' interviews). Second, despite a record of defeats for MX opponents, there remained a solid and steady core of them, at least 40 percent in the House, who remained diligent and vigilant in their scrutiny of the system. Third, even MX advocates and defense hardliners were unwilling to give their unqualified support for the Carter administration position. On the contrary, Congress continued to dictate the terms of the system's development throughout the 96th Congress. Fourth, despite a favorable reception for MX in the traditionally receptive House and Senate Armed Services Committees, the system began to receive a chillier encounter in the Appropriations Committees and a warning from the House and Senate committees with public lands jurisdiction, to which the air force would have to go for authorization to proceed with land withdrawal for MX MPS. Representative Manuel Lujan, Jr. (R-N.Mex.), for example, speaking at a seminar in Washington, D.C., in early 1980, warned that "the Interior Committee won't vote to allow the land in the Great Basin of Utah and Nevada to be withdrawn for an MX system" (*Deseret News*, April 11, 1980). Fifth, MX MPS opponents began developing a new strategy that would have more substantial payoffs during the 97th Congress. That strategy, to split up the votes on the missile and basing mode decisions, was a direct reaction to the one employed by proponents. The success of MX proponents was due in part to their ability to sell MX MPS as providing both survivability and counterforce potential. By separating out these two components, the coalition so carefully crafted by the air force and Armed Services Committees was vulnerable. Finally, this discussion demonstrates how far the MX decision-making experience deviates from the thrust of the propositions for the inner and outer layer of the bureaucratic politics argument about procurement (especially propositions 4, 5, 9, 10, and 13). The congressional arena had become central to MX decision making.

A New Administration

The 97th Congress would continue to be an important arena in the MX debate and at times an obstacle to the administration's plans, despite dramatic changes in legislative and executive personnel. For the first time in twenty-eight years, the Republicans captured the Senate, while the

Democrats retained the House. An executive administration strong on defense, cold war rhetoric, and presidential superiority in national security affairs prevailed. Furthermore, several important liberals, both in the Congress and the executive branch (ACDA), were defeated.

Although Ronald Reagan began a review of Carter's MX MPS acquisition-deployment proposal almost immediately after assuming office, the MPS basing scheme for MX remained the formal position of the U.S. government until October 1981 when Reagan rejected that alternative and offered instead an option of interim retrofitting of MX in Minuteman and Titan II silos. Thus, for the first ten months of 1981, MX MPS remained the formal acquisition and deployment proposal before the Congress and the public arena. Committees and subcommittees of Congress evaluated and debated the advantages and disadvantages of the system while government agencies proceeded with environmental impact statements and the procedural requirements for land withdrawal for MX in the Great Basin. The public debate in the Great Basin and in the nation intensified over the merits and demerits of the weapon project as well. The indecision, confusion, and internal conflict within the new administration over the basing of MX only intensified the opposition to the acquisition and deployment of MX in the Great Basin region. Ironically, it appeared to surviving liberals, arms control advocates, and erstwhile MX opponents that they might have a better chance of defeating MX with Reagan and the Republicans in control of the executive branch than with Carter.

The actions of the Reagan administration during the first ten months did nothing to alter that assessment. Candidate Reagan, prematurely in retrospect, had discredited MPS basing of MX during the 1980 campaign as being unworkably complex and expensive. In part, it had been a ploy to distinguish himself from President Carter in the defense area during the campaign. But it also reflected sincere distrust of Carter's commitment to MX. There was the suspicion in the Reagan camp that Carter had supported MX at first to gain support for the SALT II Treaty in the Senate, and later only as a gambit to make the Democratic president look stronger during the 1980 election. Following a successful reelection, Carter would junk the MPS system, and then MX, as being hopelessly unworkable (authors' interviews). Reagan was genuinely committed to the acquisition and deployment of MX. However, the manner in which Reagan and his Secretary of Defense Casper Weinberger handled the quest for a basing mode to replace MPS only added to the problems of MX especially in the congressional arena.

Two mistakes in particular would prove politically costly to the president. The first was Weinberger's refusal to avail himself of the briefings on MX MPS which Seymour Zeiberg, who remained as deputy undersecretary

171

of defense for research and engineering, had prepared for the new secretary and his defense appointees (authors' interview). This failure exacerbated a second mistake, the administration's zealous and persistent attacks on MPS basing in advance of an alternative scheme. Ironically, the MPS concept, given Reagan's commitment to developing an extended war-fighting capability, was technically the most appropriate system for it could provide a better combination of survivability and accuracy than any other land-based alternative system, at a more reasonable cost.

Having discredited the only feasible scheme and with no alternatives of its own, it was inevitable that the new administration would respond by throwing up a smoke screen to buy time; in this case, creating a blue-ribbon panel to study the matter of an invulnerable basing mode. On March 16, Weinberger announced the members of the committee, all leading defense scientists and retired senior military officers, and all pro-MX, to be headed by Charles Townes. In outlining the tasks and procedures for the panel, Zeiberg carefully circumscribed its role. Although the review group was given the ''freedom'' to make a basing mode recommendation, they were instructed that this responsibility did not include collecting new technical data that could be used to make any suggestions that would alter the direction of the MX program. Rather, the Townes's group was asked to solve the basing mode dilemma relying solely on the data assembled by the Pentagon over an eleven-year period (authors' interviews). To assist in this endeavor, Zeiberg recommended parallel briefings for Weinberger and the panel by Carter holdovers in DOD, a suggestion again rejected by Weinberger (*Deseret News*, March 19, 1981).

By limiting the panel's authority to a redundant analysis of existing data, the administration left itself vulnerable to proposals and ideas floated by the committee and others in and out of the executive branch that had been thoroughly reviewed and rejected during the previous eleven years. It also left them, as well as the entire MX program, extremely vulnerable if the Townes Commission could not discover an effective alternative to replace the MX MPS program. This is precisely what happened.

Between February and October 1981, the administration seemed to be involved in some type of ''basing-mode-of-the-month club.'' One of the most common preoccupations in Washington during that period was to speculate on which basing mode was the darling of Reagan and Weinberger at the moment. Uncertainty and dissension characterized the discussion of MX during those months (authors' interviews). All of this served to encourage critics of MX MPS.

The Coalition Opposed to MX MPS

During the Reagan administration, Mountain states conservatives became increasingly more active in defending parochial-regional interests against the national security needs of MX MPS. The intimate friendship between Senator Paul Laxalt and Reagan, and the close professional relationships among Laxalt, Garn, and the president were influential. Laxalt had been Reagan's national campaign manager. Garn had cochaired the Congressional Task Force which advised Reagan during the campaign. Senators Cannon and Hatch would eventually join the Great Basin bandwagon, following a rather strong spiritual kick in May 1981 from the Mormon church — of which the entire Utah delegation and Nevada Senator Howard Cannon are members. Although none of these individuals ever directly opposed an MX system, their constant criticism of the MPS basing mode helped erode the political credibility and feasibility of the Carter system in the minds of MX MPS advocates even within the air force and larger domain of the Pentagon.

Many other defense hawks, both within the administration and Congress, joined the coalition because of the system's complexity and expense. They suspected that Carter, for arms control reasons, had intentionally recommended an MX system so bizarre and unworkable that it would certainly be defeated by Congress. These two groups were joined by arms control advocates who were opposed to any new ICBM with ten warheads and a first strike-capability. Thus an odd three-pronged coalition emerged that would come together and fall away depending on the issue: (1) hawks and moderates suspicious of MPS basing; (2) arms control advocates opposed to MX; and (3) those from the Mountain states, with strong defense orientations, but uncomfortable with MPS basing for parochial and regional reasons.

The first group of antagonists took the Defense Department's claims about Soviet superiority, Minuteman III vulnerability, and the limited nuclear war scenario seriously. They wanted to see MX deployed in a survivable and workable basing mode as soon as possible, before the United States fell victim to "Soviet blackmail." With friends in key places, such as the congressional defense committees and the Pentagon, they exerted pressure on the Reagan administration to introduce his alternative to the Carter program (authors' interviews). It is clear now that Reagan never had an alternative in 1981 to MX MPS. But to evade such a direct legislative appeal from conservatives might hurt his proposed budget plans, particularly the massive defense buildup he envisaged. Thus, Reagan appointed the Townes Commission in part to appease conservatives, avoid political problems for his domestic programs, and develop options for the deployment of MX.

The second set of antagonists, liberal opponents of the missile itself, recognized that directly defeating the program was less likely than defeating it through delay. First, defense officials had repeatedly said that the very success of the weapon program was contingent upon its development according to a precise timetable. Any postponements in funding at the various stages would jeopardize the entire system, DOD warned. Second, any extension in the timeframe of congressional consideration of MX was an advantage to opponents, since the longer the issue dragged on, the more reluctant people became to support the administration. With each passing month more studies emerged documenting the validity of claims about the system's unworkability. Of particular interest was the release of an interim report by the Office of Technology Assessment (U.S. Congress. OTA, 1981). That report criticized the Carter plan as militarily inferior to deployment of new ICBMs on small submarines, an option enthusiastically and persistently endorsed by Mark Hatfield. The OTA report hit at the very essence of MPS when it noted that there was no guarantee that the missiles would be immune from either Soviet detection or would even survive a massive attack on all 4,600 shelters, a possibility without SALT II. On the other hand, the release of a congressionally mandated Arms Control Impact Statement for fiscal 1982 did much to deflate the rationale employed by liberals who opposed MX for arms control reasons. That report, issued in February 1981, concluded that "while there may be arms control risks involved with deployment of the MX [in a mobile system], the national, political and military risks of not doing so are even greater" (*Congressional Quarterly Weekly*, 1981:853).

Liberal opponents were significantly handicapped by their inability to convince colleagues in the other two camps to join in forming a more definitive coalition. In the first case, the goals of defense stalwarts and liberal opponents were at cross-purposes. And the third group, members of the Great Basin delegation, were reluctant to endorse the objectives of liberals for ideological and political reasons since outright opposition to MX would have been both contrary to strongly held beliefs about national defense and a political liability for some of Congress's most ardent military proponents. Despite ideological and personal differences, members of these three groups would be instrumental in deciding the fate of the missile system during the Reagan administration.

Reagan and MX MPS in the Congressional Arena

The Reagan administration received its first lesson in legislative-executive relations from defense stalwarts Ralph Regula (D-Ohio) and Bo Ginn (D-Ga.), during the House Appropriations Committee's consideration of the 1981 supplemental appropriations bill (H.R. 3512). Regula and Ginn were rankled by the air force's blatant violation of the legislative mandate in the 1981 defense appropriations bill that barred design funds from being obligated until a basing mode decision was made. Nonetheless, DOD had already spent $5 million of the $97 million appropriated for that purpose, and Defense Secretary Weinberger informed the two men that funds would continue to be spent and design contracts honored regardless of what Congress said. After voting to deny the funds for MPS construction being requested in the supplemental, the House Appropriations Committee adopted a controversial amendment by Regula and Ginn which ordered the Pentagon to cease spending the remaining $92 million in planning and design funds until a final basing mode decision was made by the Reagan administration and an EIS was completed.

Supporters of MX MPS in the Pentagon and Congress were worried. The House was asserting itself in ways that jeopardized the entire weapon system. With an IOC date for MX of 1986, each delay imperiled the actual deployment of the the new land-based ICBM system. The Appropriations Committee had pulled the plug on one of the most useful ploys the Pentagon had traditionally used to promote its weapon project: the rationale of sunk costs. Moreover, the House Interior and Insular Affairs Committee was threatening to hold up public land withdrawal, a process that could take as long as two years. Until the lands were formally released, the construction of the weapon system could not proceed. The committee's public lands and national parks subcommittee had been monitoring air force progress in conducting the various studies, including an EIS, in anticipation of the formal request for land withdrawal. Important members of the committee, such as the chair, Morris Udall (D-Ariz.), were not pleased. They had reacted angrily to attempts by the air force to fast-track the withdrawal of military lands. The formal release of DEIS III had provoked condemnation by several committee members, including Santini and Marriott. The Department of Interior's attempts in April 1981 to secure the release of public lands in advance of air force needs were met with incredulity and anger by committee members. Marriott, for one, attacked the revived efforts to fast-track the MX decision-making process "as another in a series of attempts by the Air Force to railroad the MX into Utah. . ." (News Release, May 27, 1981). The final straw was the committee's release of a bipartisan report recommending that MPS basing be dumped (House Committee Interior and Insular Affairs, 1981b).

The Senate Appropriations Committee's treatment of the supplemental bill was also disconcerting. First, the committee retained the provisions of the House bill, with the exception of the EIS requirement, which it dropped as redundant. Then it voted to delete an additional $4 million from MX planning funds and to approve $36.2 million for development of an ABM system (LoAD) for MX. Ironically, the request for ABM funds originated with the Reagan administration which, it would appear, began to seriously consider an alternative MX basing scheme vigorously promoted by Senators Garn and Laxalt, and now their Senate colleagues Harrison Schmitt (R-N.Mex.) and William Roth Jr. (R-R.I.). The alternative was to deploy MX in superhardened Minuteman silos and to protect them with an ABM system.

Congress Forces Presidential Decision on MX MPS

Legislative consideration of the fiscal 1982 defense authorization bill (S. 815) proved to be an even more decisive congressional statement on MX MPS. Perhaps legislative concern over MX was accelerated by the fact that the fiscal 1982 defense budget contained the first major financial commitment to the construction of the MPS basing mode. Congress would be moving out of R&D. The IOC date of 1986, which Congress had earlier legislated, was drawing near. Construction was to begin in 1984, and the system completed by 1989. Contracts had been let, and the momentum, already reaching steamroller proportions, would be difficult to turn back, unless legislators acted immediately. Once the construction of the system was funded, it would be almost impossible to stop, if past projects were any indication.

Senate and House floor consideration of S.815 (H.R. 3519) on July 6 became a forum on which various factions in Congress floated their particular game plans, motivated by concerns as varied as nuclear annihilation and personal friendship. Despite the variations, the cumulative effect was to nudge Reagan in the direction of an immediate decision on MX basing repudiating MPS.

Defense critic Ron Dellums, in a now annual act, tested the attitude of his colleagues with an amendment to kill the MX program outright. The bill, defeated 96 to 316, was supported by that small but persistent group of MX opponents, mostly liberals. In fact, the 1981 vote was almost identical to the 1979 and 1980 votes on Dellums's amendment to the fiscal 1980 DOD authorization bill (H.R. 4040) and the fiscal 1981 version (H.R. 6974), recorded as 86 to 305 and 82 to 319 respectively. In 1981, however, Dellums expected more. But the coalition that Dellums and his few allies had hoped for failed to materialize. During late February and early March, Dellums had even traveled to Utah to seek help from the Mormon (LDS) church in his crusade to defeat the missile, recognizing that a public statement from the spiritual leader for 2.1 million faithful in Nevada and Utah might bring some conservative Mormons to his side and make MX opposition fashionable among the hawk set. Although the LDS church publicly castigated the government for its attachment to weapons such as MX in May 1981, its statement was ambiguous enough to leave Mormons Marriott and Hansen free to vote against Dellums's bill for national security reasons.

176

At the same time, defense establishment conservatives Schmitt and Roth were trying to force the president's hand on silo basing. Their ploy was an amendment expressing the sense of Congress that the missiles be deployed in fixed silos and protected with an ABM system. Garn and Laxalt, who felt the move premature, strongly discouraged Schmitt and Roth from introducing the amendment. Perhaps Reagan had already confided in his friends from the West, and Laxalt and Garn were merely trying to avoid the appearance of Congress tying the president's hands on MX basing. Or maybe they merely wanted to take credit for the plan which they had so carefully been promoting with the administration. Armed Services Chair Tower, for quite different reasons, threatened to fight the amendment. Tower, even at this point, continued to believe that MPS basing was the best technical way to achieve survivability and a war-fighting capability.

MX opponents Senator Carl Levin (D-Mich.) and Representative Paul Simon wanted to give Congress an equal voice in the basing mode decision, a responsibility that House members came close to embracing. Both amendments would require congressional approval of an administration decision on an MX basing mode in advance of money being let for the system. While Levin's bill was tabled 59 to 39, Simon's amendment lost by only four votes (201 to 205).

To some extent, Simon's defeat can be attributed to the procedural problems involved in submitting a substitute amendment. Jim Hansen and Jim Santini had already raised the issue with their resolution giving to Congress the power to enact a resolution of disapproval within sixty days following an administration decision. On the other hand, MPS proponents saw the Simon amendment as yet another veiled attempt by liberals to actually kill the MX program through delay, and not at all the procedural tool Simon said he intended. Thus, what began as a debate on the merits of giving Congress a say in defense matters beyond the appropriations power they normally exercise, quickly became a debate on the merits of the MX and the MPS basing mode.

Conservative Representative Samuel Stratton appealed to the patriotic duty of Nevadans and Utahns to willingly embrace MX MPS for national security reasons. Stratton was at first empathic: "I can understand the people of Utah and Nevada saying," 'Do not put it in my state.'" And then pragmatic: "But unfortunately when the security of the nation as a whole is involved, somebody has got to give. . . .One state [cannot be allowed] to veto a system that is absolutely essential for our survival" (*Congressional Record*, 1981:4092). Besides, he continued, all states have made great sacrifices to national security, including New York: "We even have bombers flying over the ski runs of upstate New York and upsetting some of the ski teams. . . .but we have put up with that kind of inconvenience."

Ike Skelton's example was perhaps more credible, but no less ancillary to the topic of debate: "I represent a district that has 150 ICBM Minuteman II missiles in it. . . .I have yet to hear an unpatriotic comment from a farmer with a missile silo on his place" (*Congressional Record*, 1981:4094).

Hansen, in defense of his amendment, tried unsuccessfully to force the debate back to the procedural implications of the bill, and instead found himself defending his and his constituents' patriotism: "I would be the first to say that the people from Utah and Nevada would not back away after it was determined. . .that this is the best way to use that particular MX missile" (*Congressional Record*, 1981:4092). But wasn't it a bit premature, he queried, to obligate funds for MPS when a presidential commission (Townes Commission) was still studying several different basing modes, MPS among them?

Those who came to Hansen's and then Simon's defense, were primarily liberals who, like their conservative counterparts, used the arena to debate the merits of MX on strategic, military, economic, and environmental grounds. John Conyers (D-Mich.), who was the most loquacious, concluded with an appeal to the people to take up arms control as a "grassroots cause" and "rise up and stop the insane and obscene arms race, of which the MX is one outrageous example" (*Congressional Record*, 1981:4126).

On the one hand, it is curious that this much debate occurred over the Hansen amendment since similar, and in some cases identical, language had already been incorporated into the supplemental appropriations bill (S. 694, H.R. 3152), the House and Senate versions of the fiscal 1982 military construction authorization bill (H.R. 3455), and the Senate version of the fiscal 1982 DOD authorization bill (S. 815). In the supplemental, for example, funds were deferred pending a presidential basing decision, although Congress was given no additional legislative say such as the concurrent resolution enacted in H.R. 3419. The military construction authorization bill (H.R. 3455) restricted the expenditure of development funds for any MX basing scheme until the administration's basing mode selection was explained and justified to Congress, and sixty days had elapsed without Congress enacting a concurrent resolution disapproving the president's choice. The Senate version of the 1982 defense authorization bill contained language identical to the Hansen amendment; that is, the Senate agreed to the unqualified deferral of the release of MX funds until any basing mode decision was made and justified by the president and defense secretary, and sixty days had elapsed, without Congress enacting a concurrent resolution of disapproval. On June 4, 1981, the House passed the Hansen amendment by voice vote.

On the same day (June 4, 1981), the House passed, also by voice vote, an additional, but compatible, bill introduced by Marriott to H.R. 3455 that would withhold funding for MX until the defense secretary submitted to Congress a plan to minimize the economic, social, and cultural impacts of the weapon system on the states and communities affected by the project's deployment. This was almost the same bill that Marriott had introduced just a year earlier, but instead of public land, Marriott was now threatening to withhold funds for MX deployment.

Marriott's success in 1981 can be attributed to several factors. First, the attitude towards MX MPS in Congress was clearly changing, helped along by the confusion and indecision in the Reagan administration. More legislators were either skeptical of the massive weapon project or sympathetic to the states destined to receive it. Second, the amendment was not a direct attack on the missile system itself. Marriott continued to reason, just as he had earlier, that if Utah and Nevada were going to receive MX MPS, they needed to be forewarned of its impacts so as to better prepare for the devastation that would inevitably occur. Third, and very important, Marriott's bill, which earlier had been rejected as redundant given NEPA's EIS mandate, took on a new significance with the actual release of the environmental statement. Marriott tersely summed up the general opinion of DEIS III when he referred to it as a "joke." Finally, the formal opposition of the Mormon church to deployment of MX MPS in Utah and Nevada was a bombshell on the delegations from the Great Basin states. Although somewhat bitter about the church's formal position (authors' interviews), the LDS legislators pushed strongly to slow legislation favorable to MX deployment with the hope that Reagan would choose an alternative that would place MX elsewhere, whether in an MPS mode or not.

The fact that both the Santini-Simon and Marriott amendments were not subjected to a roll call showdown is significant to one observer who contends that House Armed Services Committee members wanted to avoid a definitive test of the sentiment of the House; sentiment that was turning against them (authors' interviews). But the test came nonetheless on the defense appropriations bill (H.R. 4241) which the House passed on September 16 in a recorded vote (382 to 24), with the entire amount requested for MX "deferred without prejudice" until the president made a basing decision.

The President Makes A Decision

On October 2, 1981, Reagan made a decision on MX that was more clearly calculated to release funds for continued development of the project than to close the so-called window of vulnerability, his administration's avowed objective. Congress, throughout the year, had made it clear that no more money could be spent unless a basing mode decision was made. Evidently, Reagan never had a proposed basing plan feasible enough to compete with the abandoned Carter plan which he claimed to have rejected for strategic reasons. Not even an illustrious group of defense experts, the Townes Commission, could discover or invent a scheme capable of closing that elusive window. Their report, which had been submitted to Weinberger in July, was never completely released to the public, except in a piecemeal manner (authors' interview).

The Reagan decision, to temporarily deploy 100 MX missiles in heavily armored underground silos until a decision for a permanent basing mode for MX was made in 1984, was also calculated to be politically expedient (authors' interviews). To the relief of Utahns and Nevadans, most prominently Paul Laxalt, their states were virtually eliminated from consideration. Moreover, the new plan was expected to have minimal impacts on the states now being considered, since the system was merely a modification of the Minuteman III and Titan schemes which already dotted Wyoming, Colorado, Montana, the Dakotas, Missouri, Kansas, and Arkansas. The proposal also circumvented many of the procedural requirements for a cumbersome EIS and public land withdrawal: procedures which had offered antagonists in the Great Basin states several opportunities to interfere with the policymaking process and, thus, delay critical decisions. In addition, with minimal new land requirements, the administration could avoid the obstacles posed by the House Interior and Insular Affairs Committee.

To those who might be offended by the technical uncertainty of the plan, well it was, after all, only a temporary solution: a solution which, Congress had already rejected as unfeasible in 1976, when they refused to authorize deployment of MX missiles in fixed silos. The administration was still committed to finding a permanent basing scheme that could prove to be the yet unfound panacea for solving the vulnerability problem for which four presidents and as many Congresses had searched in vain.

Liberals, arms controllers, and MX opponents were encouraged by the obvious difficulty Reagan was having finding a home for the ten-warhead missiles. Without a home, the missiles could not be deployed nor used, unless the missile itself was adapted to planes or submarines. If this were the case, then perhaps the missile's more onerous and anti-SALT characteristics would be deleted — its hard-target capabilities that grew out of the size of the missile. Too, those reluctant to support the program saw time as an advantage to their cause. There was however, one possible drawback with the administration's temporary plan: that efforts to superharden the launch sites might violate the unratified SALT II restrictions on the enlargement of the volume of existing missile silos.

Liberals and conservatives concerned about the enormous price tag of MX were also encouraged by Reagan's plans, which would be considera-

180

bly less costly than MPS basing. Many senior officials in the administration cited money as a key factor in the president's decision, in addition to the strategic and political ones publicly admitted to (*New York Times*, October 4, 1981).

Defense hardliners and conservatives, who had remained skeptical of MPS basing, were relieved that the missile would eventually be deployed in a feasible form. The president had mentioned three possibilities: (1) placing the missiles on planes capable of remaining aloft for days, and of mid-air launching; (2) deep underground launchers; and (3) an ABM system to protect missiles placed in conventional silos. Several members of the congressional defense committees had consistently opposed the Carter plan as a veiled attempt to kill the entire project, reasoning that the very complexity, expense, and massiveness of MPS was calculated to doom it in Congress.

Only one group expressed immediate hostility to the Reagan plan: that small congerie of MPS supporters, led by John Tower, and their friends in the air force. For three years they had toiled together to keep MPS alive. Tower sought to forestall the demise of mobile-basing with a last-minute offer to Reagan to support a scaled-down version of MPS (100 missiles in 1,000 or 500 shelters) as a compromise. Tower and Senator William Dickinson (R-Ala.) had even traveled to California during August to try and loosen the president's resolve to dump MPS. But dump it he had. Tower still had some formidable allies in Congress and OSD. Could he use these allies, his still considerable influence, and the uncompleted 1982 DOD authorization and appropriations bills to defeat Reagan?

It began to appear as much as conferees sat down to put the finishing touches on the defense authorization bill (H.R. 3519, S. 815) during November. The conference report which emerged directed that, amongst other things, a third of the $76 million authorized be used to study, incredibly, a smaller version of the shuttle system (MPS). The report also eliminated one of the three alternatives favored by the president as a possible permanent basing plan, by barring the use of research funds for the continuous airborne scheme. Finally, conferees gave Congress the option of killing the Reagan plan through a concurrent resolution before November 18. It was becoming apparent that the initial political appeal of Reagan's decision was crumbling.

Under the guidance of John Warner (R-Va.), the strategic warfare subcommittee (Armed Services Committee) held hearings during late October and early November to give the administration a forum for explaining, justifying, and defending its plan. Hearings had been used or threatened by legislators with increasing frequency during the MX missile system's uneven run through Congress, with varying success. In the hands of the Armed Services Committees and subcommittees, hearings became a rostrum from which defense officials, particularly air force personnel, could tout the benefits of a mutually favored system, MPS. In the hands of the appropriations, and public lands committees, and their subcommittees, however, hearings became an exercise in consciousness-raising for many people, who were changed by the testimony and evidence from an ever-expanding pool of professional and lay witnesses outside the executive branch.

The results of the strategic warfare panel's hearings were, by the admission of its chair, uncertain, which is to say, DOD witnesses were not convincing under the intense interrogation of Democrats Levin, J.J. Exon (Nebr.), and Sam Nunn (Ga.). In fact, the Pentagon was not even prepared to defend interim silo basing. Neither JCS nor the air force had been informed of the president's decision about MX until moments before the announcement. This means that Weinberger and Reagan had failed to generate the support of the services before making public a commitment. With no prior consultation, Weinberger then laid the unenviable task on the air force of winning congressional approval for a proposed system that had few strategic merits, as far as DOD was concerned. For one, Reagan's proposed alternative failed to address the paramount problem of survivability, although it would still have its counterforce capacity. Second, the Reagan interim proposal was similar to that of the Ford administration's 1976 proposal, which Congress had already rejected. Finally, DOD witnesses had not been primed to deflect Congress's frustrations with the endless delays in MX deployment. According to veteran observers on the Hill, DOD's incompetence cost Reagan precious congressional support (authors' interviews).

The showdown came in early December with congressional consideration of the 1982 defense appropriations bill (H.R. 4995, S. 1857). Not unexpectedly, Congress was unwilling to kill the MX missile system itself. Instead, Congress essentially registered a vote of no confidence on the Reagan MX proposal. The appropriations bill, in its final form, contained an amendment by Senators William Cohen (R-Maine) and Sam Nunn prohibiting the use of more than 5 percent of the MX R&D funds for the development of superhardened silos; and mandated that the Reagan administration adopt a permanent basing mode by July 1, 1983, rather than 1984 as planned.

Observations

Despite initial reservations, President Carter was ultimately compelled by a coalition of legislative and executive branch officials to embrace both the MX missile and MPS basing. However, the uncertainty and indecisiveness which marred the MX issue in the executive branch meant that the missile project would be controversial in the congressional arena as well. Dissension in the executive arena, particularly between DOD and the liberal forces in the State Department and ACDA, had the effect of making congressional influence more salient. Brzezinski and his allies in the Pentagon were at first successful in part because of their ability to build a coalition with key legislators in the Armed Services Committees. The traditional power of members of the military committees remained unchallenged until the strategic, foreign policy, and domestic political implications of MX MPS became more compelling.

The withdrawal of the SALT II Treaty from Senate consideration brought into question the feasibility and workability of the missile system, causing liberals to attack the project as a threat to nuclear deterrence. The Soviet invasion of Afghanistan and the Iranian hostage incident underscored the need for a stronger international military posture and a tougher foreign policy; and, thus, a truly invulnerable land-based ICBM force, to achieve both objectives. From this perspective, the technical uncertainties of MPS basing caused moderates and some conservatives to attack the missile project for its inability to close the window of vulnerability. The release of studies by the air force and legislative research agencies documenting the enormity of the environmental, socioeconomic, and cultural impacts of MX MPS deployment in the Great Basin caused some members to become sensitive to regional and constituent pressures. Although the motives provoking widespread congressional interest in the weapon system varied, they were compelling enough to counter the general pattern of disinterest in defense matters, and deference to the executive's prerogative, characteristic of past legislative behavior.

Ultimately, the technical uncertainty of the missile system, strategic (vulnerability and hard-target counterforce value), domestic political (public resistance), and foreign policy concerns (arms control and international events), and friendship influenced Reagan's decision to abandon MPS basing. While that decision did have the effect of quelling constituent protest in the Great Basin region of Nevada and Utah, Reagan's proposed interim basing plan alienated key factions in Congress. After considerable debate, Reagan's planned deployment of MX missiles in Minuteman and Titan silos was essentially given such a strong vote of no confidence by Congress that the administration eventually withdrew the plan. Thus contrary to the thrust of the bureaucratic politics literature, the congressional arena was critical in MX decision making; and strategic, foreign policy, as well as traditional constituent factors were salient.

183

The contention that Congress has become a more critical force in procurement decisions does not require that one produce evidence which shows the national legislature overturning executive branch proposals. As a corollary, if Congress agrees with the policies promoted in the executive arena, this does not constitute evidence that Congress defers to the president. What does need to be demonstrated is that Congress has been influential in directing administrative decision making. In this chapter we have explored the dynamics of legislative action on the MX missile system during the 96th and 97th congresses, and discovered legislators involved in the procurement debate in forceful ways; that is, using the power of Congress to dictate the nature and direction of the progress of the missile system's movement through R & D and acquisition. The initial effect of this activity was primarily dilatory. However, ultimately, Congress did force two presidents to modify earlier commitments. Carter embraced MX MPS, which was transformed several times in response to legislative mandates. And Reagan abandoned, at least temporarily, silo basing in March of 1982.

The MX experience during this period offers considerable support for the several additional propositions (15, 16, 17, 18, 19, and 21) suggested for testing at the end of chapter one. Strategic, foreign policy, domestic political, and technical considerations were all significant issues during MX decision-making; the president was an important participant in the procurement process; and activities within the congressional arena were decisive in affecting procurement decisions. Finally, Congress's activities also suggest the value of legislative reform during the 1970s in expanding influence over the executive branch. Consider, for example, the extensive use which legislators made of public hearings to provide a forum for their views, create a public record, and interact with the executive branch; of congressional research organizations to buttress positions with independent and scientific studies and analyses of the weapon and basing modes; and of the since challenged legislative veto. Also, the aggressive exercise of the legislative appropriations and oversight powers is clear.

The congressional arena was not the only obstacle that the Carter and Reagan administrations had to overcome in their quest for a new weapon scheme. The public arena also proved to be contentious, and a potentially more disruptive impediment than the legislative one. As members of Congress debated the merits and demerits of MX in theoretical tones, the people in the deployment areas were calculating the practical and personal costs of the missile system. It is to this part of the MX saga that we now turn.

184

Endnotes

[1] Action came on an amendment by Richard Ichord, which was accepted by voice vote.

[2] The other areas were Lake Yuma, Arizona; White Sands, New Mexico; the West Texas-Rio Grande Basin of Texas and New Mexico; the High Plains of Texas and New Mexico; the Mojave Desert, California; and the Great Basin of Utah and Nevada.

[3] See public opinion polls by Dan Jones and Associates for the *Deseret News*; and Bardsley and Haslacher for the *Salt Lake Tribune*, reprinted in the following issues: *Deseret News*, 20 March 1981, 19 November 1980, 24 November 1980, 21 April 1980; and *Salt Lake Tribune*, 1 March 1981.

[4] Interestingly, McKay's legislative assistant for MX matters later became a lobbyist for southern Utah commercial interests that supported the deployment of MX in the Great Basin.

[5] Stevens' amendment passed on November 9, 1979, 98 to 9. The same language was attached to the Military Construction Appropriations Act of 1980 (P.L. 96-130).

[6] Simon's amendment to defer R & D money from being spent for the MX basing mode before April 1, 1981, was rejected 141 to 256. Eagleton's amendment to delete the $120 million for fiscal 1981 MX RDT&E funds was rejected 12 to 65.

[7] In addition, the military construction bill mandated that the Pentagon study split-basing; refrain from using funds for site specific facilities until all of NEPA's requirements were met; consider a "point security" rather than area security system; comply with all state water, mineral, and land laws; cooperate with the states in planning the system; and consider making modifications in the MPS system that would eliminate barriers and SALT verification ports.

CHAPTER 8
THE PUBLIC ARENA AND MX

When President Jimmy Carter, in September 1979, announced a plan to rotate 200 MX missiles among 4,600 shelters in the Great Basin area of Utah and Nevada, public and official opinion were quite receptive. Governors Scott Matheson (D-Utah) and Robert List (R-Nev.) enthusiastically and unequivocally supported the massive weapon system.[1] The seven members of the congressional delegation from the region eagerly anticipated the economic benefits that generally accrue from major public works or pork-barrel projects (authors' interview). During this period, public opinion polls in both Nevada and Utah revealed that the public largely supported MX.[2]

However, as we have seen in the previous chapter, by the time Ronald Reagan assumed the presidency, public attitudes on MX had altered drastically. Both List and Matheson eventually withdrew their support for the system and assumed adversarial postures (U.S. House of Representatives, 1980a:37-49; House Interior and Insular Affairs Committee, 1980c:28). Members of the Great Basin delegation, with the sole exception of Senator Howard Cannon (D-Nev.), began to qualify their previous uncategorical defense of the deployment of MX in a MPS basing scheme in their states.[3] An unusual coalition of western landowners, environmentalists, arms control advocates, promilitary conservatives, and religious groups had emerged to actively defeat the mammoth defense installation project. In fact, by the time the Mormon church, spiritual spokesman for 2.1 million faithful in Nevada and Utah, formally announced its opposition (May 1981), organized efforts to forestall MX MPS in the Great Basin were well advanced.

The anti-MX MPS momentum, which built and spread into New Mexico and Texas following a split-basing mandate, was boosted by presidential candidate Ronald Reagan's public dissatisfaction with the Carter plan and climaxed in October 1981 when President Reagan formally rejected MX MPS. In a policy statement accompanying that announcement, the administration admitted that public opposition influenced that decision. "While it is not the determining factor, it should be noted that MPS basing has strong environmental opponents who would use every available tactic, and there are many, to delay MX deployment" (*The New York Times*, October 3, 1981). The many available tactics to which the administration was referring existed because the construction of MX MPS would have required the air force to fulfill the conditions of thirty-eight different federal laws. Each law contains procedural and substantive requirements that, if ignored, could pose potential grounds for litigation. In addition, the governors of Nevada and Utah told the air force that they expected the Pentagon to comply with all state and local regulations. Finally, several private and public interest groups, some newly formed to oppose MPS basing, were determined to bring suit against the federal government for each and every violation. When Reagan announced the abandonment of MPS basing, there were lawsuits pending that sought to delay the construction of the massive missile system. Any lengthy delay can be fatal to a project such as MX whose strategic feasibility depends upon deployment within a precise timeframe. Recognizing this, the administration elected to circumvent the obstacles posed by public opposition by recommending comparatively unobtrusive deployment schemes, silo basing and dense pack.

While immediately sidestepping the statutory and legal hurdles which can be erected by regional opponents, the Reagan administration has encountered and continues to encounter public resistance from the nuclear freeze movement. The broad objectives of this movement compel it to oppose any new weapon in the nuclear arsenal. Many of its supporting members and groups (such as SANE, Physicians for Social Responsibility, MX Information Center, and so on) were active in the MX MPS conflict, an experience which taught important lessons about fighting the military using federal statutory and legal tools. A second legacy from the MX MPS battle is the network of congressional support formed during the earlier struggle.

Although Reagan cited strategic and foreign policy factors as paramount reasons in his decision to abandon the Carter scheme, it is significant that the threats posed by citizen opposition were publicly mentioned as an ancillary concern. As the bureaucratic politics literature suggests, public opinion, when salient at all in procurement matters, merely sets the broad parameters of permissible government action (Hughes, 1978). The exceptions are in cases where economic concerns are prominent, and the interested public organize to lobby for positive action on their account. However, even in these latter situations the influence of special interest publics is mediated through the legislative branch, and less often the executive, but rarely acts as a direct constraint on governmental action. This is what distinguishes the case of the MX MPS from previous military decisions, with the exception of the ELF controversy where citizens succeeded in forestalling the construction of an extremely low-frequency communication system in Michigan and Wisconsin. In both cases public opposition was a consideration in administrative decisions to delay (ELF) or abandon (MPS) a particular military plan. In both cases the nature of the public's role in the decision-making process was at times direct and unmediated. Importantly, in each case direct citizen input was mandated by federal law. In the ELF controversy, NEPA was the primary statutory

188

vehicle available to citizen opponents seeking to directly influence decision making. The MX conflict illustrates the continuing utility of NEPA, as well as the efficacy of additional laws such as FLPMA, the Clean Air and Clean Water Acts, and so on.

In chapter 1 we sought to anticipate and ultimately explain the unique character of the public's role in the MX decision process first by considering factors and phenomena that obviate against citizen involvement. Then we extrapolated from those variables to the case study of MX in generating propositions. What follows is a brief reiteration of that discussion. First, if the public is limited in their ability to take part in weapon acquisition decisions by restricted access to critical information (often classified), then we can expect greater public interest in and concern about a project for which information is readily available. Second, if citizen activism is more likely in cases where the public has a stake in the decision, then we can expect greater public involvement in the decision process for a project that threatens to have significant, immediate, and direct impacts on people. Third, if the nature of public involvement is conditioned in part by the tools and options available to people to participate, then in cases where formal and direct participatory opportunities are present, we can expect political activism to be formal and direct; that is, nonconventional in nature. As a qualifying condition, the longer it takes the government to make a decision, the more time is available for more of the public to collect information, become aware of the stakes involved, and mobilize to influence the decision process.

Conventional wisdom explains the circumscribed nature of the public role in deciding weapon questions as resulting from the people's ignorance about and lack of interest in defense issues, the relatively limited stakes involved, and the traditionally restricted nature of lobbying and electoral power as factors in deciding acquisitions dilemmas. The conventional wisdom errs in assuming that these conditions are an *intrinsic* part of the weapon procurement process. As MX suggests, such is not necessarily the case.

This chapter demonstrates that the hurdles or obstacles to citizen involvement in weapon decisions can be overcome. In the case of MX MPS, the informational hurdle was overcome in several ways. For one, the decision to deploy the missiles in a mobile, land-based scheme raised domestic concerns, information about which is more readily available to the people. The basing mode then was used as a vehicle to attack the entire project since the missiles are essentially inert without a launching scheme. As such it was not necessary to attack the new ICBMs, information about which is highly classified for national security reasons, since by discrediting MPS basing, the project itself was jeopardized. Related to this was the

189

fact that the Freedom of Information Act (FOIA), despite a national security exemption, could be invoked to obtain unclassified information on the MPS decision. Finally, the particular scheme Carter recommended activated several federal laws and regulations, each with mandates that certain decision-making information be shared with people. Most prominently, the National Environmental Policy Act of 1969 (NEPA) requires that the federal government prepare an environmental impact statement (EIS) for any project that will have significant impacts on the human environment. An EIS must be circulated for public comment and review before any government decisions are made which advance a proposed project.

Second, the MX MPS system posed local consequences so massive that the stakes were unavoidable and apparent. Studies verified that the weapon project would transform communities and disrupt the fragile desert ecosystem in the Great Basin region. Residents also feared the consumptive potential of MX in terms of material and natural resources, and the destructive possibilities posed by the system to our "enemies," which could make the Great Basin a prime target for a Soviet strike.

Finally, the decision to deploy the missiles on public "multiple use" land brought into play additional federal, as well as state and local laws and regulations, including the Federal Land Policy and Management Act of 1976 (FLPMA), the Endangered Species Act, the Clean Air and Clean Water Acts, and so on (see Table 5.1). These statutes contain precise standards that compel federal compliance; and, in cases such as FLPMA, require that the government draw the public into the policymaking process. In the discussion that follows we examine more fully the public arena and assess the role of citizen action in the policymaking process — a phenomenon extrinsic to the propositions about procurement decision making in the bureaucratic politics literature.

The First Stage: The Incentive, Overcoming the Informational Hurdles, and Perceiving Stakes

Antinuclear groups emerged with the deployment of the hydrogen bomb and have since monitored and fought the development of increasingly sophisticated and lethal weaponry. Thus, it is surprising that a national anti-MX lobby was not formed in advance of the regional movements that ultimately helped defeat MPS basing in the Great Basin.

As indicated in chapter 5, two technically separate efforts were operating simultaneously to defeat MX MPS; a national lobbying effort, and a regional grassroots effort.[4] Although the two movements shared information and the common objective of ultimately defeating the weapon system, the activities of each were distinctive throughout the campaign. In fact, the organizational efforts to deflect the deployment of MX MAP in the South Platte Plains states, the initially preferred deployment region, were primarily regional and local. There conservative farmers, chamber of commerce groups, religious organizations, and local anti-MX groups (Stop MX Coalition), rose in opposition against the basing of MX in a system that would preempt the use of 5,000 square miles of productive farmland; and successfully pressured their congressional representatives to negotiate the missile system out of Nebraska, Colorado, and Missouri.

During 1979, with evidence that the Great Basin was now a serious contender for MX MPS, Utah state representative Frances Farley (D-S.L.C.) began her campaign to mobilize people in Nevada and Utah against the MX MPS system. The task was a formidable one since residents there are a conservative and patriotic breed, committed to a strong defense and generally deferential to presidential prerogative in such matters. To provoke the ire of such a people would require extraordinary prodding. But, the proposed MX MPS system was an extraordinary project. Ultimately, the spark that ignited the fires of protest was the realization that the system would require an exceptional personal sacrifice on the part of local residents. Moreover, the sacrifice was for a system that had uncertain strategic benefits. Residents in Utah and Nevada came to bitterly resent serving as guinea pigs in such a dangerous and precarious game.

The U.S. Air Force tried to anticipate and deflect the emerging opposition with a public relations campaign focusing on the economic benefits to be gained, and with appeals to the patriotism of area residents. But the stronger appeals were to the fears which the people had concerning the system's destructive potential, both to their immediate lifestyles and to life itself.

The public release of DEIS III in December 1980 (technically January 1981) verified the worst fears concerning MPS basing and provided substantive grounds for a battle that would be waged by citizens groups and state personnel in Nevada and Utah. In other words, until the publication of the third environmental document there was nothing definitive for antagonists to attack. Too, the draft EIS confirmed growing feelings of distrust for the air force and its handling of the MX matter, feelings which were evident as early as June 1980 when Governor Matheson commented:

> I believe that the State of Utah (and Nevada, for that matter) have been ill-served by the general unwillingness of the Air Force to promptly and candidly share all of the information which is in their possession about the MX missile system and its impacts. Indeed, process failures on the part of the Air Force are many and substantial. . . .In fact, it appears that a strategy of minimizing the impacts of MX has emerged.[5]

191

Such suspicions, which began to filter throughout the population, merely served to exacerbate the growing public concern over MX MPS (*Deseret News*, April 21, 1980). Not only would the project have tremendous and irreversible impacts on the region, but the air force was practicing deception to sell the system to area residents.

Similar attitudes were being aired by some members of the congressional delegations from Utah and Nevada, most notably by Representatives Marriott and Santini. For example, Santini, in response to DEIS III, noted that "if private industry had prepared a document as inadequate as this, it would be soundly rejected" (*Salt Lake Tribune*, Dec. 19, 1980). But unlike their South Platte counterparts, these men were unwilling to assume the role of "delegate" and unambiguously defend the regional interests of their constituents. Rather, they essentially viewed their role as decisively Burkean, a not uncommon stance for legislators to assume on military issues (See Wahlke, *et al.*, 1962). Despite apparent congruence between congressional and constituent attitudes, the Great Basin contingency maintained their independence to decide questions of national interest, unimpeded by state concerns. To those involved, this seemed the only politically feasible strategy: to couch their own equivocal positions on MX MPS in terms of national interest and avoid the pitfalls of regionalism. Consider, for example, that Marriott acted as liaison for anti-MX groups in Utah yet never publicly endorsed their cause. Or, the aloofness of Garn and Laxalt, as they sought to mobilize support for silo basing behind the scenes. Similarly, the issue of split-basing was seized upon by Great Basin senators and representatives as a safe way to register their concern with MPS basing publicly, thus casting them in the role of constituent spokesmen, while still avoiding a definitive oppositional stance to the MX system itself. Finally, despite their Burkean claims to independence, most of the legislators were willingly involved in cooperative planning efforts with their states to insure maximum congressional consideration of the federal impact aid needs of Nevada and Utah. MX state coordinators Steven Bradhurst (Nev.) and Ken Olsen (Utah) worked closely with the offices of Gunn McKay (until his defeat), Santini and Garn.

Both Senators Hatch and Cannon did not demonstrate any opposition at this stage, and served as spokesmen for defense and business interests in their respective states. In fact, even before Carter's 1979 announcement, Hatch was meeting with representatives from Thiokol Corporation, Hercules Inc., Litton, and Sperry-Univac (authors' interviews). Cannon was successful in getting the air force to open offices in Nevada and Utah to help local businessmen apply for MX construction grants. Air force officers themselves were active lobbyists at local service clubs, schools, and churchs across Utah and Nevada (authors' interviews). Groups of MX project contractors and businessmen hired political consultants to sell MX, and financed elaborate pro-MX displays, while quietly backing organizations such as Citizens for a Strong National Defense. This is interest group politics in its classic form. And, even though MX MPS never came to the Great Basin, both Thiokol and Hercules, and a few smaller companies in Nevada and Utah, have retained their MX contracts.

As soon as the Texas and New Mexico parts of the environmental statement were added rather hurriedly by the air force following a legislative mandate, people in that area began organizing against MX MPS as well. There was no ambiguity about their position. For example, a petition (quoted in *The Texas Observor*, November 26, 1980) circulated in Texas and New Mexico read: "We the undersigned citizens of West Texas and Eastern New Mexico, hereby serve notice that. . .any consideration of this area for a network of nuclear silos and targets is going to be met with fierce and determined resistance by citizens of this area through the court system and the legislative and executive branches of state and federal government. . . ." And, Senator John Tower (R-Tex.) vowed to use his new position as chair of the Armed Services Committee to prevent MX MPS from ever being based in Texas (authors' interviews).

The split-basing proposal also had the unexpected effect of activating advocates of MPS basing in the preferred deployment areas of Nevada and Utah, who had previously maintained a low profile. With the addition of Texas and New Mexico, there was the possibility of losing an operating base and, thus, the economic benefits of MX deployment, while still being in the general area where the missiles would be placed. This prompted rallies and a trip to Washington, D.C. by seventy-one citizens from Milford, Utah, to lobby for deployment of MX MPS in Utah (authors' interviews).

For the most part, early public activity, both oppositional and favorable, was primarily of the conventional nature that the bureaucratic politics propositions anticipate, albeit discount as insignificant. Although these actions served to provoke public interest in and concern about the missile system, the substantive results were primarily symbolic. In the end, when the Reagan administration aired its concerns about citizen resistance, it was not referring to the demonstrations and marches on the state capitols and federal buildings in key MX states; to the prayer vigils, peace educational programs and workshops, or services; to the several city council and county commission resolutions opposing MX MPS; nor to the speaking tours, MX exhibits, national letter-writing campaigns, or petitions. While these activities did serve to mobilize public opinion on MX, when Reagan abandoned MPS in October 1981, citing citizen opposition as an ancillary concern, he was referring to the potential power of individuals and groups to actually defeat or critically retard deployment by litigation. The visible display of grassroots politics certainly served the purpose of bringing more people into the movement, but they were not what caused Reagan, Weinberger, and the Pentagon anguish. The fear of the administration was that citizens could invoke existing laws and regulations and tie the system up in legal delays long enough to jeopardize the IOC date of 1986. As Air Force General Kelly Burke had warned: "Appreciable delay in any of these steps would be detrimental to that requirement [of reaching an IOC by the end of 1986]. Ultimately, because that IOC was established to meet a serious Soviet threat to the Nation's ICBMs which the Congress and President believe will exist by the mid-1980s, such a delay could significantly weaken the strategic defense posture of the country."[6]

The Second Stage: Implementing Strategies of Direct Action

The concerns of the president, of members of the executive branch, and of Congress about significant delays in the deployment of MX were not just idle paranoia. As soon as DEIS III was released, representatives from environmental, antinuclear, anti-MX, and peace organizations from around the country met in Salt Lake City (January 1981) to develop a unified strategy with the regional associations to defeat MX MPS. Earlier, both state governments had formed review teams for the purpose of examining and scrutinizing the environmental statement. In both situations, as people began to assess the political and legal options available to them, litigation emerged as the ultimate tool. The National Environmental Policy Act and the Federal Land Policy and Management Act appeared to be the statutes that offered the requisite grounds for such a strategy.

The National Environmental Agenda

Six months in advance of the official release of the site selection and land withdrawal/acquisition EIS (DEIS III), citizens in Nevada and Utah, concerned about the missile system's impact on their lives, were already preparing to review the largest environmental statement ever conducted.[7] Once DEIS III was publicly released, only ninety days would be available to complete the public review authorized by NEPA. Within that limited timeframe, reviewers had to find any defects in the document which, if left uncorrected, could bode disaster for the Great Basin region in the future.

To opponents of the system the public review process offered two lines of attack. The first was to disparage the government's "proposed action" of MX MPS deployment in the Great Basin region by a critical analysis of DEIS III identifying inaccuracies in the data supporting that action. Since

194

the president, in making a decision on a federal project for which an EIS is required, in part relies upon the findings of the environmental study, discrediting that document could convince the administration not to proceed with the proposed action. A second strategy was to reduce the strategic feasibility of the project through delays in construction brought on by legal action. Since NEPA provides legal remedy, lawsuits attacking the validity of the third EIS on NEPA grounds could serve to delay actual procurement until the issues were resolved.

The first strategy, pitting the states of Nevada and Utah against the Pentagon in a battle to sway administrative opinion, involved an extensive examination of DEIS III. To facilitate this endeavor, Governors Matheson and List authorized the creation of formal clearinghouses; and assembled teams of reviewers from the university systems, state and local governments, and the lay community. A total of 572 professional and lay experts actually participated in the reviews. The findings of the review teams were important in two critical ways. First, the evidence confirmed Reagan's existing discomfort with MPS basing; and second, it provoked interest in Congress among legislators previously apathetic to the issue (see chapter 7).

Of particular interest to members of Congress was the evidence presented by the reviewers suggesting that the air force was manipulating the environmental study to guarantee the selection of their preferred deployment area, the Great Basin. First, the air force, in DEIS III, was considering only four states as viable deployment regions, despite a clear mandate from NEPA that all reasonable alternatives be examined. Although an earlier study, FEIS II,[8] had studied seven deployment regions in ten states, that study did not adequately justify, at least in the reviewers' minds, the subsequent narrowing of potential sites to four. In addition, the conclusions reached in DEIS III were drafted so as to advance the selection of the Nevada-Utah site. Within the four states the air force identified eight deployment regions, six of which included the Nevada-Utah configuration. Moreover, of the eight, all of the alternatives that included the Great Basin were ranked high. What concerned reviewers was not the selection of the Great Basin per se, but the lack of sufficient evidence within the environmental statement endorsing the rank ordering.

The release of an air force classified memo, by the Sierra Club to whom it had been leaked, served to confirm the assertions of reviewers that NEPA procedures were being circumvented. In that memo, Undersecretary of the U.S. Air Force Antonio Chayes suggested to Air Force General Lew Allen that the air force begin the studies for the third environmental statement by focusing on the ''one or two significant criteria that could serve to eliminate [alternative areas] without the requirement for completing the full and highly time-consuming EIS.'"⁹ To Nevadans and Utahns, it appeared that the air force had adopted a split-basing option in DEIS III only as a subterfuge. As the rest of the memo makes clear, Chayes' suggestions were intended to promote the choice of the Great Basin, while reducing the political pressures on Matheson and List, both of whom were coming under attack for their earlier endorsement of the MPS plan.

The air force was technically responding to a legislative mandate in the FY 1981 DOD authorization act that the military consider the feasibility of split-basing the missile system in areas outside Nevada and Utah (sec. 202, 1709). The important qualifier was that the entire system could be deployed exclusively in the Great Basin if the air force could demonstrate that dispersing the system was either economically or strategically unfeasible.

The methods that the air force was using to generate and present its data were also scrutinized with care by the states' review teams. In many cases, it appeared that the air force was conducting its studies prior to or without receiving official legal authorization. Of particular concern was the timing and sequence of DEIS III, which technically was being prepared to assist the administration in making its site selection decision, and Congress in the land withdrawal process. DEIS III was the logical follow-on to FEIS II/Milestone II, which had preceded the decision to enter full-scale development in a mobile, land-based, multiple aim point (MAP) scheme. From the reviewers' perspective, two crucial and logically antecedent decisions in the policymaking process had been dealt with insufficiently. The first was the decision to narrow suitable deployment areas to Nevada and Utah, a conflict examined above. Second, was the decision to deploy the missiles in a MAP prototype.

Given NEPA's clear mandate that all reasonable alternatives to the proposed action be studied, many people assumed that the basing mode decision would be made after an examination of an airborne, submarine-launched, or stationary land-based system. On the contrary, FEIS II originally studied only alternatives within the context of the MAP prototype; but then a supplemental EIS (March 1978) was released, five months after the publication of FEIS II, which examined an air-mobile concept. According to critics the narrow construction of the analysis in FEIS II essentially anticipated critical decisions in all subsequent environmental studies, such as the third one under review. For example, the bias towards MAP immediately exempted from serious consideration several regions in the country that could support basing schemes other than a mobile, land-based one. Congress, and later the Reagan administration addressed these concerns by authorizing the Office of Technology Assessment and the Townes Commission, respectively, to examine alternative basing schemes for the new ICBMs.

The particular application of the legal technique of tiering also raised questions about whether the air force was using authorized procedures in unauthorized ways. Tiering is sanctioned in cases where the governmental decisions to be made, for which an EIS is being prepared, are multitiered ones; that is, decision making is to proceed in a successive manner. In such cases a series of environmental impact statements or analyses can be conducted on each successive issue (40 C.F.R., sec. 1508.28). This allows the authorizing government agency to make lesser decisions in advance of the major one either endorsing or opposing the "proposed action." In the case of MX MPS, tiering allowed the air force to make decisions that would successively narrow the geographic areas under study until specific sites were identified as suitable.

This process required essentially a two-tiered approach. Tier-one studies would precede selection of suitable deployment areas and operating base zones. The second level of tier analysis would anticipate the development of an operating base comprehensive plan and the selection of the actual operating base and operational capability facility (protective shelters and transportation network) areas. The Code of Federal Regulations requires that an environmental assessment (EA) of the effects of the proposed action be conducted for each tier-level decision and compared to the predictions of the EIS for the entire area (40 C.F.R., secs. 1502.20 and 1508.28). For MX MPS this meant comparing the anticipated impacts of missile deployment in successively narrower geographic areas to those predicted for the entire deployment region. The next tier of decision making can only proceed if the findings of an EA are the same or less than those of the preliminary EIS; otherwise, a more rigorous EIS must be prepared.

Reviewers accused the air force of beginning tier analyses in advance of completing antecedent ones, thus effectively presuming a decision without the appropriate documentation (an EA or EIS), in violation of NEPA.[10] By proceeding in this manner, the government risked making critical decisions without the benefit of being fully aware of the environmental problems that could accrue if the proposed action (MX MPS deployment in Nevada-Utah) was actually implemented.

These concerns took on greater significance as the air force warned of the importance of meeting program development deadlines. The possibility that the military would use project delays as an excuse to circumvent the legal requirements of NEPA was underscored when the air force tried to get Congress to pass fast-track legislation (Draft 22). (*Congressional Record*, 125:18073-76). Had it passed, Draft 22 would have exempted the military from the NEPA requirement that all reasonable alternatives to the proposed action be considered. Rather, the selection of an MX basing area could proceed following an environmental analysis in the preferred area solely.

197

The bill would also allow the military to avoid a legal confrontation on the home turf of protestants. On the contrary, the bill would give the D.C. Circuit Court of Appeals jurisdiction to hear legal challenges of FEIS III and provide for consideration of such suits in an expedited manner. Although the air force, under public and congressional pressure, did withdraw the fast-track legislation, there are enough precedents to make one cautious. For both the Trans-Alaska Pipeline and the Tellico Dam, Congress passed fast-track legislation.[11]

The bulk of reviewers' complaints concerned perceived technical and analytical problems such as data which were incomplete and in some cases inaccurate; conclusions which were faulty; mitigation measures which were unfeasible; and assessments which were improperly formulated.[12] From the standpoint of Nevadans and Utahns, these oversights were dangerous since they suggested that the government was proceeding with decision making on the missile system without being fully aware of the consequences of their decisions. If deployed, MX MPS could have impacts disastrous in nature not predicted by the legally mandated studies. For example, if, as claimed, the system's social, economic, and environmental impacts were in fact underestimated, residents in the Great Basin would not be prepared to deal with the consequences of deployment. More critically, if some of the proposed mitigation measures were, as asserted, unfeasible (for example, water recycling and sophisticated energy methods) or themselves threatened to have additional impacts not considered by the air force (for example, jeopardizing a treaty with Mexico if water from the Colorado River was extracted), the government ran the risk of having the construction of its missile system halted in midstream.

Disclosures such as these were instrumental in derogating DEIS III, the preparation of the environmental document by the military and its private contractors, and the proposed action (MX MPS deployment in Nevada-Utah) as well.[13] Some of the revelations even brought into question the strategic and technical feasibility of the system itself.[14] When the GAO, under congressional sanction, publicly released its independent analysis of the draft statement, the viability of the claims of the states' review teams were underscored. In testimony before the House public lands subcommittee (U.S. House of Representatives, 1981a), the GAO concluded that "the draft contains several questionable assumptions for selecting alternative operating base locations, determining resource availability, assessing impacts, and suggesting mitigating measures to deal with the impacts" (U.S. House of Representatives, 1981a).

Since the president ultimately has the discretion to make procurement decisions, what could possibly be the immediate effect of revelations of military malfeasance? At a minimum, the air force would be required, as

NEPA mandates, to consider and respond to the critical comments of reviewers. The Council on Environmental Quality (CEQ), which is authorized to approve EISs, could fault the document on technical grounds, deriving inspiration from the states' reviews, and compel the air force to make corrections in the final document (FEIS). An improved FEIS would put citizens in a better position to realistically anticipate the consequences of the project's construction in the area; and provide more accurate information as well. Although FEIS III was never publicly released,[15] the CEQ did in fact issue a formal condemnation of DEIS III, citing "significant omissions and weaknesses" in the study serious enough to "undermine the validity of the air force's NEPA compliance. . . ."[16] In particular, CEQ Acting Director Malcolm Baldwin cited the failure of the air force to sufficiently study (1) the feasibility of deploying the project in Colorado, Kansas, and/or Nebraska; (2) basing modes other than the MAP scheme; (3) the full-range of consequences posed by deployment in the Great Basin; and (4) alternative mitigation measures.[17] But, the critical analyses of DEIS III proved to be considerably more useful than that. In fact, the document became the basis of a major lawsuit.

The Legal Angle

Under NEPA, citizens can initiate a civil suit against the federal agents responsible for an EIS (1) for failure to conduct a legally mandated environmental study; (2) when procedural errors are committed in the preparation of the document; or (3) for substantive errors such as failure to conform to the statutory goals of NEPA (Liroff, 1981:316). However, the pattern of judicial interpretation of NEPA up to 1984 suggests that the procedural route is the most expedient one. In most cases, the predominant consequences of litigation in NEPA cases have been dilatory in nature: that is, projects have been more often delayed until the procedural errors have been corrected than blocked or modified. Of course, the MX MPS system was vulnerable to delays that could threaten the strategic feasibility of the program since the logic of the weapon project was contingent upon its closing the window of vulnerability by the end of the decade. A postponement of seven or eight months, the average delay resulting from injunctions associated with NEPA suits in 1978 and 1979 (CEQ, 1979:589; CEQ, 1980:384), could jeopardize the practicability of MX as a defense option.

The dilatory utility of a lawsuit on NEPA grounds was readily apparent to opponents of MX MPS deployment in the Great Basin. The critical analysis of DEIS III suggested two paramount grounds for attack. The first ground derives from the NEPA requirement that all "reasonable" alternatives to the proposed action be "rigorously explored," and "objectively" examined. Moreover, the government must explain and justify why certain

199

alternatives were rejected. The CEQ has called this requirement "the heart of the environmental impact statement." It is easy to see why. Failure to comply could result in an EIS which endorses the "proposed action," despite the availability of better alternatives (40 C.F.R., secs. 1502.11 and 1502.14). In the case of a defense project, such as MX MPS, failure to adopt the best option could result in disasterous consequences. One example will suffice to underscore this point.

One of the most contentious claims in DEIS III concerns the availability of water. The statement recognizes the "problem," but proposes means for supplying the precious resource nonetheless. Many reviewers felt that the air force was unduly optimistic, and that the military, in fact, would encounter a water shortage *during* construction. If that had happened, it is not difficult to predict the outcome.

Of course, opponents of MX MPS, who found litigation an attractive tool, were not necessarily motivated by an altruistic regard for the success of the air force. On the contrary, they wanted to see the project abandoned. Since under NEPA they could not directly attack the project, the only alternative was to discredit the document endorsing the proposed action. An environmental study that considered only four states as reasonable deployment regions, that limited six of the eight "reasonable alternatives" to Utah and Nevada, and that only examined MPS basing could be legally vulnerable.

The second ground of attack which NEPA suggests relates to the CEQ requirement that all environmental issues be investigated before the government takes any action towards a final and irrevocable decision. The Code of Federal Regulations also warns agencies that they cannot "commit resources prejudicing selection of alternatives before making a final decision" (40 C.F.R., sec. 1502.24). From this viewpoint, the air force's use of tiering, and the omissions and inaccuracies in the environmental document recommended further lines of legal challenge.

In June 1981 three state legislators and several citizens groups from Nevada and Utah filed a lawsuit against the federal government charging them with violating NEPA in the preparation of DEIS III and FEIS II/Milestone II (*Farley* v. *U.S. Air Force*). Plaintiffs first attacked FEIS II for being technically and procedurally flawed, primarily because of the failure in that document to consider all reasonable alternatives to a mobile, land-based, multiple aim point (MAP) strategy. After which all decisions logically consequent to the second statement were "of no legal force or effect;" that is, those made within the context of DEIS III. The air force was also faulted for its violation of a congressional mandate prohibiting the obligation of military construction funds: "for design of any site-specific facilities for the MX missile system until all terms, conditions, and requirements of NEPA. . .are met which will include a complete analysis of a split-basing alternative'' (Military Construction Appropriations Act of 1981).

Among the omissions cited by Farley, two oversights were paramount: the failure to anticipate and, thus, examine the impacts of an expansion, or enlargement, of the original 200 missile/4,600 shelter scheme; or of a Soviet strike on the system. From the perspective of the plaintiffs, both scenarios were credible ones posing predictable impacts on the human environment, which needed to be, and were not, examined in DEIS III. Finally, the inappropriate use of tiering and failure to respect NEPA mandated federal-state cooperation and coordination in the preparation of DEIS III, were cited in the suit.

The way in which the claims and charges in the suit are formulated suggests that the plaintiffs hoped to secure a court order requiring that the air force and other ''military defendants'' correct the defects in FEIS II and DEIS III to bring both statements into conformity with NEPA require-ments. With fresh evidence the federal government, plaintiffs surmised, would reconsider their previous MX decisions, now determined to be based on inaccurate data, and embrace a policy position compatible with that of the plaintiffs: to abandon MX MPS basing in the Great Basin. Barring that, an injunction ordering defendants to terminate design work and project implementation until NEPA requirements were met could serve to post-pone the system long enough to imperil it.

Although the district judge for Utah dismissed the case without prejudice after Reagan's announcement rejecting the MX MPS system, it is still important in anticipation of similar such conflicts to delineate the probable scenarios had the MX case been decided on its merits.

On the one hand, there is sufficient legal and statutory evidence to suggest that government decisions made in advance of the completion of a required environmental impact statement are invalid. For example, in *Scientists' Institute for Public Information* v. *Atomic Energy Commission* (481 F.2d. 1079, D.C. Cir. 1973) and in *Environmental Defense Fund* v. *Andrus* (596 F. 2d. 848, 9th Cir. 1979) the federal courts ruled that before the government commits itself to any decision that effectively narrows the future range of decisional options, the EIS must be completed. In addition, it is mandatory that an EIS be prepared early enough to allow the public to participate before ''an irretrievable commitment of resources.'' The CEQ regulations are also clear on this point (40 C.F.R., secs. 1502.5, 1502.2[g], and 1500.1[b]).

On the other hand, the courts do distinguish between proposed and anticipated action; that is, between federal projects which might be con-structed as opposed to those which will be unless evidence advises other-

201

wise. Only the second, "proposed actions," fall within the legal boundaries of NEPA (*Kleppe* v. *Sierra Club*, 427 U.S. 390, 1976). Most recently, in *Weinberger* v. *Hawaii* (50 L.W.:4028) the U.S. Supreme Court asserted that the government was not required to prepare an EIS before the military constructed magazines capable of housing nuclear weapons until the decision to actually place them there was made.

On the basis of these judicial patterns, what can we say about the probable outcome of the *Farley* suit? The claim that the original MAP decision (FEIS II) circumscribed subsequent decisions seems to be tenable. The counterclaim made by defendants that the mandate given the Townes Commission to study alternative basing modes returned the MPS decision to the status of anticipated rather than proposed action seems equally tenable.[18] However, if the latter is true, then the purpose of the DEIS III, to assist in site selection and land withdrawal decisions for a mobile, land-based scheme, is no longer viable.

Second, there is some evidence to support the claim that both environmental documents failed to consider fully all reasonable alternatives to the proposed action. In *Citizens Against Toxic Sprays, Inc.* v. *Bergland* (428 F. Supp. 908, 1977), the court introduced a test to assist in deciding when the government, in preparing an EIS, has violated this NEPA provision. In *Citizens* the court posed two questions: have a sufficiently broad range of alternatives been considered in the EIS, and have the alternatives been discussed in sufficient detail? Earlier, in *Natural Resources Defense Council* v. *Morton* (458 F. 2d. 827, D.C. Cir. 1972), the D.C. Circuit Court of Appeals stated that a federal agency with the responsibility for preparing an EIS could not justify disregarding alternatives by contending that "they did not offer a complete solution" (836), or fall within the agency's jurisdiction (834). These standards were later codified in CEQ regulations (40 C.F.R., sec. 1502.14[c]). Finally, in *State of California* v. *Bergland* (483 F. Supp. 465, E.D. Cal. 1980), the district court faulted the EIS prepared prior to RARE II decisions for skewing the alternatives studied in such a way as to circumscribe the decision-making process (489). It is also interesting to note that in the *California* v. *Bergland* case, the court reaffirmed that tiering cannot be used by a federal agency as a means to avoid or postpone the preparation of EAs or EISs on decisions antecedent to the major one to proceed with the proposed action.

In sum, there is sufficient judicial precedent to support a legal challenge of the environmental impact statements on procedural grounds. Although the immediate consequences are likely to be dilatory ones, the precariousness of weapon systems make them particularly vulnerable to any delays. On the other hand, the federal courts have exhibited considerable self-restraint in cases involving attacks on draft statements, deferring instead to

202

the public review and comment period provided by NEPA as the appropriate forum at this point. Of course, delaying a challenge until the final statement reduces the chances of plaintiffs securing a favorable decision, at least in cases involving military projects where time is a critical factor.

The courts' general inclination to defer to political or administrative bodies in making policy decisions means that they practice considerably more self-restraint in NEPA cases involving substantive challenges. The federal courts, of course, will consider legal challenges claiming that a government's decision is arbitrary or capricious. In addition, CEQ regulations state that "if a draft statement is so inadequate as to preclude meaningful analysis, the agency shall prepare and circulate a revised draft of the appropriate position" (40 C.F.R., sec.1502.9[a]). This provides a substantive basis for a legal challenge of the content of an environmental statement.   From a substantive perspective, the clearest omission or inadequacy in the third statement which, it can be argued, precludes a meaningful analysis of the impacts of MX MPS on the Great Basin region, is the failure to consider the consequences of any enlargement in the system. Several government studies predicted that the military project, as originally conceived, would have to be expanded. The GAO, for example, noted that "current SAC projections indicate — even within the constraints of the unratified SALT II treaty — a higher number of missiles and shelters may be required to provide the necessary survivability" (U.S. House of Representatives, 1981b:13). Similarly, the OTA estimated that "MX deployment could not be viable unless the number of shelters grew to several times the initial 4600. . . .A 12,000 RV threat in 1995 will require 12,500 shelters with 544 missiles" (U.S. G.A.O., 1981:257).

The Federal Land Policy and Management Act

In ways similar in nature, although not detail, to NEPA, FLPMA offers antagonists of a land-based government project considerable opportunities to pursue a legal challenge with the ultimate goal of defeat through delay. The *Farley* suit did invoke FLPMA as providing additional grounds for invalidating the decision-making process on MX MPS. Does that act provide for any more certainty as regards a legal challenge? Legal opinion on FLPMA is meager, making it difficult to anticipate the court's judgment in this case. However, common standards of judicial review, and two statutory aspects of FLPMA do point in the direction of a decision ultimately, although not immediately, favorable to the federal government. Again, this is the crucial point. It is unlikely that citizens can directly defeat a defense project slated for deployment in their backyard. What is possible is that they can postpone, through an injunction, the actual construction of a project long enough to defeat it in fact.

203

The first legal standard involves the courts' reluctance to make decisions that replace administrative ones. Second, courts, we have noted, have focused more often on the procedural rather than substantive aspects of congressional statutes. Both principles imply the scenario of delay discussed above. The second standard suggests an additional possibility. If, under court order, the federal government was required to go back and reexamine, according to the requirements of FLPMA, the procedures it used to reach a decision, it is possible that a different decision would emerge following procedural corrections. Plaintiffs in the *Farley* suit, for example, were hopeful that, if defendants were enjoined from proceeding with MX decision-making activities until compliance with the public participatory and public land planning requirements of FLPMA, the additional time would either force a debilitating delay or influence modifications in prior and preceding decisions.

Two statutory aspects of FLPMA are suggestive as well. Despite a strong mandate for state and local governmental involvement in all public land planning activities, FLPMA leaves a wide latitude of discretion to the secretary of interior in delineating the extent of such involvement. Several provisions specifying involvement are qualified to give the secretary the power to comply in ways which "he finds consistent with Federal law and the purposes of this Act" (43 U.S.C., sec. 1712). Finally, the broad and sweeping references to state and public involvement further the discretionary power of the interior secretary and the BLM "to define the standards on which its program will be reviewed" (Achterman and Fairfax, 1979:528).

On August 13, 1981, sheep and cattle ranchers in Nevada and Utah filed a lawsuit charging the federal government with violations of FLPMA. In an effort to circumvent the discretionary provisions of FLPMA and pinpoint violations of FLPMA with precise statutory bases, plaintiffs focused on the narrow issue of whether the activities being conducted by defendants on public land in preparation for FEIS III and public land withdrawal were legally authorized. By claiming that they were not, protestants endeavored to halt such activities until authorization was secured (*Nevada Cattleman's Association, et al.* v. *James Watt, et al.*, 1981, Civil No. C 81-0595 J., U.S. Dist. Ct., Nev.).

The activities in question were being conducted under a cooperative agreement issued by the BLM. FLPMA sanctions such agreements for purposes "similar or closely related to the programs of the secretary [of the interior]. . ." (43 U.S.C., sec. 1732). The BLM saw the activities as compatible with the interior secretary's jurisdiction over the public land withdrawal process. In contrast, the ranchers saw the activities as preconstruction and, thus, military activities, since they were advancing the *construction* of the missile system in the Great Basin. From this perspec-

204

tive, the drilling, trenching, digging, and blasting were illegal. This suit also was made moot by the Reagan administration's decision to abandon MX MPS. Even though the two judicial and two statutory caveats discussed above would likely influence the court to render a decision favorable to the federal government, the adjudicatory process for administrative appeals mandated by FLPMA does offer another, and perhaps more expedient, vehicle (see chapter 5).

FLPMA's utility as a political tool was also tested even before the legal challenges. The first major political skirmish concerned accusations that the federal government had failed to comply with Utah procedures for securing a permit to conduct environmental and geotechnic tests and surveys on state land. FLPMA requires that a federal agency comply with state and local land- use laws and regulations. During preparatory work for DEIS III, in the summer of 1979, the air force defied a Utah law requiring that an entry permit be acquired before using state lands (Utah Code Annotated, 1976:65, sec. 1-78). (It is important to note that in Nevada, a permit from the BLM automatically covers state land requirements.) The air force could hardly avoid trespassing because the area it was surveying is interspersed with state and private property. Nonetheless, the air force ignored the permit procedures twice (the second time in the fall of 1980).

Under the authority of Utah state law, the air force was fined $30,000. Utah could have taken, and, in fact, considered taking, court action charging the federal government with violations of FLPMA. However, at the time Utah was concerned with insuring federal consultation and cooperation with the state in planning for MX, not with postponing the project itself. Thus, the state yielded when the air force "promised" to consult formally with Utah on future MX matters. The air force pledged to hold periodic meetings with state officials and to use state personnel as resource persons. Although Utah and the military eventually reconciled the dispute, the "arrogance" demonstrated by the military during the incidents prompted legislative efforts in both Utah and Nevada to avoid future "misunderstandings."

Assembly Bill 383 in Nevada and Senate Bill 123 in Utah were submitted by their sponsors with the intent to compel the federal agencies involved with the MX project to comply with FLPMA requirements for intergovernmental consultation and cooperation. Each bill gave the appropriate state agencies the power to withhold state permits if a federal agency failed to first inform the state of the anticipated impacts of its activities on land and water use plans. The federal agencies were also required to submit statements detailing feasible mitigation measures in the event of intergovernmental conflicts. Finally, the attorney general in each state was empowered to take legal action to block the MX project if the above conditions were violated. The Utah bill failed to survive the "sifting" process in the House after clearing the Senate 17 to 3. On March 26, 1981, however, the Nevada bill became law (Statutes of Nevada, 1981:chap. 409).

What sorts of legal questions does the Nevada law raise.   The federal government enjoys a certain degree of immunity from state interference with federal activities. The major exceptions are where federal law specifically sanctions state interference (*McCulloch* v. *Maryland*, 4 Wheat 316, 4 L. Ed. 579, 1819). FLPMA does justify state "involvement," but does not authorize obstruction, except through provisions for judicial review. Thus, state law provisions requiring that the federal government consult and coordinate with state/local entities seem consistent with what FLPMA sanctions. However, making the issuance of state land and water permits contingent upon such consultation is tantamount to the type of obstruction that constitutional interpretation has found invalid (*Hancock* v. *Train*, 426 U.S. 167, 1976; *Miller* v. *Ark.*, 351 U.S. 948 Mem., 1956; and *Utah Power and Light Company* v. *U.S.*, 243 U.S. 389, 1917). The Legislative Counsel Bureau of Nevada, in summarizing the legal status of AB 383, concluded that "any conditioning of the exercise of the power to eminent domain on compliance with state law is impermissible."[19]

State-Federal Water Rights, and Other Statutory Provisions

If correct, this interpretation also reduces, although it does not eliminate, the utility of state control over water rights as a tool in influencing federal projects constructed on public lands. The dilatory value here lies in the provisions for public comment and review of water permit applications provided for under Nevada and Utah state law (Holland and Benedict, 1982). In both states, water allocation is a discretionary decision made by the state water engineers bounded only by considerations of availability, the "public interest," and whether the proposed use is a "beneficial" one. Public hearings are held to allow citizens to register complaints; and formal challenges can be made on the basis of the three criteria listed above. At one point during the MX MPS controversy, for example, several hundred private challenges of air force applications were pending. Resolution of the sheer number of complaints could have taken up to two years without any expediting procedures. Draft 22, if passed, would have reduced considerably the ability of citizens to delay MX decision making, through challenges of water permit applications, with a provision requiring that state and local agencies act upon any MX-related permit applications within nine months.

It is unlikely that the water engineers in either state would have denied the air force requests anyway. To invalidate a water permit application on the basis that the MX project was neither in the public interest nor constituted a proposed use of water in a beneficial way, would suggest that a political, rather than an administrative, decision was being made. Moreover, both state engineers conducted studies concluding that water availability was not a problem (Utah, 1981; Nevada, 1981).

Even a negative ruling, however, would have left the air force with several options for obtaining water (Holland and Benedict, 1982). Most notably, the air force could invoke the reservation doctrine. Second, they could purchase water rights, an option made attractive by several unsolicited offers to the air force from residents in the Great Basin region (*Salt Lake Tribune*, April 3, 1981). Moreover, when federal agencies acquire privately owned water through purchase or eminent domain, the use of such water is not subject to state laws (*Cappaert* v. *U.S.*, 426 U.S. 128, 1976). Finally, an opinion by the Solicitor of the Department of the Interior under Carter, issued to guide that Department in making claims to water rights, suggests yet another route. In that opinion, the Solicitor asserts a federal nonreserved right to unappropriated water (Anon., 1979:574-75). In essence this would have sanctioned the federal government in taking unreserved, unappropriated water for use on unreserved federal lands, without complying with state law. The opinion then extends this right to "secondary" uses on *reserved* lands. As such, this Krulitz Doctrine, as it came to be called, could have been used to secure water for ancillary uses connected to the MX project for which an original land withdrawal authorization did not apply. Although the Reagan administration, in the fall of 1982, abandoned the Krulitz Doctrine, its consideration by the executive branch underscores the tenuous status of state water rights.

The sheer number of laws and regulations that antagonists of MX MPS had at their command created a theoretical labyrinth of incredible complexity. In addition to throwing up the hurdles of NEPA, FLPMA, and state water rights, citizen opponents invoked the FOIA. They were also prepared to sue the air force under the Endangered Species Act, the Clean Air and Clean Water Acts, and the Historic Preservation Act, to name but a few. In each case, the likelihood of defeating the missile system on the grounds that it was contributing to the pollution of the air and water in the Great Basin, threatening the survival of the Bald Eagle, sage grouse, or desert tortoise, or jeopardizing the integrity of ancient Indian relics, was recognized as slim. But, temporarily postponing the actual construction of MX MPS by tying the project up in litigation was viewed as a definite possibility.

Consider the case of the FOIA as an illustration. The FOIA was invoked in spring of 1981 by MX opponents who sought to secure information about the process preceding the decisions to deploy MX MPS in the Great Basin, in order to document that the air force was, in fact, violating both NEPA and FLPMA. Under the provisions of the act, an agency must legally respond to a FOIA request within ten working days, unless the materials are difficult to amass (5 U.S.C., secs. 552[a], [b]). Almost two months after the request, the air force sent 75 percent of the requested materials, but withheld the remainder under the act's national security exemption. Protestants responded with a series of appeals in which the air force was reminded of their legal obligation to "segregate and supply the portions of the document [requested] that are not subject to legitimate classification, deleting and withholding only that portion that is legitimately classified."[20] The remaining documents were never released. This was hardly surprising since as early as November 1979, State Senator Farley had applied through the FOIA for a *nonclassified* map detailing the deployment scheme for 4,600 shelters in the Great Basin. The air force did not respond.

Under the FOIA, opponents could have enlisted the help of a federal court to decide the validity of the information's classified status. Had they done so, the court would most likely have defended nondisclosure absent a compelling reason to the contrary. Nonetheless, the action of bringing suit could have involved the air force in another lengthy legal battle.

Several Indian tribes in the vicinity of the MX MPS zone were prepared to take legal action as well. For example, the Western Shoshone Sacred Lands Association threatened to invoke international law, since a third of the missiles would be deployed on lands they consider sacred. Moreover, ranchers and public officials in Nye County, Nevada, were successful in getting the BLM to refuse to allow the air force to conduct MX test blasts in Tonopah, after the Public Lands Legal Foundation filed suit in March 1981. Likewise, a federal district court judge issued a temporary restraining order barring Rocketdyne from further testing of a fourth stage of the MX missile, following a suit filed by Alliance for Survival in February 1981. In addition, two state legislators in February 1981 introduced a "dummy bill" (H.B. 626) making it a felony to place MX missiles on productive farmland in New Mexico. Finally, a suit challenging the security system proposed to protect MX MPS as "an unconstitutional form of military rule heretofore unprecedented in our legal system," followed an article by investigative reporter Mark Shapiro in June 1981. These are just a few of the actions which were undertaken in efforts to forestall MX MPS deployment.

Observations

We cannot definitely measure the extent to which public opposition influenced the Reagan administration's decision in October 1981 not to deploy MX in an MPS mode in the Great Basin. But it is definite that a role the public did play. While citing strategic and foreign policy reasons as paramount considerations, the president did mention the threat of lawsuits as an ancillary concern. Similarly, Weinberger, in a series of public statements, admitted that the administration was apprehensive about the specter of litigation. Even more significant is the fact that the proposals endorsed by the Reagan administration have been characteristically unprovocative to most regional interests. All three basing plans — interim silo basing, closely spaced basing, and Peacekeeper — would be deployed on relatively small plots of mostly private or military lands, with socioeconomic, cultural, and environmental impacts deemed manageable by most area residents; and, thus, would avoid many, although not all, of the hundreds of federal, state and local laws and regulations that MPS basing in the Great Basin activated.

We, therefore, believe that the public arena was a significant factor in the decisions made for MX in 1980 and 1981. The evidence in this chapter thus supports four of the additional propositions suggested at the end of chapter 1 — propositions 17, 18, 20, and 21. More precisely, environmental considerations and socioeconomic issues did have a significant impact on MX decision making; and the public arena was very significant in MX deliberations between 1979 and 1981. The bureaucratic politics approach is insufficient for explaining this dimension of MX procurement policy. The propositions for the inner and outer layer for procurement decision making need restatement to take into consideration the conditions that are likely to activate the public arena.

Has the Reagan administration, by promoting relatively unobtrusive basing modes for MX, successfully circumvented the obstacles of citizen resistance? More importantly, can future administrations avoid encounters with the public over nuclear weapon systems? The environmental impact statement prepared in anticipation of the most current administration basing plan, silo basing in Wyoming and Nebraska, has been examined and commented upon by affected citizens. Public opinion polls suggest majority support for the project. However, those residents in southeastern Wyoming and western Nebraska who have attended the public hearings have been overwhelmingly critical. In Torrington, Wyoming, for example, where the first missiles will be placed, one hundred residents aired concerns with regard to the future integrity of ranching and farming in the area, receiving adequate federal impact assistance, and surviving a boom-bust phenomenon if the MX is deployed (*The Salt Lake Tribune*, November 3, 1983). Western Solidarity, an umbrella coalition of western opposition to MX, has been working with opponents in Wyoming and Nebraska, providing them with legal assistance in preparation for a challenge of the current environmental document. Many of these activists are veterans of

209

the battles in Nevada, Utah, New Mexico, and Texas. They are also members of the national anti-MX movement, where work continues on two fronts: (1) encouraging active regional resistance to actual deployment; and (2) lobbying Congress to cut off MX funds.

Can the federal government avoid future political hassles by recommending military projects that are structurally unprovocative? To some extent the answer is yes, since the reaction to MX MPS can be explained in part by the unique nature of that missile system: its enormous size, cost, environmental disruption, and lethality; and, the strategic implications of its capacity to be a first-strike weapon. There is, however, a problem with this assessment. The current plan, Peacekeeper, does not solve the problem of vulnerability. Ironically, that challenge could require mobile, land-based schemes as threatening as the Carter one. Current predictions anticipate the deployment of Midgetman in a MAP prototype. To do otherwise would require substantial modifications in our current strategic policies. In particular, if we were to abandon land-based systems, this would require that we also abandon the nuclear triad. To renounce land-mobile systems, we would have to discover a way to superharden stationary silos to enhance their ability to withstand a direct hit from increasingly more accurate Soviet missiles, or else adopt a launch-on-warning policy. Finally, to forsake large MIRVed ICBMs would require substantially new technology, or an arms limitation agreement with the Soviet Union.

There is also an important legacy of the battle over MPS basing, which continues to play a critical part in the ongoing saga: the nuclear freeze movement. Future administrations may be able to defuse regional opposition with less obtrusive weapon systems. But can they deflate the growing national resistance to the nuclear arms race itself? The public debate over MPS basing that began as an isolated regional issue grew into a national controversy, and then expanded into an examination of the validity of the need for new weapons such as MX. This helped incite the emergence of a national freeze movement. Despite attempts by the Reagan administration to discredit the sincerity of those who advocate disarmament, the movement continues to gain adherents. So important has public concern over nuclear weapons become that several younger members of Congress have embraced the issue as potentially expedient (authors' interviews).

The concerns raised by anti-MX groups and individuals that later infected Congress helped to create a mood in the national legislature that laid to rest the first two basing plans submitted by Reagan, before a third one was finally given equivocal endorsement by Congress. It is to a discussion of that tumultuous period of the Reagan administration that we now turn.

Endnotes

[1]See appendices A and B.

[2]Opinion polls covering the period between the president's announcement of his plan to place a land-based ICBM in the Great Basin region through the 1980 election show a public opinion in Utah and Nevada that is committed to MX, but substantially divided on the issue of its deployment in Utah and Nevada. Polls show a dramatic shift against the system between October 1979, when 69 percent of Utahns surveyed said they were "not personally bothered" by the decision, and April 1980, when opposition rose in Utah to 60.2 percent and in Nevada to 37 percent. Those who supported the project were 31.5 percent and 35 percent in Utah and Nevada respectively. A year later, after Reagan's inauguration, public opinion in the Great Basin states shifted again, with polls showing a dramatic decline in the number of those Utahns opposed to MX (49 percent to 41 percent in favor), and a lesser decline in Nevada. However, a clear majority remain opposed or undecided. An equally dramatic shift took place after the LDS church's public statement in opposition to the MX in May 1981. Opposition reached a high of 75 percent in Utah. After that, opinion stabilized, with a significant majority (65 percent) clearly opposed to deployment in the Great Basin, but committed to the MX to secure national defense. Polls were conducted by Dan Jones and Associates, Salt Lake City, Utah, and reprinted in the *Deseret News* (Salt Lake City). See, in particular, the following issues: 20 March 1981; 19 November 1980; 21 April 1980; 24 November 1980.

[3]See chapter 7 for a discussion.

[4]The authors are grateful to Stan Holmes for clarifying some of this information.

[5]Quoted in a pamphlet distributed by Citizens Call, Salt Lake City, Utah, at the May 1981 public hearing on DEIS III.

[6]Statement of Lt. General Kelly H. Burke, *Farley, et al.* v. *U.S. Air Force, et al.*, 21 August 1981.

[7]Some of the analysis in the section that follows on NEPA appears in Holland (1984).

[8]The final decision to produce and deploy the advanced missiles in a certain launching scheme and a specific geographic area originally was to follow a series of four environmental impact statements. Two studies prior to DEIS III had concluded that the MX missile system should be built (FEIS I), and should enter full-scale development in a mobile, land based, multiple aim point format (FEIS II). The third study was to be used in selecting deployment areas (both missile and support facility sites), and for land withdrawal and acquisition purposes for a mobile system. A fourth study was to precede the actual production and deployment decision.

[9]The memo was made public by the Sierra Club on 3 April 1981.

[10]This information was supplied by Ann Keegan, MX Coordinator, Utah State Office. Interview by the authors, Salt Lake City, Utah, 29 April 1982.

[11]See for example, the Trans-Alaska Pipeline Authorization Act, P.L. 93-153, sec. 203(d).

[12]Among the major criticisms were the air force's failure: (1) to employ the most recent data available, particularly in estimating construction labor force size; (2) to consider the impacts of two competitive synthetic and fossil fuel development projects, and the construction of an electric coal generation plant, near the MX area; (3) to document generalizations such as the one that MX deployment would bring economic advantages to the region (a boom) which would ameliorate the disadvantages (the bust); (4) to consider the results of MX being decommissioned; (5) to provide data supporting some claims such as the one that sufficient water for the project would be available; and (6) to include "adequate" maps. See "State of Nevada Official Response to the United States Air Force Deployment Area Selection and Land Withdrawal/Acquisition Draft Environmental Impact Statement," and "State of Utah Comments on the Air Force DEIS on the Proposed MX Missile Project" (Hereinafter called The State Reviews).

[13]The issue of water is illustrative. The Great Basin area is one of the driest in the nation with an average of four to ten inches rainfall. Almost all of the water is allocated. In FEIS II, the Air Force failed to consider either water availability or control as "geotechnic requirements" in selecting deployment regions. In DEIS III, the air force concluded that the water problem was critical but "solvable." First, this assurance was attacked by the Council on Environmental Quality, the Office of Technology Assessment, the General Accounting Office, and the Department of Interior, all of which took issue with the assumptions in DEIS III. Second, reviewers pointed to (1) the failure of the air force to consider the impacts of the competition for water by other energy projects in the area; (2) the fact that many of the mitigation measures cited relied upon technology as yet developed; (3) probable conflicts with Mexico and other western states if water was drawn from the Colorado River, as suggested; (4) the failure to consider the water needs of an expanded MX MPS system; and (5) the failure to anticipate a drought in the area. As the Bureau of Land Management concluded, water "is probably the most critical resource, to both the project itself and the other users in the area." See, for example, House Committee on Interior and Insular Affairs, The MX Missile System, 96th Congress., 1st & 2d sess., 1980, 28; U.S. Air Force, "Deployment Area Selection and Land Withdrawal Draft EIS," vol 3:10-12; and The State Reviews.

[14]See Lauren Holland and Robert Hoover, "Congressional-Executive Relations: the Case of the MX Missile System," paper delivered at the 1984 Western Political Science Association Convention, Sacramento, California.

[15]A final EIS was to have been completed and publicly available by May 1982. It is not obtainable.

212

[16]These comments were made in a letter from Baldwin to Air Force Secretary Vern Orr, dated 30 April 1981.

[17]*Ibid.*

[18]In March of 1981, Defense Secretary Caspar Weinberger appointed a committee of nongovernment experts headed by Dr. Charles Townes, to assist him in conducting a review of available basing modes.

[19]Letter from George Postrozny, Nevada Deputy Legislative Counsel to Assemblyman Paul V. Prengaman, March 5, 1981.

[20]William J. Lockhart, Attorney for Frances Farley, to Secretary of the Air Force, 4 August 1981, p. 2.

CHAPTER 9
THE REAGAN BASING-MODE-OF-THE-MONTH CLUB

Conventional wisdom suggests that a president derives extraordinary prestige and power from the preeminent position of that office in foreign affairs and defense matters. Some scholars have even suggested that there are really two presidencies paralleling the distinctive issue areas of international and domestic affairs; and that most presidents are more comfortable and actually spend more time with the former (Wildavsky, 1968). Conventional wisdom also indicates that the executive branch acts as a more cohesive institution than Congress in the issue area of national security policy. As a corollary, it is asserted that the national legislature is better equipped to legislate in the domestic area because the very institutional, constitutional, and behavioral factors that limit its ability to compete with the executive branch on foreign and defense policy issues matter less on domestic ones.

Again, the case of MX from the fall of 1981 through the summer of 1983 only partially vindicates conventional wisdom, especially the thrust of the propositions for the bureaucratic politics approach for procurement. Most importantly, the experience of those two years contradicts proposition 9 while it tends to support propositions 15 through 21. Specifically, during the Reagan administration Congress has continued to show its traditional reluctance to defeat the missile system outright. It has maintained its pattern of tying its support for the missile dimension of the MX program to concessions from the president on the basing mode. The linkage became so strong that the future of MX was seriously in doubt by late 1982. With the missile system in dispute, U.S. efforts to commit the West European governments to accept the Pershing II and cruise missile programs were complicated. Eventually, the Reagan administration was forced to reevaluate the MX project and reformulate its basic strategic and defense posture in order to win congressional support for the weapon system.

During much of its first two years the Reagan administration was as divided, if not more so, than Congress as to how to proceed with the MX project. In contrast to the theme that the executive branch and Congress are monolithic institutions, the Reagan administration and the national legislature were active arenas in which contending coalitions of participants maneuvered to influence MX policy.

The most remarkable illustration of executive-legislative relations described here is the bargain negotiated by a coalition of executive branch officials, congressional participants, and nongovernmental specialists that rescued the entire MX program from the threshold of defeat during the spring and summer of 1983. In return for congressional support for the deployment of the ten-warhead MX in Minuteman silos, the president abandoned both the concept of the window of vulnerability and much of the logic of his strategic program, and agreed to commit his administration, although rather vaguely, to a more far-reaching arms control platform.

Congressional treatment of the Reagan administration's three basing mode proposals — interim silo basing, closely spaced basing, and the Peacekeeper/Midgetman compromise — illustrates that legislators can be far more committed to a thorough evaluation and scrutiny of weapon systems programs, under certain conditions than proposition 10 indicates. In the case of MX, two conditions were paramount. The first was the extraordinary costs associated with the development and deployment of a new nuclear weapon system coming at a time of staggering budget deficits. This condition was complicated by a second one, the controversial, and uncertain strategic utility of the proposed basing schemes for the missiles.

Finally, while it is widely contended on the Hill that Congress rejected both interim silo basing and dense pack for strategic and technical reasons, political factors such as constituent pressures associated with the nuclear freeze movement were very important. In fact, the coalition that formed to push passage of the Peacekeeper/ Midgetman package was preeminently a political one. As we will see, the Scowcroft package of recommendations was formulated for the purpose of being politically attractive to Congress, the arena that was now the greatest obstacle to the president's plans.

Interim Silo Basing

As is clear by now, protracted debate over the MX system has revolved primarily around finding an acceptable basing mode. In this respect, by 1981 Congress had established the conditions for "acceptability" by repeatedly underscoring two prerequisites: the mode had to be survivable and politically viable (i.e., be reasonably priced, pose minimum environmental and societal problems, and be compatible with certain arms control objectives). Against these criteria, Reagan's first MX proposal, interim silo basing, was unacceptable. His second proposal, closely spaced basing (also known as dense pack), was equally inadequate when measured against these standards.

In retrospect, it is remarkable that the Reagan administration would recommend a basing proposal, even on an interim basis, that defied the rule of survivability; particularly one that resembled so closely the Ford proposal for interim basing rejected by Congress in 1976. However, the im-

216

mediate deployment of the new missiles was imperative for the administration. As suggested in chapter 8, Reagan and his key appointees in the Pentagon and ACDA saw MX as the hard-target killer necessary to implement their damage limitation strategy (see chapter 2). Thus, strategic factors were clearly a driving force. Furthermore, MX was seen as a key to the administration's START strategy; and the desire to negotiate from a position of strength. Finally, a quick deployment of MX was vital if Western Europe was to accept Pershing IIs and the cruise missiles. A wavering on the MX program by Reagan could further erode the rather tenuous commitment in Europe to the missiles, particularly given the growing political opposition there. The administration saw the interim silo basing proposal as the best approach to a series of interrelated political, strategic, and foreign policy problems. The proposal had the threefold advantage of representing the earliest deployment date for MX, postponing debate about the complex basing choices to a later time, and avoiding the environmental and socioeconomic problems generated by MX MPS.

Congress was at first sympathetic; however, after the initial enthusiasm for the basing mode settled and Congress had time to evaluate the president's strategic arms plan, the vulnerability of silo basing, both strategically and politically, surfaced. The plan to deploy the ten-warhead missiles at an enormous cost in existing but superhardened Minuteman and Titan silos provided little additional protection for the missile from a Soviet first strike. The validity of the superhardened concept was widely questioned (authors' interviews). In the end, a majority in Congress felt the expenditures were not justified given the limited payoffs in survivability.

Nevertheless, traditional congressional reluctance to defeat weapon systems outright, and dissension within both the executive and legislative branches over the utility of the proposed weapon system and the foreign policy consequences of its immediate rejection, led Congress to pick at the interim silo basing proposal for the next six months. In the fiscal 1982 defense appropriations bill, Congress voted to cut substantially, but not completely delete, funds for superhardening the silos (P.L. 97-114). The action had the effect of undercutting the critical feature of the basing proposal — immediate superhardening for interim basing. The appropriations act as passed also called upon the president to recommend a permanent basing mode to Congress by July 1, 1983, instead of Reagan's promise of 1984. In effect, Congress was forcing an agenda for MX decision making onto the executive branch. In response, Reagan abandoned the superhardening option in February of 1982, and then the entire interim solution in anticipation of legislative defeat on the fiscal 1983 defense authorization bill (H.R. 6030). (For all bills cited in this chapter see Table 9.1.)

217

TABLE 9.1

Lists of Acts and Bills Cited

Fiscal Year	Department	Title	House/Senate Number	Public Law Number
1982	Defense	Appropriations Act	H.R. 4995	P.L. 97-114
1983	Defense	Authorization Act	H.R. 6030	P.L. 97-252
1983	Defense	Appropriations Act	H.R. 7355	P.L. 97-269
1983	Defense	Military Construction Appropriations Act	H.R. 6968	P.L. 97-323
1984	Defense	Authorization Act	H.R. 2969	P.L. 98-94
1984	Defense	Appropriations Act	H.R. 4185	P.L. 98-212

Blunders

Ironically the problems that the Reagan administration confronted after it proposed interim basing of MX were to a large extent a product of their own blundering. For one, the president had failed to develop a consensus within his own administration, let alone within the congressional arena, for the interim basing proposal. Ultimately, the administration managed to alienate key groups in the Pentagon, Congress, and the specialized strategic community. The Pentagon, particularly the air force, was offended because no effort had been made by Secretary of Defense Weinberger to involve them in the preliminary decision making preceding the October 1981 announcement (authors' interviews). In fact, the president's decision overruled the recommendations of senior military officers who were informed of the decision for interim silo basing just before Reagan's speech announcing his strategic program and the MX decision. This also bothered key legislators both in the Senate and the House who rely upon and are deferential to military expertise in defense matters. John Tower, for

218

example, caustically remarked that Reagan's decision was made "within a small circle, without the coordination of the best military expertise" (*Congressional Quarterly Weekly*, 1981:1890). Then without sufficient forewarning, the Pentagon was given the unenviable and unwanted task of selling a system to the same institution, Congress, that had already rejected a similar proposal in 1976. Thus, many in Congress were already suspicious of the program. Furthermore, there was limited time to build a technical defense for the interim proposal. The silo basing decision was a crucial error that ultimately cost the administration the confidence and support of Congress on the MX issue.

In defense of interim silo basing the administration touted the merits of an immediate deployment of the missiles. The strategic, foreign policy, and political advantages of the scheme were also underscored (see chapter 4). Taking definitive action would convey a message to the Soviets that the United States was committed to redressing the "strategic imbalance" in offensive capability. It was also argued that a quick deployment of the new missiles would enhance the U.S. bargaining position at the START talks. As an aside, it is of interest to note that after Reagan agreed to abandon superhardening, the air force argued that the questionable arms control features of interim basing had been ameliorated. In addition, deployment of MX was necessary if the West Europeans were to continue to allow U.S deployment of Pershing II and cruise missiles. Finally, the administration emphasized that the social and environmental impacts of this proposal would be minimal, and the costs, while large (approximately $28 billion), were less than that estimated for MPS basing — $40 billion (Medalia, 1982:4).

Nevertheless, key members of Congress were appalled by the incredibly poor job the Pentagon and the White House were doing in selling the plan. Under questioning, the logic of interim silo basing began to evaporate and so did legislative support for MX, particularly among members of the Senate Armed Services Committee. According to one congressional participant the magnitude of the Defense Department's poor performance on Capitol Hill in selling the interim MX plan is unprecedented. Members of the MX office in the Pentagon candidly admitted that selling interim silo basing to Congress after more than five years of debate about missile vulnerability was an impossible task (authors' interviews).

Two other problems plagued the administration's efforts to sell silo basing to Congress. For one, the government was faced with enormous projected budget deficits, and the president's insensitivity to the fiscal problem, as illustrated by the recommendation of a costly but uncertain system, was unnerving to many in Congress. In fact, the MX's massive acquisition costs became a pivotal issue in the congressional controversy between the Democrats and Reagan's Republicans over how to trim the budget, during the debate on the FY 1983 DOD authorization bill (authors' interviews).

In addition, the proposal did nothing to address the concerns of arms control advocates who view increased ICBM vulnerability as destabilizing (see chapters 2 and 3) for two reasons. It could encourage a Soviet first strike in a crisis situation (i.e., the classic "use them or lose them" problem), and the adoption by the United States of a launch-on-warning strategy to offset the Soviet first-strike incentive. Thus, the interim silo basing proposal accelerated growing concern among arms control supporters about the administration's commitment to arms limitation. As the nuclear freeze movement began to generate broadly based political support for bilateral arms control, congressional interest in the issue grew (authors' interviews).

The Defeat

In May of 1982, after affirming the strategic need for the missile itself, the Senate, following the lead of John Tower and the Armed Services Committee, voted to cancel MX R&D funds for interim silo basing (H.R. 6030, S. 2248). The release of the Armed Services Committee's report on H.R. 6030 indicates that the House was prepared to dump silo basing as well (U.S. House of Representatives, 1982:24-25). On July 19, two days before the full chamber was to vote, Reagan abandoned the interim silo basing plan and announced that a permanent mode would be adopted by December 1, 1982.

In retrospect, the president's move was premature since the House refused to delete funds for the interim plan (Simon amendment), voting instead to "fence" the RDT&E monies earmarked for the basing mode pending a presidential decision on a "long-term" scheme (Stratton amendment) (July 27, 1982). Then the House, following the Senate's lead, narrowly approved production of the first nine MX missiles (212 to 209), but also "fenced" those funds. On September 8 the fiscal 1983 defense authorization bill became law with 90 percent of MX basing procurement funds occluded until thirty days after Congress had been informed of a presidential decision. The fiscal 1983 military construction appropriations bill (H.R. 6968) became law on October 13 (P.L. 97-323) with all base-specific funding fenced until a permanent mode was accepted.

Veteran observers of the weapon procurement process on the Hill are convinced that the administration was setting up Congress to take "the rap" for killing MX; that, in fact, Reagan proposed a plan that was guaranteed to doom MX and implicate the Democrats in the process (authors' interviews). Reagan's presidential campaign attacks had focused

220

on the Carter administration's inadequate defense programs; but, the new Republican administration was making little if no progress in its efforts to find a suitable alternative to MPS. It was widely believed that if MX was not built, blame for its defeat would be shifted to Democrats in Congress (authors' interviews).

But Democrats, in the House especially, were unwilling to play that game. They were particularly reluctant to take any action that would interfere with the success of the START negotiations, such as denying the president the MX as a bargaining tool. On the other hand, majorities in both houses refused to liberate MX from the chains of its basing mode. The defense bills that Congress passed for fiscal 1982 were expressions of legislative intent that the missile would not survive without an acceptable basing mode. By 1982 it was beginning to appear as if no basing mode could ever appeal to the disparate factions in Congress, and that the new weapon project was doomed. In fact, dense pack, the second in a series of three Reagan MX basing proposals, was crippled in less than two weeks.

From the time of the Reagan proposal for interim silo basing to his withdrawal of that proposal in July 1982, the congressional arena was again setting the agenda for MX decision making. This pattern of affairs is clearly contrary to propositions 9 and 10 for the outer layer of procurement decision making. That pattern did not change when the president proposed a second basing mode for MX. In fact, the lengthiness of the missile controversy forced onto the legislative agenda strategic questions about the very need for MX itself. Discussions now also began to center upon alternatives to a large multiple warhead ICBM, able to achieve the still illusive combination of hard-target counterforce capability and survivability (author's interviews). This too is contrary to the thrust of the bureaucratic politics literature.

Dense Pack: "Our Last Time at Bat"

In desperation, Weinberger, who had spearheaded the drive for silo basing, turned to the Pentagon to provide a technical solution to the MX basing dilemma; that is, one which would satisfactorily address the issue of survivability. The administration neglected, however, political considerations and thus virtually ignored one of the two preconditions of congressional acceptance of the MX system. Not unexpectedly, closely spaced basing (CSB) or dense pack was a technical solution with few political attributes.

While the air force did not "discover" dense pack until 1982, the idea actually had originated in the 1970s with a young air force captain doing some preliminary work on fratricide. It was even considered as an alterna-

221

tive to MPS basing in the Carter administration (authors' interviews), which eventually discarded CSB because of uncertainties about its technical feasibility; ironically, the same concern would undermine its credibility in 1982.

Closely spaced basing was revived as an alternative for housing MX in 1982 by Air Force Major Mike Harvey. It ultimately won the support of key scientists in the Pentagon and officers in the Pentagon MX office (known as the Peacekeeper Office after July 1982), the secretary of defense, and the national security advisor. The Townes Commission also gave qualified support. However, the most influential advocate became the president's science advisor, George Keyworth (authors' interview).

Problems Confronting Dense Pack

The feasibility of dense pack rested upon three technical features, all of which defy conclusive verification: (1) the workability of fratricide; (2) the ability to superharden silos enough to allow them to withstand multiple Soviet strikes; and (3) the failure of the Soviet Union to develop ways to circumvent fratricide (Medalia, 1982:6).

The administration's technical case for CSB was severely hampered by the prohibitions on atmospheric testing in the 1963 Nuclear Test Ban Treaty. To a large extent, the technical logic of dense pack was contingent upon demonstrating the viability of the concept of fratricide; i.e., the phenomenon by which the explosions of an attacking nuclear weapon would destroy, or degrade the accuracy and effectiveness of those which followed. Without being able to actually test the multiple burst concept, the air force was forced to proceed on the basis of *ex post facto* analysis of old testing data — atmospheric nuclear tests conducted twenty to twenty-five years earlier with different purposes in mind. Of course, such *ex post facto* analysis raised crucial validity problems in the minds of many people.[1]

Without conclusive scientific tests, efforts by the air force to describe the sophisticated scientific theories behind fratricide served to further alienate skeptics. The opposite descriptive tactic, to simplify the system's workability, made dense pack appear ridiculous: bunching all one's advanced ICBMs in a small area and relying upon Soviet missiles to destroy each other as they exploded seemed risky (authors' interviews). Second, if the technical advantages of closely spaced basing were theoretical, then the possibility that the Soviets could develop ways to circumvent fratricide, while also theoretical, were equally plausible. Three procedures had been mentioned by technical opponents: (1) the ''spike'' attack in which the explosion of incoming warheads was timed to avoid fratricide; (2) warheads designed to burrow underground, and then explode; or (3) pin-down strikes (see chapter 3).

222

In addition to technical problems, the air force was hampered by the question of how to translate a bizarre theoretical concept into a practicable plan. The dense pack proposal submitted to the president by the air force included three options with two additional defensive alternatives (authors' interviews).

1. 100 MX in 100 superhardened silos deployed in a closely spaced based configuration;
2. 100 MX in 300 superhardened silos deployed in a closely spaced based configuration with an MPS concept included;
3. 100 MX in 500 superhardened silos deployed in a closely spaced based configuration with an MPS concept included;
4. an active defense of either of the first three options by a ballistic missile defense;
5. a passive defense of the first option and perhaps the other two as well by deep basing of the MX.

Options two and three were especially appealing to Tower and SAC. A mobile protective shelter concept had gained wide acceptance in the Armed Services Committee as technically the most effective way to hedge against ICBM vulnerability. Thus, a closely spaced basing concept that included MPS compensated for the technical uncertainty of dense pack.

To a large extent, the Pentagon's options in selecting a basing mode were constrained in advance by legislative mandate and by what the executive branch would accept. Of the permanent alternatives that Reagan had announced in October of 1981 as possible deployment schemes — air-mobile, deep basing, and missile defense — Congress forced the administration to withdraw all three. The air-mobile mode was dropped by the administration after pressure from critical members of both Armed Services Committees and the Pentagon who saw it as extremely costly and highly dubious as to its invulnerability.[2] Deep-underground basing was attacked in both the Congress and the executive branch because of uncertainties related to the time it would take for the missiles to be launched.[3] An ABM system was criticized for the political consequences of abrogating the 1972 SALT I Treaty with the Soviets, and the system's technical uncertainty. Of the ABM schemes under consideration at the time of Reagan's announcement, LoAD and "layered defense," the first had been designed especially for an MPS system and the second was "frontier technology" (Medalia, 1982:6).

In the executive branch, the White House and the secretary of defense were opposed to linking MPS to closely spaced basing. Mobile-deception plans raised again land acquisition problems, EIS questions, and the greater financial costs of superhardening additional silos, of which at least half would always be unused. These factors in turn could produce grave political problems for dense pack. Consequently, the White House chose the first option with the fourth alternative (100 MX in 100 superhardened silos deployed in closely spaced based configuration with exploration of an active defense). Of course, without mobile-deceptive characteristics, it was likely that dense pack would be unfavorably received by even conservatives such as John Tower, long a supporter of the MPS approach and now the chair of the powerful Senate Armed Services Committee.

On November 22, 1982, Reagan recommended the deployment of MX in a dense pack scheme in southeastern Wyoming. No one was terribly surprised by the announcement. The White House had decided in May to explore formal acceptance of dense pack and the idea had been floating around ever since. Interestingly, the Townes Commission report, in an executive summary released in March 1982, had mentioned closely spaced basing as a possible long-term option (authors' interview).

Just as he had done with the interim scheme, and as he would do again with the Peacekeeper MX/Midgetman program in 1983, Reagan was careful to couch the basing mode proposal within the context of broader strategic issues. In this instance, Reagan tied MX to arms control, a tactic intentionally gauged to defuse the growing sentiment for a nuclear freeze. In fact, during the 97th Congress, U.S arms control policy and the nuclear freeze were two of the most important issues on the legislative agenda. They were also issues that Congress could not avoid since there was widespread public interest in them. The fear of nuclear war and the belief that such a war was becoming more likely, fueled the dramatic growth of the grassroots movement that emerged in the New England states during 1980 (authors' interviews).

Thus, Reagan's speech had to address these fears while still defending the need for a new weapon system more lethal than anything in our nuclear arsenal. He did this by making two contentious assumptions. The first was that peace could only be maintained through a balance in nuclear weapons between the United States and the Soviet Union; but, the Soviets were ahead, justifying our need to "catch up." Second, the Soviets would not negotiate a workable arms control treaty unless they were convinced that "we are determined to match their military capacity with a buildup of our own. The prevention of conflict and the reduction of weapons are the most important public issues of our time," pronounced the president. And "the United States wants deep cuts in the world's arsenal of weapons. But unless we demonstrate the will to rebuild our strength and restore the military balance, the Soviets, since they are so far ahead, have little incentive to negotiate with us" (*Congressional Quarterly Weekly*, 1982:2933-35).

The reactions from MX opponents and nuclear freeze advocates, most prominently Edward Kennedy, Mark Hatfield, and Alan Cranston, were predictable. They denounced both assumptions as vacuous. These liberals argued that, on the contrary, our ability to levy a destructive second strike was enough of a deterrent; and, strengthening our first-strike capacity would be destabilizing, encourage the Soviets to follow suit, and, thus, discourage an arms control agreement. They also found the president's decision to call MX the "Peacekeeper" ironic. Most importantly, though, they were not convinced that Reagan was sincere in his commitment to arms control. Gone were Reagan references to a limited war scenario and the tough talk and combative tone of earlier speeches. But, although the president's rhetoric was toned down, the scheme still raised serious problems of compatibility with the SALT I and II treaties. Opponents were concerned about the fact that dense pack might violate the SALT agreements' ban on new fixed ICBM silo launchers and could eventually require an ABM system, something that would undermine the U.S. commitment to SALT I. *Pravda* had responded to the president's announcement by condemning it as inconsistent with "one of the central provisions of the SALT I and SALT II accords: an obligation not to create additional silos for intercontinental missiles" (Medalia, 1982:18).

Significantly, many moderates and conservatives, who previously had supported MX, were now thrown into a quandary by the president's selection of dense pack. Their immediate reaction was to be cautious, and hope that the administration could build a viable case for the basing scheme; although some, such as Larry Pressler (R-S.Dak.) adopted an adversarial position. However, even administration supporters conceded that Reagan's proposal would have a rough time in Congress (*Congressional Quarterly Weekly*, 1982:2922).

This time, at least Reagan could count on strong regional support. The entire congressional delegation as well as Wyoming Governor Edward Herschler and local public officials endorsed the system that was slated for deployment in their state. However, the societal impacts of dense pack were predicted to be small since the system was expected only to consume 10 to 15 square miles of military land and require 100 miles of road (Medalia, 1982:9).

The caution and patience of administration supporters of MX in Congress proved to be futile. There was no strategy for selling the Pentagon's plan since it was widely assumed that Congress would defer consideration of the issue until the next legislative session (*Congressional Quarterly Weekly*, 1982:2922; authors' interviews). For this reason, the air force and Reagan defense officials were once again ill-prepared to defend dense pack when the House moved quickly and unexpectedly to tie the appropriations

225

vote on acquisition of the new missile to dense pack approval during the lame duck period.

The Pentagon was confronted with the problem of selling an extremely complex and bizarre theoretical concept to an already highly suspicious group of legislators without a reliable data base, and with only a week to do so. In that time the air force conducted personal briefings for over two hundred people, and one for the Senate Armed Services Committee, but not the House Armed Services Committee. The pictures of mushroom clouds and the charts illustrating fratricide that the air force used in its lobbying campaign were so graphic that they engendered perhaps more opposition than support (authors' interviews).

The problem of time was compounded by the atmosphere in Congress, especially in the House that December. It was a lame duck session. The results of the 1982 election were interpreted by many in both the Senate and House as a negative statement about the Reagan administration. The charged partisan environment in conjunction with the perception of dense pack as a zany idea resulted in a movement in the Democratically controlled House to fence off funds for MX until the executive branch proposed a basing mode that would be invulnerable and politically acceptable.

In addition to the partisanship in the Congress that December, the Pentagon was handicapped in its efforts to sell dense pack by another dimension of the congressional mood: frustration over the failure of both this and other administrations to resolve the MX dilemma. It was widely acknowledged after the interim silo basing fiasco that the air force had but one more chance to find an acceptable mode for the missiles. And dense pack was, as several executive branch officials conceded, a last-ditch effort to keep the MX missiles alive. If dense pack failed to fulfill congressional expectations, then the MX program was likely dead (authors' interviews).

Representative Jack Edwards (R-Ala.) expressed the frustration that many of his colleagues felt when he told Under Secretary for Research and Engineering Richard De Lauer: "I am supposed to be one of the hawks on the [Appropriations] Committee, I guess, but I swear the more I sit here and listen to this, the more I wonder what in the world we are up to. . . . This whole world has got to be foolish. . . . This sounds like Dense Pacman" (quoted in Paine, 1983:4). Representative Norman Dicks then warned the air force and defense witnesses that their description of dense pack was so incredible that the U.S. people would never accept it. "If you think you had problems with Multiple Protective Shelters this thing is going to be much more difficult, because it sounds stupid, quite frankly" (Paine, 1983:6). One observer of the hearings noted that "trying to make sense of the administration's case for the 'Peacekeeper' [was] like trying to nail Jello to the wall" (Paine, 1983:5).

226

The final blow to an already precarious case for MX was the split by the Joint Chiefs of Staff on support of dense pack. The army was concerned about the validity of the fratricide theory in the absence of conclusive data, while the navy raised questions about the theory of hardening the silos. The administration failed to anticipate the damage to dense pack that would result from such a division. After the public announcement of the split was made by Chairman of the JCS, General John Vessey, on December 8, the system "took a nose dive." The case for closely spaced basing appeared to be lost.

Once again, Congress demonstrated its reluctance to kill the weapon system outright, voting instead in effect to postpone definitive decisions. On December 7 the House voted to accept an amendment by Addabbo (181 to 121) to deny procurement funds for the MX missiles while retaining R&D monies (245-176) (H.R. 7355). However, to gain even that legislative concession the White House had engaged in a vigorous lobbying campaign that included intercontinental telephone calls to Congress from the president and secretary of state Shultz in Brazil, and Weinberger in Belgium. The day before the House vote on the 1983 defense appropriations bill (H.R. 7355) Reagan sent a letter to all members reminding them, "We must move forward with the MX to have any hope of achieving meaningful progress at the arms negotiations in Geneva" (*Congressional Quarterly Weekly*, 1982:2953). At the same time, Tower entreated his colleagues to postpone the decision in similar correspondence. On December 8 General Vessey testified that the Chiefs of Staff of the Marine Corps, Navy, and Army were opposed to dense pack. The House then decided to fence the funds allocated for the basing mode until April 30, 1983.

In combination, the two sets of votes — the one on missile procurement and the other on basing mode development — transmitted a clear message to the president: the House still supported MX, was uncertain about dense pack, and was unwilling to fund missile procurement in advance of an acceptable basing mode. There was another implicit message that Reagan could hardly avoid: Republicans and conservative Democrats were willing to break ranks both with the administration and with a long tradition of deference to the Pentagon. Their paramount concern in opposing the president had been strategic in nature. In addition to strategic concerns, MX had become for many a "symbol. . .of the costliness of the Reagan military budget," according to Representative Sydney Yates (D-Ill.). The red ink was also of vital concern to constituents. As Carroll Hubbard, Jr. (D-Ky.) described it: "Right or wrong, the words 'Here come the Russians' nowadays do not scare Kentuckians half as much as 'Here come the creditors'" (*Congressional Quarterly Weekly*, 1982:3004).

After the House vote, many Senate MX opponents realized that their chances of deleting MX funds were less certain than securing a postponement similar to that achieved by the House. Reagan read the House vote as precarious support for his defense plan. The air force read it as the death of the MX project itself. These attitudes provided the basis for the deal that was cut between the Senate and the White House. On December 14 Reagan and senior senators from both parties met to work out the proposal under which Congress would fund MX procurement, but bar expenditures pending a basing mode choice (authors' interviews). The bargain was formally introduced as an amendment by the late Henry Jackson to H.J. Res. 631,[4] which passed 56 to 42 (P.L. 97-377). Staunch opponents, who had refused to join the coalition, were appalled. When Alan Cranston introduced an amendment to delete all of the funds authorized for MX procurement and to prohibit any R&D funds from being expended on dense pack, an open breach in the liberal camp occurred. Mark Hatfield was outraged since he felt that a large defeat on the Cranston amendment would send the wrong signal to House-Senate conferees and jeopardize efforts to gain concessions in conference. As Hatfield expected, Cranston's measure was tabled 70 to 28.

In the final bill, Congress agreed to eliminate all funds for MX procurement, prohibit flight testing of MX,[5] and fence R&D funds for the basing mode until congressional acceptance through concurrent resolution. To enhance Congress's oversight role in this capacity, the president was also required to submit at the same time a technical assessment report of dense pack and alternative basing modes as well as an evaluation of alternative ICBMs. Finally, the act delegated to the Appropriations Committees, and not the Armed Services panels, jurisdiction over the basing mode resolution (*Congressional Record*, 1982:15694). Despite its tone, the bill contained enough loopholes that the air force could still build as many as twelve missiles with the R&D funds, making the MX operational at the same time a basing decision was made; thus allowing the air force to actually circumvent the proposed delay of full implementation of the weapon system.

Nonetheless, the president had barely survived the battle over dense pack. The mood in Congress was becoming increasingly more antagonistic, and a growing number of people were beginning to question the assumption that a technically and politically acceptable basing mode could in fact be found. First, there were those who had come to embrace a smaller and more mobile, single warhead ICBM as the only way to solve the basing mode problem; and, for arms control reasons. Second, some members, who doubted that the ICBM vulnerability problem existed, began searching for other ways to achieve the kind of strategic and foreign policy goals associated with MX. Finally, long-time opponents of MX's damage limitation implications, but supportive of the missile for strategic and foreign policy reasons (see chapter 2), sought to construct a coalition to promote a compromise that would advance their interests, especially those associated with arms control. They would become instrumental in the "miracle" of 1983 that resurrected MX from the dead. That miracle was the Scowcroft Commission recommendations, which gave MX a new lease on life.

Contrary to propositions 9 and 10, Congress was a significant arena in MX decision making in 1982. In that year as well, decisions within the executive branch were far more sequential than incremental — something quite contrary to proposition 6. Finally, a coalition was forming composed of executive branch officials, members of Congress, and Washington strategic and media specialists to influence MX deliberations in both Congress and the presidency. Once again, the propositions for the outer layer for procurement cannot fully capture the activities in that year.

The Scowcroft Commission Compromise

One congressional staffer suggests that legislators approach decision making about weapon procurement in the same ways they approach domestic ones. They arrive at a decision through a process in which they consider their consciences, constituent concerns, party pressures, and the issue's utility as a bargaining lever in gaining concessions on other more salient issues (authors' interviews). By 1983 the Reagan administration came to this same conclusion: that the MX missile issue had become hopelessly politicized. Three political realities were paramount considerations in the search for a basing mode. First, any new proposal on MX could not originate with either the White House or the Pentagon, both having lost credibility on the interim solution and dense pack debacles. Second, Congress while previously restrained, was in a position and a mood to bury the MX program. Finally, a growing number of legislators were no longer convinced that MX was necessary given their growing doubts about the justification for the missile system; namely that deterrence, invulnerability, and war-fighting capability were linked.

The Appointment of the Scowcroft Commission

On January 3, 1983, the president, on the advice of Robert McFarland, deputy national security advisor, created yet another bipartisan commission to study the MX "problem" — the President's Commission on Strategic Forces or the Scowcroft Commission as it became known. The move reflected the administration's "better-late-than-never" sensitivity to the political realities discussed above. First, by creating an "independent"

229

commission, the administration avoided "tainting" a basing mode recommendation. Second, as part of its mandate, the panel, headed by retired general and former national security advisor Brent Scowcroft,[6] was told to coordinate and consult with Congress. In effect a consensus was to be reached, if possible, before the Scowcroft Commission released its report. Third, the president gave the members a broad mandate to study the total array of the country's nuclear deterrence. Although the maintenance of the land-based leg of the nuclear triad was explicit in their mandate, the commission was given just enough discretion to allow them to alter basic strategic policy and force posture assumptions.

Whether the president actually expected them to do so is questionable, as two factors suggest. For one, the panel was told to report to the president by February 18 (although, they did not issue their report until April 11, 1983), giving them but a month and a half to deliberate and recommend a policy course on a subject that had stumped Washington for over a decade. Moreover, the men selected as panel members, while respected for their military policy expertise and technical knowledge, were "safe," i.e., all had been advocates of the MX in the past.[7] According to several Hill staff members, it was widely believed that the president's ulterior motive in establishing the commission was to provide a rationale for MX in a dense pack mode (authors' interviews).

The White House emphasized to the Scowcroft Commission members that the critical test of their proposal would be its success in passing review in Congress (authors' interviews). Thus, any package of recommendations would need to be a compromise worked out in advance with key members in Congress and the executive branch, which addressed the disparate concerns of the various legislative and executive factions. Importantly, wooing liberal and moderate House Democrats and Senate moderates was viewed as imperative. Thus, several of the commission appointments were directed toward the recruitment of needed Democratic votes in Congress; notably, former Carter Secretary of Defense Harold Brown, a prominent Democratic scientist, and Carter White House advisor Lloyd Cutler, the consummate Democratic politician. Their support and later lobbying for a package of proposals about MX were critical in attracting congressional Democrats.

The ultimate success of the Scowcroft Commission would be to erase the blunders that Reagan had made in the first two attempts to acquire and deploy MX. The fact that the commission was successful is nothing less than incredible and attests to the political skills of Scowcroft and others on the commission.

The Scowcroft Commission Strategy

The commission determined immediately to develop a clearly stated and easily understood rationale for the basing proposal adopted for MX. Consequently, the panel began a new review of basing ideas with an eye towards the political viability of the various options, and a sensitivity to the vulnerability debate. The commission members were assisted in this activity by continual consultation with key legislative actors. For example, Representative Les Aspin (D-Wis.) and Senator Sam Nunn (D-Ga.) were among many in Congress who visited frequently with members of the commission about the direction the proposal was taking, often providing corrective advice from the perspective of what would likely draw the most legislative support.

To better accomplish its tasks, the commission split into two groups: the technical committee and the information committee. The objectives of the technical committee were to outline the strategic problem facing the United States, to develop an appropriate strategic response, and to choose a basing mode for MX that would be invulnerable, politically acceptable, and square with the strategic rationale. The objective of the information committee was to keep all interests and important groups in both the executive branch and Congress abreast of the direction of the technical committee's work, and to provide input into the choices for those outside government. The outside groups included important reporters in the Washington print media and strategic specialists with influence on the Hill. After Midgetman became prominent in these discussions, liaison activity with defense corporations increased (authors' interviews).

The Scowcroft Commission announced its recommendations on April 11, 1983. Delivered as a package, the panel made three interrelated proposals, all to attract a potential majority of legislators. At the center of the recommendations was endorsement of the deployment of 100 MX missiles (Peacekeepers) in existing Minuteman silos with the continued exploration of a more permanent home for MX. At the same time, the commission called for the development of a new, smaller single warhead missile, Midgetman, to shift away from MIRVed ICBMs. Third, the commission urged the United States to negotiate a strategic arms limitation agreement with the Soviets to reduce mutually the number of warheads in the inventory of the two superpowers. In other words, the commission urged that the United States develop a new approach in its arms limitation policy — return the emphasis to missiles with single warheads as opposed to multiple, or MIRVed, ones. Within this context, the idea of "build-down" was offered (Talbott, 1984).[8] The commission was adamant that their proposals be viewed as an integrated package for "no one part. . .can

231

accomplish it [the objective of reducing the risk of war] alone'' (*Congressional Quarterly Weekly*, 1983:756).

The president endorsed the commission's recommendations eight days later (April 19). In accepting the Scowcroft package, the administration was signaling its resolve to make major changes in the nation's nuclear strategy. Most notably, in accepting the commission's arguments the president implicitly acknowledged that the vulnerability problem was not urgent. Two lengthy statements in the commission's report laid the window of vulnerability argument to rest at least for the near future.

> The different components of our strategic forces would force the Soviets, if they were to contemplate an all-out attack, to make choices which would lead them to reduce significantly their effectiveness against one component in order to attack another. For example, if Soviet war planners should decide to attack our bomber and submarine bases and our ICBM silos with simultaneous detonations — by delaying missile launchers from close-in submarines so that such missiles would arrive at our bomber bases at the same time the Soviet ICBM warheads (with their longer time of flight) would arrive at our ICBM silos — a very high proportion of our alert bombers would have escaped before their bases were struck. . . .If the Soviets, on the other hand, chose rather to launch their ICBM and SLBM attacks at the same moment (hoping to destroy a higher proportion of our bombers with SLBMs having a short time of flight), there would be a period of over a quarter of an hour after nuclear detonations had occurred on U.S bomber bases but before our ICBMs had been struck. In such a case the Soviets should have no confidence that we would refrain from launching our ICBMs during that interval after we had been hit. It is important to appreciate that this would not be a "launch-on-warning," or even a "launch under attack," but rather a launch *after* attack — after massive nuclear detonations had already occurred on U.S. soil. (*Report of the President's Commission on Strategic Forces*, 1983:8)

And later the report suggested that

> the vulnerability of such silos in the near term, viewed in isolation, is not a sufficiently dominant part of the overall problem of ICBM modernization to warrant other immediate steps being taken such as closely-spacing new silos or ABM defense of those silos. This is because of the mutual survivability shared by the ICBM force and the bomber force in view of the different types of attacks that would need to be launched at each, as explained above [the preceding excerpt]. In any circumstances other than that of a particular kind of massive surprise attack on the U.S. by the Soviet Union, Soviet planners would have to account for the possibility that MX missiles in Minuteman silos would be available for use, and thus they would help deter such attacks. To deter such surprise attacks we can reasonably rely both on our other strategic forces and on the range of

232

operation uncertainties that the Soviets would have to consider in planning such aggression — as long as we have underway a program for long-term ICBM survivability such as that for the small, single warhead ICBM to hedge against long-term vulnerability for the rest of our forces. (*Report of the President's Commission on Strategic Forces*, 1983:17)

The thrust of these two statements was intended to change the terms of the debate over short-term vulnerability, i.e., U.S. ICBMs were invulnerable until at least the Soviet Union deployed ICBMs with terminal guidance capability. A mobile Midgetman was the hedge against that long-term possibility. Although this argument was by no means accepted by everyone (e.g., several important officials within the Pentagon as well as legislators did not accept that argument according to authors' interviews), it was attractive to a large number of analysts and political officials within Congress who had developed grave doubts about the operational assumptions of a Soviet strike on U.S. ICBMs.

A second major modification in nuclear strategic policy associated with the Scowcroft recommendations was the rationale for the MX missile itself. For years the new generation of ICBMs were viewed by many as imperative for achieving an effective war-fighting capability. Now the commission was hinting that the ten-warhead missiles be endorsed as trade bait to lure Soviet concessions in strategic arms limitation negotiations (authors' interviews). The commission reasoned in its report that the Soviets could only be compelled to negotiate a build-down warheads proposal seriously if they were convinced that, in lieu of substantive progress in the arms control talks, the United States had the resolve and capacity to match and even surpass the nuclear strength of the Soviet Union. "A credible capability for controlled, prompt, limited attack on hard targets [would cast] a shadow over the calculus of Soviet risk talking" (*Report of the President's Commission on Strategic Forces*, 1983:16-17).

Reagan's acceptance of the Scowcroft package seemed to imply the acceptance of very different strategic and arms control objectives than those established by him two years earlier. However, as recently as December 14, 1982, Reagan had stated emphatically: "This [the MX] is not in the sense of a bargaining chip that somebody could say, well you're building it just to tear it down. No. We need modernization. Even if we get the reduction of arms. . .this would not be the missile that would be taken out of circulation" (Paine, 1983:5). Thus, confusion over what the administration was actually accepting in endorsing the Scowcroft Commission report would materialize and plague efforts to secure congressional passage of the missile system.

The administration, having learned from its mistakes with two previous proposals, had already forged a formidable coalition of congressional allies in advance of the announcement of the commission's recommendations. At the center of the Scowcroft alliance were House Armed Services Committee member Les Aspin (D-Wis.), an influential colleague respected for his defense expertise, and James Woolsey, who served during both the Nixon and Carter administrations in a variety of national security posts, and a personal friend of Aspin and McFarlane. Although pundits continue to speculate about whether Aspin's motives were strategic or personal, he joined with the Scowcroft team to produce a sellable MX package, and worked as the chief House strategist (Drew, 1983:49). However, the architect of the package which bore the name of the Scowcroft Commission was James Woolsey. The central feature of the Scowcroft package that emerged from the panel was the deal which Aspin and Woolsey were instrumental in forging: legislative support for MX (Peacekeeper) in return for administration concessions on arms control (Midgetman; de-MIRVing). Thus, a coalition was being fostered in both the legislative and executive arenas in support of an MX package by people with no formal responsibility or executive branch title (authors' interviews).

The task of securing an administrative commitment to arms control as a centerpiece of the Scowcroft package might have been harder if the president had not acted decisively this once to curtail internal dissension within the executive branch on the issue. As late as March 12, 1983, SAC Commander General Davis and presidential science advisor George Keyworth were still publicly promoting dense pack as the leading alternative in the executive branch. (These comments were made at a meeting of the Air Force Association in Chicago.) Assistant Secretary of Defense Richard Perle and START negotiator Edward Rowny also remained chief holdouts (authors' interviews). But, the political astuteness of the White House and the good tactical sense of the president led the administration to side with the Scowcroft Commission package of proposals, thus preempting the discussion within the executive branch.

The Scowcroft Package in the House

The dissension within the legislative branch was not as easily quelled. Despite the care taken in forging a winnable package of MX proposals, liberals and some moderates were immediately and irreversibly opposed to the Scowcroft recommendations. Long-time opponents such as Hatfield and Cranston saw the so-called virtues of MX — its accuracy, firepower, and hard-target kill capability — as deficits that would operate to merely exacerbate Soviet-U.S. tensions. Some moderates such as Senators J. James Exxon (D-Nebr.) and Mark Andrews (R-N.D.) were concerned about the commission's failure to resolve the issue of vulnerability, that, after a decade, was suddenly abandoned. To others, the general strategic logic of the recommendations seemed facile and coincidental. Finally, many legislators were suspicious of Aspin's active and zealous involvement, given a public record of opposition to the various MX basing plans.[9]

As the chief promoter in the House, Aspin employed a three-pronged strategy to win approval for the Scowcroft proposals. First, working with Albert Gore (D.-Tenn.), with whom the arms control idea of build-down was associated, he put together a formidable coalition of moderate Democrats and Republicans to support the Scowcroft Commission package. Second, he managed to convince House Speaker Tip O'Neill not to formally oppose the recommendations. If O'Neill had chosen such a route, MX would have become a party issue. This was a critical part of Aspin's strategy — to block an attempt by liberal opponents to capitalize on the controversial nature of the MX and congressional discomfort with the Reagan defense buildup, and mobilize formal party opposition. Eventually, the entire democratic leadership, with the exception of O'Neill who continued to doubt Reagan's sincerity on arms control, would support MX on the first vote, although that support disappeared on the following two votes (authors' interviews).

Finally, Aspin ensured that the commission's announcement was carefully timed and staged to maximize congressional support. For one, Aspin counseled the administration to promote the commission's recommendations as a set of compromises — a package of concessions — to deflect the criticism of opponents who could invariably find fault with at least one of the several proposals. Second, Aspin urged the White House to postpone formal announcement until after congressional consideration of two other contentious issues: the president's nomination of Kenneth Adelman as director of ACDA and the freeze resolution. In the first case, Aspin reasoned that legislative skeptics would conclude from a zealous endorsement of the Scowcroft Commission by its members that the administration had engineered a major coup, rather than a mutually beneficial compromise. It was imperative that Congress get the impression that everyone had made concessions. On the second issue, by postponing the announcement, a vote on MX would also be delayed, giving "doves," particularly in the Senate, a chance to calculate the political risks involved in opposing the Scowcroft package. "The usual pattern of this place," argued Aspin, "is that people begin to get a little uncomfortable if they've gone too far one way, and start looking for a way to pop back the other way" (Drew, 1983:55). Aspin hoped that opponents of Adelman, and supporters of the freeze, would "pop back" and support the Peacekeeper/Midgetman compromise.

Convincing people that President Reagan was sincere in endorsing the Scowcroft proposals as a package deal, particularly that he would seriously pursue arms control, was the most significant problem that Aspin and his legislative allies Gore, House Majority Whip Thomas Foley (D-Wash.), Norman Dicks (D-Wis.), Vic Fazio (D-Calif.), and Richard Gephardt (D-Mo.), encountered in selling the Scowcroft recommendations. Liberals in particular were suspicious of the "great actor's" motives and intentions. Although the president had toned down considerably his combative rhetoric and cavalier attitude toward a war-fighting nuclear strategy, and the role of MX in that scenario, the president's nomination of Adelman and Reagan's strong denunciation of the nuclear freeze movement, reaffirmed liberals' beliefs that arms control was not a paramount concern of the current administration. Downey warned his colleagues about the trap that Reagan was setting for them: "Oh, you are dreaming, my colleagues, if you think that the MX is going to get you Midgetman. You are sadly, sadly mistaken" (*Congressional Record*, 1983:32-33).

Downey and AuCoin were at the forefront of a drive to defeat Peacekeeper/Midgetman. They led a coalition of House liberals originally mobilized by Representative Toby Moffett (D-N.Y.) during 1982. Downey, AuCoin, Moffett, and others began meeting to plan an opposition to the Scowcroft Commission report even before the panel released its findings. The catalyst was the rumored Aspin-Gore cooperation with the Scowcroft Commission (authors' interviews). Their strategy was to underscore both Reagan's untrustworthiness, with evidence of the president's past callous attitude towards arms control, and the lopsidedness of Aspin's rather vague "bargain." At the same time, specific appeals to vote against MX were made to those in the House concerned about either the impending budget deficits or the continued vulnerability of MX.

In advance of the first of three crucial votes on the Scowcroft plan, in an effort to shore up support for the package of proposals, Aspin and eleven other key legislators in both chambers sought Reagan's written assurances of a sincere commitment to arms control and Midgetman. A House letter bearing nine signatures read: "Statements in the press — attributed to 'high-ranking officials' in the Department of Defense and others — have already raised a suspicion that there are some in the Administration who embrace the Scowcroft report, not in its entirety, but only as a means to the end of securing Congress' approval for the deployment of MX." A similar letter was sent to Reagan by Senators Cohen, Nunn, and Percy. Both letters made the point that current START proposals needed to be revised to square them with the Scowcroft's arms control recommendations. Both sought a formal commitment by Reagan to develop and deploy Midgetman. Finally, the two letters specifically linked support for MX by the signatories to substantive evidence of arms control progress by the administration. House and Senate Democrats had even considered inserting a provision in the 1984 DOD authorization bill that would legislate this latter bargain by setting a ceiling on the MX force. Removal of the ceiling would be contingent upon evidence of arms control progress (*Congressional Quarterly Weekly*, 1983:890).

In his written responses, the president did promise to revise his current arms reduction proposals to promote movement towards small, single warhead ICBMs; to tie the number of MX missiles deployed to arms control progress; to abandon efforts to develop the capacity to launch a debilitating surprise attack on the Soviets; and to develop Midgetman.[10] The president also gave an ambivalent commitment to study the build-down idea.[11] However, as if to underscore the opacity of Reagan's promises, Weinberger (quoted in Drew, 1983:64), in a television appearance following the exchange of letters, expressed surprise over congressional doubts about the president's sincerity on arms control. "I don't really understand. . .what it is additionally that is wanted from the President. The President has been the leading advocate of arms reduction, drastic arms reduction, down to the point of equality, and that would be fully verifiable from the beginning. . .that is exactly the position he's always had."

Reagan's letters were a pivotal part of the congressional debate over the Scowcroft proposals; particularly to the issue of the administration's arms control commitment. The first round of the debate was precipitated by legislative consideration of the defencing of funds for MX flight testing and basing mode development imposed earlier (P.L. 97-377); and it would end with consideration of the 1984 defense authorization and appropriations bills.

Opponents in the House, led by Addabbo, AuCoin, and Downey, hammered away at the argument that lifting the previous bans (i.e., defencing the funds) would commit Congress to MX production and, thus, give the president the authority to proceed without the reciprocal arms control concessions sought in the Scowcroft package. "There has been no strategic weapon that has passed this stage of funding that has ever been permanently cancelled," AuCoin reminded his colleagues. "This, my friends, is the moment in which the genie leaves the bottle unless we decide to exercise our good judgment and keep it inside" (*Congressional Record*, 1983:3220). As an ancillary point, to win support from defense moderates and hardliners, the issue of MX vulnerability was raised (*Congressional Record*, 1983:3221f).

Aspin, Gore, and Dicks, who had been instrumental in eliciting the Reagan letters, countered by focusing on the value of MX as a necessary leverage to force Soviet concessions in the START negotiations. They underscored the fact that there would be later opportunities for Congress to kill MX if the president failed to comply with the Scowcroft bargain. As

Aspin (*Congressional Record*, 1983:3193) put it: "We have tried with a number of carrots. . .to get the Soviet Union to abandon the SS-18s and SS-19s. . .which we found so threatening. We were totally unsuccessful. We cannot seem to get their attention unless we start to do the similar thing to them."

Liberals found Aspin's logic unconvincing for two reasons. For one, there was no historical evidence to suggest that the results of advances in nuclear weaponry by the United States had been Soviet conciliation. "History has shown that the weapons we have deployed have driven the Soviets to the production line, not to the bargaining table," warned Edward Markey (D-Mass.). Second, the so-called "bargain" was not what Congress was being asked to decide. "There is no package in this resolution" asserted Addabbo. "Do not kid yourselves. That is what you are voting for this afternoon — the procurement of MX missiles and the deployment of MX missiles" (*Congressional Record*, 1983:3270). The fallacy of the "bargain," Addabbo warned, was that Congress was required to register formally its consent to MX production while the president was only asked to make a "promise" to arms control. Nonetheless, the House voted affirmatively on both flight testing and the development of silo basing, with the approval of Concurrent Resolution 113 (239 to 186) on May 25, 1983.

In the House, Aspin's strategy had worked. The margin of victory was provided by those liberals and moderates who had been wooed by prospects for improvements in arms control. Although, it was rumored that domestic and military porkbarrel had been traded by a now experienced White House with key legislators (authors' interviews). Ironically, the president almost shattered the tenuous thread of support which Aspin had built. At a White House dinner the evening before the House vote, according to one attendee among the sixty lawmakers, the president's personal display of virtual ignorance on the elements of the Scowcroft recommendations left many allies in both the House and Senate confused (authors' interviews).

It took less than a month for some of the legislators in Aspin's coalition to begin having second thoughts about the "deal" they had cut with the White House and air force. The pro-MX coalition began to come apart. In the two months preceding legislative consideration of the 1984 defense authorization bill (H.R. 2969), virtually no progress was made by the administration at developing a new START position, one that would be more negotiable. This despite a July 8 announcement by the administration to the contrary. Opponents of Peacekeeper viewed the lack of progress in START as a vindication of their warning: the president could not be trusted to deliver on his promises (authors' interviews). House members with reputations as arms control specialists who had voted with the administration in May became visibly uncomfortable, particularly under now intensive constituent and Democratic party pressure to defect from the Aspin coalition.

Jim Bates (D-Calif.) had organized a Democratic caucus following the May vote to discuss the upcoming defense authorization bill. Although in recent times Democratic House caucuses seldom have been effective in working out a party position on an issue, most participants were surprised by the level and intensity of bitterness toward O'Neill and especially toward Wright. O'Neill had succumbed to Aspin's request to avoid making the Scowcroft package a partisan issue; and Wright had voted to defence MX funds in May, despite the fact that two-thirds of the House Democrats had voted against the measure. Several angry young representatives at the caucus indicated that leadership positions would be contested (authors' interviews).

The House leadership seized upon the idea of using the authorization vote on MX to bargain with the administration on the tax bill; that is, as one way of restoring their image. Specifically, Wright and O'Neill sought adjustments in the tax bills toward greater equity and reduced budget deficits. Unless the president compromised on the tax bill issues, the speaker and majority leader would vote against the authorization of the first group of MXs. Wright spent an hour to no avail with the president before the votes on MX and the tax bill (authors' interviews). Thus, the MX issue was now linked to two new issues: equity in government spending cuts and a reduction in deficits.

On July 20 the House narrowly agreed (220 to 207) to authorize funding for the procurement of the first twenty-seven MX missiles. The vote, which came on an amendment by Charles Bennet (D-Fla.) and Nicholas Mavroules (D-Mass.) to delete the $2.6 billion in MX funds, was nonetheless significant for two reasons. First, the House came within eight votes of denying procurement funds. Second, twenty lawmakers, who in May had voted in favor of MX, were now opposed. Importantly, critical members of the Aspin coalition had broken ranks, including Majority Leader Wright.

The lobbying engaged in by the White House and its House allies was effective to the extent that MX barely passed. However, the message was clear: without more substantive evidence that progress was being made at the START talks, the appropriations battle in the fall could be the death knell of the missile program. During floor debate, Aspin's Democratic allies emphasized that there had been "movement" in the START talks. But even they were skeptical, as evidenced by two amendments ultimately adopted by the House on voice votes. The first, submitted by Armed Services Chair Price, prohibited the procurement and deployment of Peacekeeper from outrunning the development of Midgetman (*Congressional Record*, 1983:5314). The second by Gore and Dicks cut the number of MX missiles authorized from twenty-seven to eleven (*Congressional Record*, 1983:5338-39).

The Scowcroft Package in the Senate

The members of the Scowcroft Commission and the Pentagon engaged in a parallel lobbying effort for MX in the Senate. Close to 80 percent of the membership of the Senate was reached by the commission's "impressive dog and pony show" that Max Friedersdorf coordinated. The key senators in this lobbying effort were Tower, Cohen, and Percy on the Republican side of the aisle and Nunn on the Democratic side (authors' interviews).

Individuals in the Senate contend that Nunn, Cohen, and Percy, the moderates who led the negotiations for the Senate side, were successful in securing more tangible concessions from the president than Aspin and his colleagues in the House. The president eventually agreed to emphasize the build-down concept in nuclear warheads in the new START instructions for Ambassador Rowny; to appoint Woolsey to the START delegation; and to proscribe limits in Midgetman weight and total warheads, to make it truly mobile (authors' interviews).[12]

However, in the short-run Nunn, Cohen, and Percy were barely able to negotiate in time the compromise with the White House that saved MX. In a meeting between the president and the three senators at the White House, without staffs, in advance of the Senate vote to defence MX funds, an agreement was negotiated that had so many loopholes from the subsequent perspective of the senate staffs that the negotiations were reopened. This time the staffs were included and an agreement was reached that formally specified the conditions in a letter to the senators from Reagan. In that letter, the three senators had sought and received, in a written reply, from Reagan a commitment to the Scowcroft package; that is, to the development of Midgetman and to the concept of build-down. Originally advanced by Nunn and Cohen as an alternative to the nuclear freeze, build-down would commit the U.S. and Soviet Union to retire two existing nuclear warheads for each new one deployed.

On May 25 the Senate voted to defence MX funds for flight testing and silo basing, with approval of Concurrent Resolution 26 (59 to 39). Following the vote nineteen Republicans, whose support for MX was contingent upon the administration's commitment to START, informed Reagan that their support would be reversed unless real arms control progress was forthcoming (authors' interviews).

Nonetheless, with no substantive movement in the START talks, the Senate, in the July vote on the fiscal 1984 defense authorization measure, turned back the liberal attempt to defeat the production of the first twenty-seven missiles. A filibuster orchestrated by presidential candidate Gary

Hart (D-Colo.) to gain extended debate on the MX issues and build a case against the massive missile system, succeeded only in postponing the vote for two weeks. On July 26 the Senate registered support for the administration's MX program, in defeating an amendment by Hart and Hatfield to delete MX procurement funds from the authorization bill (S. 675) (defeated 41 to 58). In contrast with the vote in the House, the Senate vote essentially mirrored the one in May to approve flight tests. Hardline Democrats and Republicans once again made up the pro-MX majority, and liberal arms control advocates composed the anti-MX minority. The same people voted in the same ways for the same reasons. Opponents emphasized the destabilizing consequences of deploying MIRVed ICBMs in a vulnerable basing mode, both in terms of the United States adopting a launch-on-warning strategy, and the Soviets following suit. "There is one and only one inescapable conclusion that the Soviet strategic planners could come to," warned Dale Bumpers (D-Ark.). "And that is that [MX] is not a weapon to deter [but] a weapon which will be used as a first strike weapon" (*Congressional Quarterly Weekly*, 1983:1545). "I defy any senator to cite one weapon system we have built that has brought the Soviets closer to the bargaining table," challenged Hart. "There are not any" (*Congressional Quarterly Weekly*, 1983:1545). Nonetheless, proponents argued that the strategic threat of MX missile deployment would encourage the Soviets to negotiate the eventual abolition of MIRVs; and, that the MX was not as threatening nor vulnerable as critics argued.

The Final Round?

With the passage of the fiscal 1984 DOD authorization bill, anti-MX forces in Congress had but one last chance to decide the fate of Peacekeeper/Midgetman before the end of the legislative year. Lacking movement on the START talks, the Reagan administration watched as their thin margin of support began to evaporate in the summer of 1983. So optimistic were members of the anti-MX coalition by August that they predicted MX's defeat on the upcoming appropriations vote (authors' interviews). During the summer the Moffett/Downey group had been particularly active in supporting a grassroots and congressional lobbying campaign engineered by Common Cause, SANE, Friends of the Earth, the Federation of American Scientists, and other antinuclear weapons groups. Certain House members were targeted, and a barrage of letters and personal calls made, in a final effort to turn the tide against MX. Then, as if to give substance to Reagan's rhetorical claims of Russian cruelty, the Soviet Union shot down a South Korean passenger jet, killing all 269 people aboard.

241

The impact of this incident on the MX debate is, of course, uncertain. However, in conjunction with the timely announcement of changes in the U.S. START negotiating position, the Korean airline debacle may have motivated the return of defectors back into the bipartisan groups headed by Aspin and the Senate triumverate. In the end, Congress voted to fund the production of the ten warhead missiles (P.L. 98-21, H.R. 4185).

The president's October 4 announcement of a new START position was again carefully orchestrated by legislative allies. Aspin, Gore, Dicks, Percy, Cohen, and Nunn had watched with dismay the declining congressional support for MX during the summer. Meeting in late September, with national security advisor William Clark and members of the reformed Scowcroft Commission, the six legislators threatened to withdraw the support of their coalitions unless the administration made specific changes in advance of the resumption of the START talks on October 6. The changes they secured were intended to address the concerns of colleagues now ambivalent on MX. For one, build-down would be one of the new arms control proposals to be introduced by the United States. In addition, the administration was receding from its previous insistence upon drastic reductions in the Soviet ICBM force, thus giving Rowny a more flexible negotiating position. Finally, James Woolsey, a Democrat attractive to many in his party and an important lobbying figure in the Scowcroft Commission, was appointed to the START team.

On November 1 and 7 respectively, the House and Senate catapulted the MX missiles over their last legislative hurdle prior to production, with approval of $2.1 billion for the purchase of the first eleven weapons. Also approved were R&D funds for Midgetman. Phoenix-like, the MX had survived four presidential administrations, thirty different basing modes, legal threats, popular demonstrations, legislative obstacles, and multiple lobbying pressures. Still there was no guarantee that the program would survive the annual scrutiny that Congress would execute during the authorization and appropriations battles in the years to come.

With the new generation of ICBMs in production, however, it will become increasingly more difficult to turn back the system's deployment. As contracts are let, the number of people with a vested stake in the survival of the weapon system will proliferate and the pressures on the congressional and executive branch arenas to sustain the program will multiply. Although the future fate of the MX missile system remains uncertain, the likelihood that Congress will continue to play a critical role in the MX drama is great. Whether that institution will also become more involved in other such weapon system is an assessment we address in the next chapter.

Observations

The discussion of MX procurement decision making between 1981 and 1983 suggests that again the bureaucratic politics model is of limited utility in explaining the decision making for this weapon. Specifically, propositions 7, 9, 10, 12, and 13 are only partially supported by the experience of MX decision making during this period. For example, as is obvious, the congressional arena was the center of MX decision making during this period in contrast to proposition 9. Moreover, porkbarrel was not the motivating factor in congressional involvement in contrast to proposition 10. In addition and despite the fact that President Reagan's first two proposed basing modes were the cheapest systems available, and chosen partially for their "economy," they were rejected (contrary to proposition 12). Finally, the Congress did in fact cause the president to alter the chosen basing mode, again something contrary to proposition 13.

On the other hand, the evidence does support several of the additional propositions suggested for testing at the end of chapter 1 — propositions 15 through 21. Strategic, foreign policy, environmental, and socioeconomic considerations were important factors in MX procurement decision making during these three years, in both the executive branch and the congressional arena. The president was a central actor in MX negotiations sometimes acting contrary to the advice of the Pentagon. And, again, the congressional arena was the central forum during this period. Finally, the administration's success in securing legislative approval of MX was tied to its success in forging a coalition with key legislative actors. Consequently, the bureaucratic politics model requires modification to be an effective explanatory device for procurement.

Endnotes

[1] The crucial question concerned whether or not conclusions about fratricide based on analysis of data drawn from tests in the 1960s with purposes other than the testing of fratricide were in fact valid.

[2] Congressional conferees in their report to S. 815, but not in the bill itself, barred research on the air-mobile alternative.

[3] Actually, two alternatives were studied, deployment in hard rock or sand. The first, called the "pencil pusher" variant, would be quite costly, and the missiles difficult to evacuate. The "sandy silo" alternative would be relatively cheap.

[4] Because the Senate was in special session, the 1983 defense appropriations bill was considered as part of the second continuing resolution.

[5] The action came on an amendment by Gary Hart.

[6] See Talbott (1984) and Drew (1983) for discussions of the Scowcroft Commission.

[7]See Drew (1983:46) for an interesting discussion of this point.

[8]For the most thorough discussion of the concept of build-down, see Frye (1983).

[9]Apparently in return for his support for MX, Aspin received promises from the Scowcroft Commission, however vague, that it would urge the administration to revamp the START proposals, to deploy a small, mobile, single warhead ICBM, and to limit MX to very small numbers in the years ahead, perhaps to less than 100 (authors' interviews).

[10]The letters, dated April 19 and 20, also contained the classified report by DOD on strategic force modernization required by P.L. 97-377.

[11]For Reagan to really embrace the idea, would require him to retire twenty warheads for each Peacekeeper deployed.

[12]Ironically, in the long run, the Midgetman, given its presumed role in the nuclear arsenal, could raise the same problems as MX MPS did, such as cost (as much as $100 billion over twenty years); manpower needs (at least 50,000 people); verifiability problems; and so on. For an interesting discussion of Midgetman, see Rich (1984).

CHAPTER 10
CONCLUSIONS

In setting ourselves the task of testing the validity of the bureaucratic politics perspective as the appropriate paradigm for describing, explaining, and, perhaps, predicting procurement decisions centered around the MX system, we have of course erected a straw man. Our purpose in doing so was to direct the attention of students of defense politics to elements of the policymaking process previously ignored or underrated. Analysts who attempt an examination of the weapon procurement process without recognizing that under certain circumstances the public and congressional arenas will be active ones, and that strategic, foreign policy, and domestic political forces can be salient, even within the executive branch, will miss the full richness and complexity of the decision-making process. It remains then to delineate the conditions under which we can expect a weapon project to provoke reactions similar to those we found in studying the MX system. We do this within the context of a brief summary of our findings.

Summary of Findings

We began this study by examining the bureaucratic politics perspective. We selected this paradigm for two reasons. First, it was and remains the most often used approach to describe and explain the weapon procurement process. Thus, it seemed reasonable to assume that it's utility would extend to an analysis of current weapon decisions. Second, and importantly, despite its shortcomings, the paradigm contains within its several propositions the seeds of a new approach. For example, by asserting that the role of Congress in procurement decisions is limited, the paradigm challenges us to look at Congress's role and see whether this is still the case. In fact it may be that the assumptions are no longer correct and need reformulation.

During the early years, from the late 1960s to the decision in June 1973 to proceed with full-scale research, development, and testing of MX, critical decisions were made in ways that do conform to the propositions of the bureaucratic politics approach; in particular, the propositions for the inner layer of procurement activity. (The summary of our findings is presented in Table 10.1.) The idea for a new experimental missile was a response to the desire of the air force to develop a third generation of ICBMs as a logical follow-on to Minuteman. The movement of the MX and its basing mode through the design and development stages was influenced by the interplay of organizational doctrine (the air force and SAC), technological opportunities, and projections of the enemy threat in the late 1970s and 1980s. Thus, during this phase of procurement activity, decision

Table 10.1

SUMMARY OF CONCLUSIONS

Proposition	Evaluation
A. Propositions for the inner layer:	
1. Ideas for new weapons or refinements of old weapons are seldom the result of deliberate strategic policy analysis. Rather they are the product of organizational doctrines, technological opportunities, perceptions of enemy threat, and/or incomplete and often vague strategic attitudes. More accurately, these ideas involve the interaction of engineering groups of the Director, Defense Research and Engineering (DDR&E), design labs in industry, engineering elements in think tanks, and the subunit of the military service with ultimate responsibility for the use of the new or refined weapon.	MX experience confirms proposition
2. During the design, research, development, and testing stage, procurement decisions about weapon ideas continue to be determined by the interaction of engineering groups of the DDR&E, design labs in industry, engineering elements in think tanks, and the subunit of the military service with ultimate responsibility for the use of the new or refined weapon being the most significant actor.	MX experience only partially confirms proposition
3. The mission of the subunit of the military service with the ultimate responsibility in the military for the use of the new weapon along with the power of that subunit are more important factors in the success of a weapon system (i.e., the attractiveness of the weapon to draw support within the Pentagon as compared to other alternatives) than the	MX experience rejects proposition

246

larger strategic and force posture considerations of U.S. national security policy.

4. Senior political officials outside the Pentagon may disturb decisions at this layer of action on procurement but rarely control it.

    MX experience rejects proposition

5. Political officials outside the executive branch as well as extra-governmental individuals will seldom seek to influence the inner layer procurement decisions, let alone disturb or even control them.

    MX experience rejects proposition

6. The hundreds of interrelated yet individual decisions during design, research, development, and testing cause the character of procurement decisions in this layer of activities to be incremental rather than synoptic.

    MX experience only partially confirms proposition

7. The likelihood that a weapon idea will reach design, research, development, and testing depends on the effectiveness of its advocates to continually promote the economic and political well-being of their project, for the longer a new weapon system survives during this inner layer of procurement activities the greater the momentum that builds for the weapon. The repeated individual choices begin to establish an irresistible bureaucratic inertia.

    MX experience confirms proposition

B. Propositions for the outer layer:

8. When the decision for a weapon program reaches the point of acquisition and deployment, the number of participants with interests in a particular weapon system tends to increase significantly, especially inside the executive branch.

    MX experience confirms proposition

9. During the acquisition and deployment stage, more actors from the congres-

    MX experience rejects proposition

247

sional and public arena are activated. However, the congressional and public arenas remain indirect and peripheral to the decision process for weapon procurement.

10.	The principal factor for producing what congressional involvement there is in procurement is porkbarrel.	MX experience rejects proposition
11.	The acquisition and deployment of a weapon program continues to depend on the capability of its advocates to promote the economic, strategic, and political well-being of their project.	MX experience confirms proposition
12.	Those weapon systems being considered for acquisition and deployment most likely to engender significant support (i.e., that will be least controversial) are those where	MX experience confirms proposition

    a) the missions of the organization responsible for the new weapon converges with the capability of the weapon;

    b) technological opportunity converges with a consensus on national policy;

    c) the strategic requirements or foreign policy needs converge with the weapon system's capabilities;

    d) the cost of deploying the weapon system in domestic terms (i.e., money, land, environmental impacts, and jobs) are likely to be relatively less than other alternatives; and

    e) the advantages of deploying the weapon system in domestic terms (i.e., contracts and jobs) are likely to be relatively greater than other alternatives.

13.	Weapon programs are seldom slowed or overturned once initial approval of acquisition is achieved in the executive	MX experience only partially confirms proposition

248

branch, and only a presidential directive is likely to slow or overturn that decision. However, the decision to modify, while executive based, may be made in anticipation of public or congressional resistance deemed threatening enough to warrant change.

14. The "rules of the game" introduced by the secretary of defense and the president shape how and by whom acquisition and deployment decisions will be made within the executive branch.

MX experience confirms proposition

15. Strategic policy considerations will be significant factors in procurement decisions in cases where the weapon system's strategic advantages are uncertain.

MX experience confirms proposition

16. Foreign policy considerations will be significant factors in procurement decisions in cases where the weapon system's foreign policy advantages are uncertain.

MX experience confirms proposition

17. Environmental considerations will be significant factors in procurement decisions in cases where the weapon system will be environmentally costly.

MX experience confirms proposition

18. Socioeconomic considerations will be significant factors in procurement decisions in cases where the weapon system will consume large amounts of resources (material and financial) and be socially costly.

MX experience confirms proposition

19. The president will be a decisive participant in cases where the strategic, foreign policy, and/or domestic considerations of the weapon system are in conflict with administrative policies.

MX experience confirms proposition

20. Congress will be an important arena in cases where the strategic, foreign policy, and/or domestic considerations of the weapon system are in conflict with

MX experience confirms proposition

249

constituent and/or personal policy preferences.

21. The public arena will be an important   MX experience
one in cases where the costs and/or   confirms proposition
benefits of deploying the weapon system pose a clear and present threat to the
interests of individuals.

---

making was dominated by engineering groups in DDR&E, the design labs of defense industries (especially TRW), engineering elements of think tanks (RAND Corporation), and SAC. Moreover, the decisions about research, design, development, and testing of MX were incremental rather than synoptic; the result of hundreds of separate yet interrelated actions by individuals in the above groups. Finally, SAC was the dominant force during the early stages of MX development. Consequently, the early evolution of MX was similar to that suggested by propositions 1 and 2.

Despite a pattern of conformance, however, during this period the shadows of a different experience for MX as compared to most other procurement decisions were already beginning to appear. Foreign policy considerations, particularly the SALT agreement, complicated the basing mode decisions after 1972. For strategic reasons, moreover, OSD, senators, and staffers were actively involved in resisting proposed characteristics for greater warhead accuracy and yield improvements in the new missile. This would have meant greater counterforce lethality. Therefore, after 1973, strategic questions about the missile's first-strike potential, technical questions about the survivability of MX, and the financial costs of the weapon system brought into the decision-making process additional individuals and groups, expanding the narrow confines of the procurement community.

It is in the period after 1974, and especially between 1979 and 1983, that the propositions associated with the bureaucratic politics paradigm provide insufficient insight into MX decision making. In general we find the number of actors involved in MX decision making increasing at an almost exponential rate, both inside and outside the executive arena; legislative and public actors exercising influence in ways not anticipated by the propositions; foreign policy, strategic and domestic political factors affecting the MX debate in significant ways; and key decisions on MX delayed, modified, and blocked by forces outside the inner circle of important Defense Department officials normally dominant over such matters.

Moreover, after 1975, the pattern of MX decision making was more synoptic than incremental. With the increasing dominance of strategic, foreign policy, and domestic political issues in the MX debate, the preeminent position of SAC declined, and the influence of senior national security officials, especially the president, increased. At the same time, actors in Congress and the public arenas had begun testing their power and forcing reconsideration of basing decisions. Between 1976 and 1983 the MX received five fresh basing mode reviews and many less broad reexaminations by three presidents and their senior officials.

In fact, between 1979 and 1983, the fate of MX was increasingly decided on the floor of the Senate and the House; and in the offices of the lawyers for the Sierra Club and Nevada Cattlemen's Association. These latter organizations, together with others in the public arena, were the first to fully use the participatory options available for defeating through delay a major weapon project. The Reagan administration, particularly sensitive to the role of both the public and members of Congress, deliberately selected basing modes that would reduce opposition to MX on financial, environmental, and socioeconomic grounds; and which offered concessions on arms control to recalcitrant legislators. Finally, the longer the debate over MX prevailed, the more important coalition building became, to such an extent that no decisions concerning MX today can be made without coalition politics; coalition politics that transcend branches of government. The quintessential example, of course, is the Scowcroft Commission. The realization by members of the panel that the game of procurement decision making had changed at least for weapon systems like MX saved the missile project from oblivion in 1983. Thus, propositions 1 through 14 provide incomplete and occassionally misleading explanations of MX decision making after 1975; whereas propositions 15 through 21 offer better insights.

If we can identify the reasons for these deviations from the conventional wisdom, we can begin to build a case for anticipating similar decision-making patterns in future weapon programs. Most obviously, both the missile and the several basing modes proposed to house MX were different than for most previous weapon programs. The strategic and foreign policy implications of deploying a ten-warhead, 190,000-pound missile, as well as the socioeconomic, cultural, and environmental consequences of making the missile mobile, were unprecedented. To some extent, then, the case of the MX system is unmatched. However, if this were the total picture then the controversy over MX would have subsided after Reagan's decision to abandon MPS basing. On the contrary it has accelerated. Moreover, just because a weapon system is controversial does not guarantee that actors outside the executive branch can actually influence its direction. Thus, we need to look elsewhere for our answer to the question of why MX is different.

251

In addition to the strategic, foreign policy, and domestic political concerns that the missile and its various basing modes raised was the fact that uncertainties always characterized the system from its origins. The most obvious example was the elusive search for a basing mode capable of closing the window of vulnerability. It has never been found. The alternative promoted by the Scowcroft Commission was the denial that it had ever really existed. Thus, despite the fact that MX was compatible with the organizational doctrine of SAC, and that the technology was available, the system faced critical strategic uncertainties that seriously delayed, if not prevented, its deployment.

The uncertainties over the strategic value of the various basing modes, and conflict over the foreign policy consequences of the new missile system inevitably produced dissension within the executive branch. To this day the battle between those in the State Department and NSC, with concern over the arms control implications of MX's hard-target capability and the threats to the SALT regime posed by certain basing modes, and the Pentagon, whose singular interest is with a new missile with greater hard-target capability, has never been resolved. The debate is currently being fought on the floor of Congress. At various points, and contrary to the conventional wisdom, several presidents (Ford, Carter, Reagan) and their senior political advisors (Schlesinger, Brown, Weinberger) have been brought into the fray to settle disputes in the executive branch. Their involvement proved decisive, at least temporarily until the next crisis, in shaping the character of both the missile and basing mode.

Fourth, the controversial nature of MX and dissension within the executive branch have expanded the arena of conflict to include actors outside the executive branch. As the strategic, foreign policy, and domestic political implications of the missile system's deployment became more compelling, the actors in the public and congressional arenas were brought into the debate in ways not anticipated by the conventional wisdom. For example, it was Congress, motivated by strategic concerns, that forced the Ford administration to postpone its plan to temporarily retrofit the MX in Minuteman silos; that compelled the Carter administration to effect changes in the MPS basing mode; that blocked the Reagan administration's efforts to deploy the missiles in a dense pack scheme; and that has postponed indefinitely the full deployment of the missile.

However, the character and level of public and congressional involvement in the MX decision-making process would not have been possible unless three additional forces had been operating. For one, the magnitude of the direct and indirect effects of MX on the people of the proposed region of deployment was such that the missile system was of vital concern to residents and their representatives in the South Platte Plains states, the

252

Great Basin, the High Plains and most recently, Wyoming, Colorado, and Nebraska. Second, the decision to deploy the missiles in a land-based mode meant that several domestic laws came into play, with provisions mandating the direct and formal participation of the people, and requisite intergovernmental consultation and cooperation. Third, the legislative reform movement of the 1970s gave members of Congress the tools to influence procurement policy in ways previously not possible.

More specifically, part of Congress's success in influencing MX decisions was the strategic expertise of its committees, now equipped with additional information available through both additional staff and the expansion of its research outlets such as the OTA and GAO. The public's role has been greatly enhanced by the availability of the land withdrawal procedures and the environmental impact process mandated by FLPMA and NEPA respectively.

In sum, then, the case of policymaking for MX illustrates the interplay of several factors that may never converge again: (1) a weapon system capable of massive and irreversible impacts, both nuclear and nonnuclear; (2) a lack of consensus on the foreign and strategic policy objectives that inform the development of a weapon system; (3) a system that is technically flawed or unsatisfactory; (4) a project so controversial that consensus building is difficult in the executive and congressional arenas; (5) congressional and public actors equipped and willing to use their power to influence the nature and direction of procurement policymaking; (6) a project for which a movement of opposition has mobilized and operates in several decision-making arenas simultaneously; and (7) a system so expensive that it threatens to preempt other domestic goals.

On the other hand, it is not inconceivable to imagine these forces operating in future weapon procurement decisions, although not perhaps to the degree of intensity as that for MX. For example, to reverse the current trend towards ever larger and more lethal nuclear weapons would require major modifications in our strategic and foreign policy objectives. The development of a deployment mode for our ICBMs capable of providing invulnerability comparable to that of the 1960s would require discovering technology that has previously eluded four administrations and a freeze in comparable improvements in Soviet technology. To forestall controversy over further nuclear weapon systems would require the development and deployment of unobtrusive projects that offer definite solutions to clearly delineated problems that are accepted as such by political and administrative actors; and either carry a reasonable price tag, or are promoted during periods of economic prosperity. To circumvent any obstacles that the public and Congress might seek to erect in efforts to influence the nature and direction of future weapon systems would require the reversal of

253

congressional reforms and revisions in domestic laws such as NEPA and FLPMA. To quell the public's current concern over nuclear war would require a national lobotomy.

The broad consensus about foreign policy objectives that characterized the pre-Vietnam period has been replaced by a clear division within the United States about national security policy. Congress is better equipped to assume an active role in procurement decisions. The enormity of the projected deficits over the next six years guarantees that budgetary and defense politics will collide. The increasing sensitivity of large groups of people to the quality of life make federal installation projects portending vast socioeconomic and environmental side effects potentially controversial. The increasing democratization of the federal administrative process, i.e., the expansion of participatory opportunities, provides the means for public actors to become involved in the decisions concerning the construction of massive weapons of destruction. Finally, the lines delineating the arenas of power will continue to be breached by groups and individuals seeking allies in their efforts to dictate the direction of our procurement policy.

Thus, if the case of the MX system is indicative of important future trends for certain types of weapon procurement, the system by which our society decides to research, develop, build, and deploy its weapons is becoming far more open. What this means is that all of us are now implicated in the decisions to deploy nuclear weaponry. Are we prepared to assume that responsibility? This of course raises important normative questions.

The Normative Questions

Implicit in the bureaucratic politics literature is the belief that procurement decisions are best made within the "competitive" environment of the executive arena. Advocates of the bureaucratic process see significant utility in factional disputes among the various organizations and interests in the executive branch, especially in the second layer of decision activities. They believe that the procurement decision-making process as described above exists and its effects are quite healthy for U.S. national security policy. It produces a robust competition that causes a more complete review of the advantages and disadvantages of different decisions concerning national security policy, and in particular, procurement alternatives. This vitality of competition helps delineate the probable costs and benefits of a potential policy or weapon program and acts to constrain an administration from adopting policy positions without a careful evaluation of the various alternatives. There is also the assumption that this competition will prevent a single, narrow perspective from dominating the procurement process, something counterproductive to good policy.

However, normative critics of the bureaucratic politics paradigm contend that rather than good policy, the bureaucratic politics process produces decisions that lack coherence, continuity, and consistency; and therefore, our security policy is unable to facilitate the realization of our foreign policy goals. According to Henry Kissinger, referring to the procurement process during the Nixon administration, the policy that emerges from such a process is most often a broad compromise of the vested interests of the parochial concerns of the organizations that make up the executive branch, rather than a response to the external needs of the international environment. "The nightmare of the modern state is the bigness of the bureaucracy, and the problem is how to get coherence and design into it," contends Kissinger (quoted in Destler, 1974:3).

A third set of analysts views the competition within the executive as incomplete. The competition over procurement that does take place among sets of actors within the executive branch is actually too narrow to produce good policy. Thus, certain side effects of a weapon decision, such as environmental, social, and economic costs, are seldom considered in the procurement decision-making process since certain topics are virtually excluded from the process. The experience of the Vietnam War and Watergate suggest to these critics that greater diversity within the executive branch is not sufficient to counter the president's national security powers. Thus, these analysts argue that the variety of ideas and vitality of competition necessary for good policymaking can only be introduced from outside the executive bureaucracy. These analysts call for institutional changes that would provide greater access to the procurement process for a larger number of actors.

The MX decision-making pattern illustrates that the process by which certain types of procurement decisions are made has changed; and, that this change has been in the direction of expanding the arena of conflict. Whether this dispersion of power will create good policy is a two-edged sword. On the one hand, competition, it is said, breeds compromise that guarantees that the "best" decision — however we define the term — will not be made. On the other hand, there is the argument that any decision that is the product of the democratic process will be a decision that has been more fully examined, scrutinized, considered, and weighed. It may not, however, be the most technically appropriate policy option available; but it could be the most rational policy in the long run.

It is 1984, the time when our ICBM force was supposed to be most vulnerable to a Soviet first strike according to the proponents of MX in the mid-1970s. From one perspective, the democratic process has prevented

255

the government from adequately guaranteeing the national security that the U.S. Constitution mandates. However, in doing so, the democratic forces have postponed the deployment of the most lethal weapon in the history of mankind and one that may not have offered any real advantages in the strategic sense envisioned a decade ago.

EPILOGUE

The Scowcroft compromise of MX, the Midgetman, and arms limitation as the core of the Reagan administration's strategic policy has faced several problems since its initial successes in 1983. On February 1, 1984, the U.S. Air Force released the final copy of its $8 million environmental impact statement, thus eliminating one more obstacle in the way of deployment of MX in Minuteman silos in Nebraska and Wyoming. FEIS III, which responds to 1,500 individual issues raised at the public hearings held in the deployment areas and the written comments of 400 concerned citizens, anticipates the construction of the support facilities for the missile system, which is to be completed by 1986. As of this writing (June 1, 1984), citizens in Nebraska, Wyoming, and Colorado are preparing both a legal and political campaign to defeat Peacekeeper. Western Solidarity, a coalition of fifty anti-MX groups in eight midwestern and intermountain states, has mobilized its 50,000 members to work on its effort to qualify a ballot (initiative) proposition for the November election to halt MX deployment in Wyoming, and in anticipation of the filing of a lawsuit during the summer. The suit will claim that FEIS III fails to fulfill the requirements of NEPA and other applicable statutes and will seek an injunction halting MX preparatory work in Nebraska. Ultimately, Western Solidarity hopes to delay work on the support facilities for the missile system long enough to give the national anti-MX lobby a chance to defeat the weapon project in Congress.

Despite the recent vote on the fiscal 1985 defense authorization bill funding fifteen additional MXs, opponents are optimistic. In March Governors Ed Herschler of Wyoming and Bob Kerney of Nebraska formally requested that Reagan delay for one year the deployment of the MX system, to send a "clear message to the Soviet Union of our desire for peace and a more stable world" and to help reduce federal spending (*Desert Sun*, March/April 1984). Reagan refused. All three candidates for the Democratic presidential nomination, Gary Hart, Jesse Jackson, and Walter Mondale, publicly declared themselves opposed to any funding of the weapon system.

Finally, the General Accounting Office (GAO), in the most recent in a series of continuing oversight reports on the MX, condemned the missile project for its estimated cost ($26.4 million) and for being technically flawed. Three findings in the report are of paramount concern. First, the air force has modified the missile with the addition of a heavier warhead, the Mk 21. The air force had to reduce the amount of propellant used on MX to compensate for the heavier warhead. This the GAO claims, may affect the

257

missile's range performance. Second, the report claims that intelligence information indicates that the Soviets have achieved a threefold increase in the hardness of its silos since 1979, thus placing in jeopardy the viability of MX. Third, the GAO criticizes the air force for producing component parts for the missile without first testing them, and for planning deployment in advance of flight-testing. The air force has responded by indicating that the intelligence data the GAO was working with is inaccurate and that the parts referred to are "low-risk components" (*Salt Lake Tribune*, 12 May 1984).

Even the House vote on MX in May was encouraging to opponents who read in it the continuation of a clear pattern of declining support for the MX weapon project; despite the most recent of the compromise deals negotiated by Les Aspin with the White House. On May 16, 1984, the House of Representatives, by a six-vote margin, first defeated an amendment by Nicholas Mavroules and Charles Bennett to cut off all funds for MX in the fiscal 1985 defense authorization bill. That margin represents a consistent decline from a fifty-three-vote edge in the critical May 1983 decision. The House then voted to accept the compromise that Aspin had reached with the president: legislative endorsement for MX in a number significantly less (fifteen) than the president sought (forty), and the money ($1.8 billion) for the additional missiles fenced until April 1, 1985, to give the Soviets a chance to return to the bargaining table. The House vote essentially called Reagan's bluff. It tells the president that he will lose the MX missile program if the Soviets *do* return to the bargaining table, thus responding directly to his bargaining chip theme. The Catch-22 is that Reagan also views the MX as a critical component of his defense modernization program. As many journalists have already commented, however, the Soviets are unlikely to respond favorably to what essentially constitutes blackmail. "The Aspin compromise, which assumes that the Soviet Union can be bought for a mere fifteen additional intercontinental ballistic missiles, is ridiculous" (*Salt Lake Tribune*, 20 May 1984). Since the Soviets abandoned the arms talks because of the deployment of U.S. missiles in Western Europe; and since the first missiles, funded by Congress last year, have yet to bring the Soviets back to the arms table, it is highly unlikely that fifteen more advanced, ten-warhead ICBMs will do so. More importantly, the Russians have threatened to retaliate for MX and the other arms programs that Congress approved in May (*New York Times*, 18 May 1984).

At the state and local levels citizens prepare to battle the MX in their regions. At the national level, legislators and interest groups together continue the National Campaign To Stop The MX. Fifty organizations, including SANE, Common Cause, Council for a Livable World, labor unions, and legislators led by Tom Downey wage the battle on the congressional front. Although the national lobby so far has failed to achieve its ultimate objective of "zeroing" the missiles requested in the 1985 defense budget, and deauthorizing the unspent portion of the $2.1 billion appropriated last year, they did succeed in cutting back the number of missiles slated for procurement, and once again slowing down the procurement process. Conceding eventual defeat in the Republican controlled Senate on the authorization measure (as of this writing, the Senate Armed Services Committee's strategic warfare subcommittee had adopted a proposal to limit production funds to twenty-one missiles, according to the *Salt Lake Tribune*, 20 May 1984), opponents point out that there will still be two more authorization and appropriations votes, and one election before the first MX missiles become operational.

While the MX controversy continues, the debate over Midgetman has intensified. The air force is examining lands in the southwestern region of the United States, including areas in Nevada and Utah, as possible deployment sites for 1,000 Midgetman missiles, in a mobile, land-based scheme. Current estimates suggest that, if built as presently conceived, the Midgetman program will consume 12,000 to 38,000 square miles of land, and cost as much as $100 billion (*Salt Lake Tribune*, 25 March 1984). Already eighteen contracts have been awarded for research and development of the system that is expected to consist of launchers capable of moving on and off roads, of withstanding 30-psi overpressure, and of being reached by mobile command. The air force expects the first Midgetman to be operational in 1992. In a recent examination of the Midgetman, Johnathan Rich (1984:6) suggests:

> As presently envisioned, the Midgetman will be about 44 feet in length and four feet in diameter, with a range of 6,000 nautical miles. A payload capacity of approximately 1,000 pounds will allow it to carry one Mk 21, a 300 to 500 kiloton warhead, ten of which are designed for each MX. The air force is using a lightweight version of the Advanced Inertial Reference Sphere (AIRS) employed on the MX as the baseline guidance system. Alternative systems, such as ring-laser gyroscopes and terminal guidance are also being pursued.

Part of the "complexity, expense and development time" of Midgetman results from a combination of actions by Congress and interests of the air force. Congress amended the defense authorization bill in 1983 to require development and testing of Midgetman before the deployment of MX in 1986. By that time, the air force must complete guidance and propulsion tests for Midgetman systems. Congress also set an "upper limit of 33,000 pounds on the weight of the missile to assure its mobility" (Rich, 1984:6). The air force also wants the Midgetman to have hard-target capability so that the deployment of 1,000 small missiles in conjunction with MX and Minuteman III will put Soviet ICBMs at risk. The congressional require-

259

ment concerning weight clashes with the present AIRS and Mk21 size. Consequently, considerable advancement quickly in these systems for Midgetman is necessary in order to allow MX to be deployed. Meanwhile, veterans of the MX battle in Nevada, Utah, New Mexico, Texas, and Colorado are anticipating that if Midgetman is deployed in their states, the land, public interface, and technical problems that will arise can once again provide grounds for defeating the next generation of land-based nuclear missiles.

The third dimension of the Scowcroft compromise involves strategic and theater arms limitation. In November 1983, following the initial deployment of 572 U.S.-built cruise and Pershing II missiles in West European countries, the Soviets walked out of both sets of negotiations in Geneva. In March 1984, the President's Commission on Strategic Forces (the Scowcroft Commission) released its final report to the president. They reaffirmed that the goal of strategic stability could only be achieved if all three elements of its original recommendations are pursued: the deployment of MX, the development of Midgetman, and arms control. They encouraged the administration to be more aggressive in the arms limitation dimension of the program.

It is unlikely that any of the issues which now divide the nation on the MX system will be resolved in the near future. The weapon continues to carry the first-strike capability which frightens arms control advocates, the enormous price tag which concerns fiscal conservatives, and the counterforce potential which enamors war-fighting strategists. The end of the MX controversy is nowhere in sight.

SELECTED BIBLIOGRAPHY

Books

Allison, Graham T. (1971) *Essence of Decision: Explaining the Cuban Missile Crisis*. Boston, Massachusetts: Little, Brown and Company.

Anderson, Frederick A. (1973) *NEPA in the Courts: A Legal Analysis of the National Environmental Policy Act*. Baltimore, Maryland: Johns Hopkins University Press.

Ball, Desmond. (1980a) *Developments in U.S. Strategic Nuclear Policy Under the Carter Administration*. Los Angeles, California: UCLA, Center for International and Strategic Affairs.

_____. (1980b) *Politics and Force Levels: The Strategic Missile Program of the Kennedy Administration*. Berkeley, California: University of California Press.

Beard, Edmond. (1976) *Developing the ICBM: A Study in Bureaucratic Politics*. New York: Columbia University Press.

Brezezinski, Zbigniew. (1983) *Power and Principal*. New York: Farrar, Straus, Giroux.

Brodie, Bernard. (1959) *Strategy in the Missile Age*. Princeton, New Jersey: Princeton University Press.

Cantril, Hadley. (1971) *Gauging Public Opinion*. Port Washington, New York: Kennikat Press.

Crabb, Cecil V., and Pat M. Holt. (1980) *Invitation to Struggle*. Washington, D.C.: Congressional Quarterly Press.

Dahl, Robert A. (1956) *Preface to Democratic Theory*. Chicago, Illinois: University of Chicago Press.

Davis, Jacquelyn K., *et al*. (1980) *The Soviet Union and Ballistic Missile Defense*. Cambridge, Massachusetts: Institute for Foreign Policy Analysis.

Davis, Vincent. (1967) *The Politics of Innovation: Patterns In Navy Cases*. Denver, Colorado: Monograph Series in World Affairs, The University of Denver Press.

Destler, J.M. (1974) *Presidents, Bureaucrats and Foreign Policy*. Princeton, New Jersey: Princeton University Press.

Dexter, Lewis Anthony, Raymond A. Bauer and Ithiel de Sola Pool. (1963) *American Business and Public Policy: The Politics of Foreign Trade*. New York: Atherton Press.

261

Edwards, John. (1982) *Super Weapon: The Making of MX*. New York: W.W. Norton and Company.

Frank, Thomas and Edward Weisband. (1979) *Foreign Policy By Congress*. New York: Oxford University Press.

Freedman, Lawrence. (1982) *The Evolution of Nuclear Strategy*. New York: St. Martin's Press.

Frye, Alton. (1975) *A Responsible Congress: The Politics of National Security*. New York: McGraw-Hill Book Company.

George, Alexander L. and George Smoke. (1974) *Deterrence in American Foreign Policy: Theory and Practice*. New York: Columbia University Press.

Goure, Leon. (1976) *War Survival in Soviet Strategy: U.S.S.R. Civil Defense*. Miami, Florida: University of Miami Press.

Gray, Colin S. (1981) *The ICBM and National Security*. New York: Praeger.

Greenwood, Ted (1975) . *Making the MIRV: A Study of Defense Decision Making*. Cambridge, Massachusetts: Ballinger Publishing Company.

Halperin, Morton. (1974) *Bureaucratic Politics and Foreign Policy*. Washington, D.C.: the Brookings Institution.

_____., and Arnold Kanter. (1973) *Readings in American Foreign Policy: A Bureaucratic Perspective*. Boston, Massachusetts: Little, Brown and Company.

Hammond, Paul. (1963) *Super Carriers and B-36 Bombers: Appropriations, Strategy, and Politics*. Indianapolis, Indiana: Bobbs-Merrill Company, Inc.

_____. (1961) *Organizing for Defense: the American Military Establishment in the Twentieth Century*. Princeton, New Jersey: Princeton University Press.

Henkin, Louis. (1972) *Foreign Affairs and the Constitution*. New York: W.W. Norton and Company.

Hilsman, Roger. (1967) *To Move A Nation*. New York: Delta Book.

Hodgden, Louise. (1981) *The MX Missile System: The Decision Making Process and Implications for Arms Control*. Santa Monica, California: The California Seminar on International Security and Foreign Policy.

Hoover, Robert A. (1982) *The MX Controversy*. Los Angeles, California: Regina Press.

Hughes, Barry B. (1978) *The Domestic Context of American Foreign Policy*. San Francisco, California: W. H. Freeman and Company.

262

Huntington, Samuel P. (1961) *The Common Defense*. New York: Columbia University Press.

International Institute of Strategic Studies. (1982) *The Military Balance, 1981-82*. London, Britain: Adlard and Son Ltd, Bartholomew Press.

Kahan, Jerome H. (1975) *Security in the Nuclear Age*. Washington,D.C.: The Brookings Institution.

Kaplan, Fred. (1983) *The Wizards of Armageddon*. New York: Simon and Schuster.

Kissinger, Henry. (1982) *Years of Upheaval*. Boston, Massachusetts: Little, Brown, and Company.

Klessig, Lowell L., and Victor L. Strite. (1980) *The ELF Odyssey: National Security Versus Environmental Protection*. Boulder, Colorado: Westview Press.

Korb, Lawrence J. (1979) *The Fall and Rise of the Pentagon: American Defense Policies in the 1970s*. Westport, Connecticut: Greenwood Press.

Lapp, Ralph. (1970) *Arms Beyond Doubt: The Tyranny of Weapons Technology*. New York: Cowles.

Legault, Albert and George Lindsey. (1974) *The Dynamics of the Nuclear Balance*. Ithaca, New York: Cornell University Press.

Morris, Roger. (1977) *Uncertain Greatness: Henry Kissinger & American Foreign Policy*. New York: Harper and Row.

Neustadt, Richard E. (1970) *Alliance Politics*. New York: Columbia University Press.

———. (1964) *Presidential Power*. New York: John Wiley and Sons.

Newhouse, John. (1973) *Cold Dawn: The Story of SALT*. New York: Holt, Rinehart, and Winston.

Nixon, Richard M. (1973) *U.S. Foreign Policy for the 1970s: Shaping A Durable Peace*. Washington D.C.: Government Printing Office.

Platt, Alan. (1978) *The U.S. Senate and Strategic Arms Policy*. Boulder, Colorado: Westview Press.

———, and Lawrence Weiler. (1978) *Congress and Arms Control*. Boulder, Colorado: Westview Press.

Quester, George. (1971) *Nuclear Diplomacy*. New York: Dunellen.

———. (1966) *Deterrence Before Hiroshima*. New York: John Wiley and Sons.

Russett, Bruce M. (1970) *What Price Vigilance: The Burdens of National Defense*. New Haven: Yale University Press.

Sapolsky, Harvey M. (1972) *The Polaris System Development: Bureaucratic and Programmatic Success in Government*. Cambridge, Massachusetts: Harvard University Press.

Scheer, Robert. (1982) *With Enough Shovels: Reagan, Bush and Nuclear War*. New York: Random House.

Schelling, Thomas C. (1960) *The Strategy of Conflict*. New York: Oxford University Press.

Schilling, Warner, William T.R. Fox, Catherine M. Kelleher, and Donald Puchala. (1973) *American Arms and a Changing Europe: Dilemmas of Deterrence and Disarmament*. New York: Columbia University Press.

————, Paul Hammond, and Glenn Snyder. (1962) *Strategy, Politics and Defense*. New York: Columbia University Press.

Scoville, Herbert J. (1981) *MX: Prescription for Disaster*. Cambridge, Massachusetts: MIT Press.

Smith, Gerald C. (1981) *Doubletalk: The Story of SALT I*. New York: Doubleday and Company, Inc.

Snyder, Glenn H. (1961) *Deterrence and Defense: Toward a Theory of National Security*. Princeton, New Jersey: Princeton University Press.

Spanier, John and Eric M. Uslaner. (1978) *How American Foreign Policy is Made*. New York: Holt, Rinehart and Winston.

Talbott, Strobe. (1979) *End Game*. Boston, Massachusetts: Little, Brown, and Company.

Wahlke, John C., *et al*. (1962) *The Legislative System*. New York: John Wiley and Sons.

Wolfe, Thomas W. (1979) *The SALT Experience*. Cambridge, Massachusetts: Ballinger Publishing Company.

Articles

Achterman, Gail and Sally Fairfax. (1979) "The Participation Requirements of the Federal Land Policy and Management Act." *Arizona Law Review* 21, no 2: 501-39.

Aderman, Gary. (1979) "The MX Missile—There's More to It Than Just Salt." *National Journal* 11 (August):1323-25.

Allison, Graham T. (1969) "Conceptual Models and the Cuban Missile Crisis." *American Political Science Review* 43 (September):689-718.

———, and Frederic Morris. (1976) "Armaments and Arms Control: Exploring the Determinants of Military Weapons." In *Arms, Defense Policy, and Arms Control*, edited by Franklin A. Long and George W. Rathjens. New York: W.W. Norton and Company.

———. (1972) "Bureaucratic Politics: A Paradigm and Some Policy Implications." In *Theory and Policy in International Relations*, edited by Raymond Tanter and Richard H. Ullman. Princeton, New Jersey: Princeton University Press.

Anderson, J. Edward. (1981a) "First Strike: Myth or Reality?" *The Bulletin of Atomic Scientists* 37 (November):6-11.

———. (1981b) "Missile Vulnerability: What You Can't Know." *Strategic Review* 9 (Spring):38-41

Anonymous. (1981) "MX The Weapon Nobody Wants." *The Defense Monitor* X.

———. (1981) "USAF Analysis Attacks Airmobile MX Concept." *Aviation Week and Space Technology* 115 (17 August):30-31.

———. (1980) "Congress Challenges MX Basing Plan." *Science* 19 (30 May):1007.

———.(1979). "Federal Water Rights of the National Park Service, Bureau of Reclamation and the Bureau of Land Management." *Interior Decisions* 86.

———. (1971) "Environmental Law: Public Participation in the Environmental Impact Statement Process." *Minnesota Law Review* 61:363-81.

Art, Robert J. (1973) "Bureaucratic Politics and American Foreign Policy: A Critique." *Policy Sciences* 4 (December):567-90.

Aspin, Les. (1975) "The Defense Budget and Foreign Policy." In *American Defense Policy* 4th edition, edited by John E. Endicott and Roy W. Stafford, Jr., 4th ed. Baltimore, Maryland: Johns Hopkins Press.

Ball, Desmond. (1982-83) "U.S. Strategic Forces: How Would They Be Used?" *International Security* 7 (Winter):31-60.

———. (1981) "Counterforce Targeting: How New? How Viable?" *Arms Control Today* 11 (February):1-2, 6-9.

———. (1979) "The Road to Strategic Flexibility: The Schlesinger Doctrine." In *Nuclear Strategy: Flexibility and Stability*, edited by Keith B. Payne, C. Johnson Conover, and Bruce W. Bennet. Los Angeles, California: California Seminar on International Security and Foreign Policy.

Barlow, Jeffrey G. (1981) "MX Deployment: Inadequacies of Air and Sea Based Options." *Heritage Foundation Backgrounder* 150 (31 August):1-28.

Baugh, William H. (1980) "Deceptive Basing Modes for Strategic Missiles: An Exercise in the Politics of an Ambiguous Nuclear Balance." *Western Political Science Quarterly* 33 (June):247-59.

Blair, Stewart. (1982) "Question for Strategic Modernization: Why 'Ride Out' a Soviet Attack?" *Strategic Review* 10 (Spring):44-52.

Brandon, Henry. (1963) "Skybolt." In *Readings in American Foreign Policy: A Bureaucratic Perspective*, edited by Morton Halperin and Arnold Kanter. Boston, Massachusetts: Little, Brown and Company.

Brodie, Bernard. (1946) "The Weapon." In *The Absolute Weapon: Atomic Power and World Order*, edited by Bernard Brodie. New York: Harcourt, Brace.

Caldwell, Dan. (1977) "Bureaucratic Foreign Policy-Making." *American Behavioral Scientist* 21 (September/October):87-110.

Center For Defense Information (CDI). (1980-81) "The MX Missile: Boom or Boondoggle." *Business and Society Review* 35 (Winter):46-52.

Davis, Jacquelyn K. (1978) "End of Strategic Triad?" *Strategic Review* 6 (Winter):36-44.

Davis, Vincent. (1973) "The Development of a Capability to Deliver Nuclear Weapons by Carrier-Based Aircraft." In Halperin and Kanter.

Davis, William, Jr. (1980) "Ballistic Missile Defense Into the Eighties." *National Defense* 64 (September/October):55-63.

Dine, Thomas A. (1978) "Military R & D: Congress' Next Area of Policy Penetration." *Bulletin of Atomic Scientists* 34 (February):32-37.

Draim, John E. (1980) "Move MX Missile Out to Sea." *National Review* 32 (12 December):1527.

Drell, Sidney. (1979) "SUM." *Arms Control Today* 9 (September):1-8.

Drew, Elizabeth. (1983) "A Political Journal." *New Yorker* 59 (20 June):39-75.

Engdahl, David E. (1976) "State and Federal Power over Federal Property." *Arizona Law Review*, 18:283-384.

Freedman, Lawrence. (1976) "Logic, Politics and Foreign Policy Processes: A Critique of the Bureaucratic Politics Model." *International Affairs* 52 (July):434-90.

Frye, Alton. (1983) "Strategic Build-Down: A Context for Restraint." *Foreign Affairs* 62 (Winter):293-318.

Garwin, Richard L. (1979-80) "Missile Vulnerability Reconsidered." *International Security* 4 (Winter):117-39.

Goetz, Lall Betty. (1976) "Arms Control Impact Statements: A New Approach to Slowing the Arms Race?" *Arms Control Today* 6 (July/August):1-3.

Gold, David. (1980) "MX and the American Economy." *Arms Control Today* 10 (February):3-5.

Gray, Colin S. (1982) "Strategic Forces: The Reagan Story." *International Security Review* (Winter):1-3.

_____ and Keith Payne. (1980) "Victory is Possible." *Foreign Policy* 39 (Summer):14-27.

_____. (1979) "Nuclear Strategy: A Case for a Theory of Victory." *International Security* 4 (Summer):54-87.

_____. (1977) "The Future of Land Based Missile Forces." *Adelphi Papers, no. 144.* London, Britain: International Institute for Strategic Studies.

Haas, Richard. (1979) "The Role of the Congress in American Security Policy." In *American Defense Policy* 5th edition, edited by John Reichart and Steven Sturn. Baltimore, Maryland, Johns Hopkins Press.

Haslam, Elizabeth. (1978-79) "Federal and State Cooperation in the Management of Public Lands." *Journal of Contemporary Law* 5 (Winter): 149-62.

Henderson, Wallace D. (1982) "Launch Under Attack: Counterforce Disincentive." *Astronautics and Aeronautics* 20 (March):32-37.

Hershman, Robert. (1980) "The Great Basin: First Casualty of the MX?" *Atlantic Monthly* 245 (April):4-13.

Holland, Lauren. (1984) "The Use of NEPA in Defense Policy Politics: Public and State Involvement in the MX Missile Project." *Social Science Journal* 21 (July):53-71.

_____ and Robert Benedict. (1982) "Life After MX: Federalism and Water Policy." *Nevada Public Affairs Journal* 2 (Fall):39-44.

_____ and Robert Benedict. (1981) "The Role of the State in Defense Policy: The Case of MX." Paper delivered at the 1981 meeting of the American Political Science Association.

Ikle, Fred Charles. (1982) "The Reagan Strategic Defense Program: A Fuse on the Strategic Imperatives." *Strategic Review* 10 (Spring):11-18.

Jacob, Walter. (1980) "It's Not Only The Russians Who Regard the MX as a Threat." *National Journal* 23 (August):1400-02.

Kincade, William H. (1981) "Missile Vulnerability Reconsidered." *Arms Control Today* 11 (May):1-8.

Koshland, James M. (1978) "The Scope of the Program EIS Requirement: The Need for a Coherent Judicial Approach." *Stanford Law Review* 30 (April):767-802.

Krasner, Stephen D. (1972) "Are Bureaucracies Important? (Or Allison Wonderland)." *Foreign Policy* 7 (Summer):159-79.

Kurth, James. (1971) "A Widening Gyre: The Logic of American Weapons Procurement." *Public Policy* 19 (Summer):373-404.

Laurence, Edward J. (1976) "The Changing Role of Congress in Defense Policy-Making." *Journal of Conflict Resolution* 20 (June):213-50.

Leacacos, John P. (1971-72) "Kissinger's Apparat." *Foreign Policy* 5 (Winter):3-27.

Liroff, Richard. (1981) "NEPA Litigation in the 1970s: A Deluge or a Dribble?" *Natural Resources Journal* 21 (April):315-30.

Marsh, Robert T. (1982) "Strategy Missiles Debated: Missile Accuracy — We Do Know." *Strategic Review* 10 (Spring):35-37.

Marshall, Eliot. (1981) "A Question of Accuracy." *Science* 21 (11 September):1230-31.

Mueller, John. (1971) "Trends in Popular Support for the Wars in Korea and Vietnam." *American Political Science Review* 65 (June):358-75.

Nacht, Michael. (1982) "ABM ABCs." *Foreign Policy* 47 (Spring):155-74.

Nathan, James A. and James K. Oliver. (1978) "Bureaucratic Politics: Academic Windfalls and Intellectual Pitfalls." *Journal of Political and Military Sociology* 6 (Spring):81-91.

Nitze, Paul H. (1979) "Preserving the ICBM Leg of the Triad." *National Defense* 64 (July/August):30-34.

Notes. (1976) "Program Environmental Impact Statements: Review and Remedies." *Michigan Law Review* 75, no. 1 (November):107-47.

Pipes, Richard. (1977) "Why the Soviet Union Thinks It Could Fight and Win a Nuclear War." *Commentary* 64 (July):21-34.

Porro, Jeff. (1981) "BMD Technology — A Layman's Guide." *Arms Control Today* 11 (April):2-9.

Ricciuti, Edward R. (1979) "Salting the Desert with ICBMs." *Audobon* 81 (November):162, 164, 166-67.

Rich, Jonathan. (1984) "Midgetman: Superhero or Problem Child?" *Arms Control Today* 14 (May):1, 6-9.

Robinson, Clarence A., Jr. (1981) "Layered Defense System Pushed to Protect ICBMs." *Aviation Week and Space Technology* 114 (9 February):83-86.

_____. (1980) "Carter Strategic Policy Under Scrutiny." *Aviation Week and Space Technology* 113 (11 August):22.

Roherty, James M. (1974) "The Office of the Secretary of Defense: The Laird and McNamara Styles." In *New Civil Military Relations*, edited by John Lovell and Philip Kronenberg. New Brunswick, New Jersey: Transaction Books.

Rosenbaum, Walter A. (1974) "The End of Illusion: NEPA and the Limits of Judicial Review." In *Environmental Politics*, edited by Stuart S. Nagel. New York: Praeger.

Schell, Jonathan. (1982a) "The Fate of the Earth: A Republic of Insects and Grass." *New Yorker* 58 (1 February):47-113.

_____. (1982b) "The Fate of the Earth: The Second Death." *New Yorker* 58 (8 February):49-109.

_____. (1982c) "The Fate of the Earth: The Choice." *New Yorker* 58 (15 February):45-107.

Shapiro, Mark. (1981) "The Electrifying MX Security System." Prepared for the Center for Investigative Reporting. Oakland, California.

Slocombe, Walter. (1981) "The Countervailing Strategy." *International Security* 6 (Spring):18-27

Smith, Jeffrey R. (1982) "An Alternative to the MX: The Answer to America's Current Strategic Dilemma May Lie Offshore." *Science* 21 (May):828:30.

Snow, Donald. (1980a) "MX: Maginot Line of the 1980s." *The Bulletin of the Atomic Scientists* 36 (November):20-25.

_____. (1980b) "The MX-Basing Mode Muddle." *Air University Review* 31 (July/August):11-25.

Steinbruner, John and Thomas Garwin. (1976) "Strategic Vulnerability: The Balance Between Prudence and Paranoia." *International Security* 1 (Summer):138-81.

Stockton, Paul N. (1982) "Arms Development and Arms Control: The Strange Case of the MX Missile." In *American Politics and Public*

Policy, edited by Allan P. Sindler. Washington, D.C.: Congressional Quarterly Press.

Sweet, William. (1981) "MX Missile Decision," In *Editorial Research Reports.* Washington, D.C. Congressional Quarterly.

Tammen, Ronald L. (1981) "The Reagan Strategic Program." *Arms Control Today* 11 (December):1-3, 5-6.

Tsipis, Kosta. (1981) "Precision and Accuracy." *Arms Control Today* 11 (May):3-7.

Ulsamer, Edgar. (1979a) "MX Entering Home Stretch?" *Air Force Magazine* 62 (September):21-22.

_____. (1979b) "MX Status Report." *Air Force Magazine* 62 (May):22-25.

_____. (1978) "The MX Enigma." *Air Force Magazine* 61 (December): 21-22.

Walker, Paul F. (1979) "New Weapons and the Changing Nature of Warfare." *Arms Control Today* 9 (April):1-9.

Warnke, Paul C. (1982) "Dare We End the Arms Race?" *Arms Control Today* 12 (May):4-5, 8-9.

Weinstein, John M. (1982) "Soviet Civil Defense: The Mine Shaft Gap Revisted." *Arms Control Today* 12 (July/August):1-2, 7-9.

Westervelt, Donald R. (1974) "The Essence of Armed Futility." *Orbis* 18 (Fall):689-705.

Wildavsky, Aaron. (1969) "The Two Presidencies." In *The Presidency* edited by Aaron Wildavsky. Boston, Massachusetts: Little, Brown and Company.

Wohlstetter, Albert. (1959) "The Delicate Balance of Terror." *Foreign Affairs* 37 (January):211-34.

York, Herbert. (1973) "Multiple-Warhead Missiles." *Scientific American* 229 (Nov.):18-25.

Government Documents

Congressional Record. (1973-83) Washington, D.C.: Government Printing Office.

Congressional Quarterly Weekly Reports. (1973-83) Washington, D.C.: Congressional Quarterly Press.

House of Representatives. Committee on Interior and Insular Affairs. (1981a) "Hearings." 97th Cong., 1st sess. Washington, D.C.: Government Printing Office.

————. Committee on Interior and Insular Affairs. (1981b) "Basing the MX Missile." Staff report. 97th Cong., 1st sess. Washington, D.C.: Government Printing Office.

————. Committee on Interior and Insular Affairs. Subcommittee on Public Lands and National Parks. (1981a) "The MX Missile System." 97th Cong., 1st sess. Washington, D.C.: Government Printing Office.

————. Committee on Interior and Insular Affairs. Subcommittee on Public Lands and National Parks. (1981b) "OTA Assessment Briefing." 97th Cong., 1st sess. Washington, D.C.: Government Printing Office.

————. Committee on Interior and Insular Affairs. Subcommittee on Public Lands and National Parks. (1981c) "Hearings." 97th Cong., 1st sess. Washington, D.C: Government Printing Office.

————. Committee on Interior and Insular Affairs. Subcommittee on Public Lands and National Parks. (1980) "Oversight Hearings." 96th Cong., 1st and 2d sess. Washington, D.C.: Government Printing Office.

————. House Appropriations Committee. Military Construction Subcommittee. (1980) "Military Construction Appropriations for 1980: MX Missile Deployment." 96th Cong., 1st sess. Washington, D.C.: Government Printing Office.

————. House Appropriations Committee. Defense Subcommittee. (1980) "Hearings." 96th Cong., 1st sess. Washington, D.C.: Government Printing Office.

————. Report 1097, 96th Cong., 2d sess. (1980). Washington, D.C.: Government Printing Office.

————. Office of Technology Assessment (OTA). (1981) MX Missile Basing: Summary. Washington, D.C.: Government Printing Office

————. Senate. (1980) Report 931. 96th Cong., 2d sess. Washington, D.C.: Government Printing Office.

————. Hearings Before the Committee on the Armed Services. (1980) Department of Defense and Authorization for Appropriations for Fiscal Year 1981: Part VI - Research and Development, Civil Defense. 96th Cong., 1st sess. Washington, D.C.: Government Printing Office.

————. Hearings Before the Committee on the Armed Services. (1979) Department of Defense Authorization for Appropriations for FY 1980: Part VI - Research and Development. 96th Cong., 1st sess. Washington, D.C.: Government Printing Office.

_____. Hearings Before the Committee on the Armed Services. (1977) *Fiscal Year 1978 Authorization for Military Procurement, Research and Development, and Active Duty, Selected Research and Civilian Personnel Strengths: Part X - Research and Development*. 95th Cong., 1st sess. Washington, D.C.: Government Printing Office.

_____. Hearings Before the Committee on Armed Services. (1975) *Fiscal Year 1975 Authorization for Military Procurement, Research and Development, and Active Duty, Selected Reserve and Civilian Personnel Strengths*. 94th Cong., 1st sess. Washington, D.C.: Government Printing Office.

_____. Hearings Before the Committee on Armed Services. (1974) *Fiscal Year 1975 Authorization for Military Procurement, Research and Development, and Active Duty, Selected Reserve and Civilian Personnel Strengths*. 93rd Cong., 2d sess. Washington, D.C.: Government Printing Office.

_____. Hearings Before the Committee on Armed Services. (1973) *Fiscal Year 1974 Authorization for Military Procurement, Research and Development, Construction Authorization for Safeguard ABM and Active Duty and Selected Reserve Strengths*. 93rd Cong., 1st sess. Washington, D.C.: Government Printing Office.

Medalia, Jonathan. (1981) "Antiballistic Missiles." *Library of Congress Congressional Research Service* (2 February).

_____. (1980a) "Domestic Considerations Affecting the Deployment of a Multiple Protection Structure Basing System for the MX Missile." Washington, DC.: Congressional Record Service.

_____. (1980b) "MX Intercontinental Ballistic Missile Program." Issue Brief No. IB 77080. Washington, D.C.: Congressional Record Service.

State of Nevada. State Engineer's Office. (1980) *Water for Nevada*.

State of Utah. Department of Natural Resources. (1981) *Water for Utah*.

U.S. Council on Environmental Quality. (1980) *Environmental Quality: 11th Annual Report*. Washington, D.C.: Government Printing Office.

_____. (1979) *Environmental Quality: 10th Annual Report*. Washington, D.C.: Government Printing Office.

U.S. Department of Air Force. (1980) "Deployment Area Selection and Land Withdrawal Draft EIS." Washington, D.C.: Government Printing Office.

U.S. Department of Air Force. (1978) *Final Environmental Impact Statement, MX: Milestone II*. Washington, D.C.: Government Printing Office.

U.S. General Accounting Office. (1981) *The MX Weapon System: Issues and Challenges*. Washington, D.C.: Government Printing Office.

U.S. Office of Technology Assessment. (1981) *MX Missile Basing*. Washington, D.C.: Government Printing Office.

_____. (1974) *The Effects of Nuclear War*. Washington D.C.: Government Printing Office.

APPENDIX A

Telegrams authored by Governor Matheson of Utah to President Carter and Defense Secretary Brown

From: Scott M. Matheson, Governor, State of Utah, State Capitol, Salt Lake City, UT 84114

To: The Honorable Jimmy Carter, President of the United States of America, White House, Washington, DC/ZFF-1

Dear President Carter,

I am advised that you will soon receive from Defense Secretary Brown a request that the U.S. Air Force begin research and development of the MX Missile System. As governor of the state in which development may eventually occur, I want to assure you of my support for this weapon system.

The State of Utah has worked closely with the Air Force in the review of Environmental Impact Statements for all phases of the project and the probable impact on the state if a decision to deploy is made. As I have indicated in previous correspondence with the Department of the Air Force, there are no adverse environmental impacts associated with either the missile launching sites or the engineering and production of the missile components.

I have been extensively briefed by Air Force officials of this proposed project, and it is my conclusion that the MX Missile based on multiple productive shelters will comprise a vital and necessary part of our national defense capability.

Sincerely,

Dr. Harold Brown, Secretary, Dept. of Defense
The Pentagon
Washington, DC 20301

Dear Secretary Brown:

I want to indicate to you my complete and unequivocal support for the MX Missle System as a vital and necessary part of our national defense capability. The State of Utah has worked closely with the Air Force in the review of the Environmental Impact Statement for all phases of the project and the probable impact on the state if a decision to deploy is made. There are no adverse environmental impacts associated with either the missile launching sites or the engineering and production of the missile components. I have previously indicated my support of the MX Missile System to President Carter and want to affirm that support with the Department of Defense.

Sincerely,

Scott M. Matheson, Governor of Utah

APPENDIX B

Letter authored by Governor List of Nevada to the President of the United States. Entered into the *Congressional Record* on September 13, 1979.

Dear Mr. President:

I would like to take this opportunity to express my viewpoints regarding the possible development of the MX system in Nevada. United States Air Force officials have extensively briefed members of the Nevada Legislature as well as myself regarding all aspects of the project. During early phases of the environmental impact investigation when an "area security" approach was being considered some concerns were raised as to the possible adverse affects on minerals, exploration, and development and on other uses of the land. We have since been assured that the more recent "point security" approach would minimize any such limitations.

Although I know that additional details would be developed concerning the impact of the installation and while I feel that a full opportunity for public comment should then be allowed, it now appears that adverse environmental impacts associated with the missile launching sites in Nevada would be minimal. It is my belief that the multiple protective shelters deployment system for MX is essential to the future of our national defense capability. As governor of Nevada I wish to convey to you the willingness of the state of Nevada to do its part in the development of such a system should the decision be made to deploy it here.

GLOSSARY*

Air-Launched Cruise Missiles (ALCM): Small unmanned airplane-like vehicles armed with nuclear weapons.

Antiballistic Missile Defense: All measures to intercept and destroy hostile ballistic missiles or otherwise neutralize them. Equipment includes weapons, target acquisition, tracking and guidance radars, plus ancillary installations.

Arms Control: Explicit or implicit international agreements that govern the numbers, types, characteristics, deployment, and use of armed forces armaments.

Arms Race: A competitive relationship between two or more nations that results in weapons proliferation, an increase in the virulence of weapon-systems, and a quantitative and qualitative growth in the armed forces of those nations.

Arms Stability: A strategic force relationship in which neither side perceives the necessity for undertaking major new arms programs in order to avoid being placed at a disadvantage.

Assured Destruction: A highly reliable ability to inflict unacceptable damage on any aggressor or combination of aggressors at any time during the course of a nuclear exchange, even after absorbing a surprise first strike.

B-52: A heavy intercontinental range strategic bomber deployed by the United States. B-52 bombers can be equipped with gravity bombs, short-range attack missiles, or air-launched cruise missiles.

Ballistic Missile Defense (BMD): Systems for defense against missiles which follow trajectories resulting from gravity and aerodynamic drag following termination of powered flight. This term is used interchangeably with ABM systems.

Breakout: As used in connection with discussion of the LoADS ABM system, breakout refers to the rapid deployment of the LoADS defense unit by use of explosive charges to break through the top of the protective shelter permitting the defense unit to activate its radar and launch its interceptor missiles.

Circular Error Probable (CEP): A measure of the accuracy with which a weapon can be delivered. It is the radius of a circle around a target of such size that a weapon aimed at the target has a 50-percent probability of falling within the circle.

Command, Control, and Communications (C^3): The systems and procedures used to ensure that the president, senior civilian and military officials, and U.S. strategic nuclear forces remain in communication with each other, able to plan for the use of nuclear weapons, to choose among options, to deliver orders to the forces in the field, and to receive word that the forces have executed or attempted to execute their orders, during the course of peacetime or wartime operations.

Containment: Measures to discourage or prevent the expansion of enemy territorial holdings and/or influence. Specifically, a U.S. policy directed against Communist expansion.

Controlled Counterforce War: War in which one or both sides concentrate on reducing enemy strategic retaliatory forces in a bargaining situation and take special precautions to minimize collateral casualties and damage.

Controlled Response: Response to a military attack by military action that is deliberately kept within certain definable limits for the purpose of avoiding all-out nuclear war.

Countercity Strategy: Strategy of nuclear warfare implying that the attacker will strike at the enemy's population and industrial centers.

Counterforce: The employment of strategic air and missile forces to destroy or render impotent military capabilities of an enemy force. Bombers and their bases, ballistic missile submarines, ICBM silos, ABM and air defense installations, command and control centers, and nuclear stockpiles are typical counterforce targets.

Counterforce Strike: Attack, thermonuclear or other, of a strategic nature, conducted with the aim of destroying an enemy's strategic means of attack and any of the military installations pertaining to his offensive capabilities.

Counterforce Strategy: Strategy specifying the targeting of enemy forces, particularly those which it could use in retaliation. At Ann Arbor in 1962, Secretary of Defense McNamara stated that, in the event of a nuclear war, the principal military objective should be the destruction of enemy military forces, not his civilian population.

Countervalue: The concepts, plans, weapons, and actions used to destroy or neutralize selected energy population centers, industries, resources, and/or institutions. See also Counterforce.

Cruise Missile: A pilotless aircraft, propelled by an air-breathing engine, that operates entirely within the earth's atmosphere. Thrust continues throughout its flight. In-flight guidance and control can be accomplished remotely or by onboard equipment. Conventional and nuclear warheads are available. Although both the United States and the Soviet Union deploy cruise missiles, technological asymmetries separate the cruise missile systems of the two powers.

Damage Limitation: Active and/or passive efforts to restrict the level and or geographic extent of devastation during war. Includes counterforce actions of all kinds as well as civil defense measures.

Dash-On-Warning: A concept in which MX missiles on vehicles are dispersed rapidly upon receipt of warning that an attack appears underway to a nearby shelter where the MX missile is quickly inserted.

Detente: Lessening of tensions in international relations. May be achieved formally or informally.

Deterrence: Steps taken to prevent opponents from initiating armed actions and to inhibit escalation if combat occurs. Threats of force predominate.

> Type I Deterrence: Deterrent power inhibiting a direct attack against the United States.
>
> Type II Deterrence: Deterrent power inhibiting serious infractions short of attacks against the United States, i.e., aggression against friends and allies.
>
> Type III Deterrence: Deterrent power inhibiting aggression by making limited provocations unprofitable.

Endoatmospheric Defense: ABM systems which operate inside the earth's atmosphere, typically at altitudes from the ground to 100,000 ft.

Exchange Ratio: The number of nuclear weapons that must be used by an attacker to destroy one nuclear weapon belonging to an adversary.

Exoatmospheric Defense: ABM systems that operate outside the atmosphere.

First Strike: The launching of an initial strategic nuclear attack before the opponent has used any strategic weapons himself.

First-Strike Strategy: Strategy based on the notion that only by striking first can a nuclear power gain the advantage and prevent defeat.

Flexible Response: A strategy predicated on capabilities to act effectively across the entire spectrum of war at times, at places, and in manners of the user's choosing.

Fractionation: The division of the payload of a missile into a larger number of warheads with smaller individual yields.

Fratricide: The destruction or degradation of the accuracy and effectiveness of an attacking nuclear weapon by the nearby explosion of another attacking nuclear weapon. This phenomenon would decrease the effectiveness of an attack on closely spaced targets, such as missile silos.

Hard Target: A point or area protected to some significant degree against the blast, heat, and radiation effects of nuclear explosions of particular yields.

Heavy ICBM: The 1972 SALT I Interim Agreement on the limitation of selected strategic offensive systems identified heavy ICBMs as those having a volume significantly greater than that of the largest light ICBM. The U.S. Titan II and the Soviet SS-7, SS-8, SS-9, and SS-18 are heavy ICBMs.

Intercontinental Ballistic Missile (ICBM): A land-based, rocket-propelled vehicle capable of delivering a warhead to intercontinental ranges (ranges in excess of about 3000 nautical miles). Agreed interpretations of the SALT I agreement define ICBM as strategic ballistic missiles capable of ranges in excess of the shortest distance between the northeastern border of the continental United States and the northwestern border of the continental USSR (about 300 nm).

An ICBM consists of a booster stage, one or more sustainer propulsion stages, a reentry vehicle (s), possibly penetration aids, and, in the case of a MIRVed missile, a post-boost vehicle. The U.S. Minuteman III and the Soviet SS-11 are examples of ICBMs.

Kilotons (Kt): Equivalent to 1,000 tons of TNT.

Launch-On-Warning (LOW): A strategic doctrine under which a nation's bombers and land-based missiles would be launched on receipt of warning (from satellites and other early-warning systems) that an opponent had launched its missiles. Sometimes recommended for use when there is uncertainty over the ability of fixed-site ICMBs to survive an attack.

Launch-Under-Attack (LUA): A doctrine for strategic forces requiring their launch upon receipt of an attack on the United States.

LoADS Defense Unit: This consists of radar, interceptor launchers, and interceptors mounted on a mobile unit and deceptively deployed in conjunction with MX missile deployments.

Low Altitude Defense System (LoADs): A system proposed by the Army as an endoatmospheric antiballistic missile defense.

Maneuvering Reentry Vehicle (MARV): A ballistic missile reentry vehicle equipped with its own navigation and control systems capable of adjusting its trajectory during reentry into the atmosphere.

Megaton Weapon (Mt): A nuclear weapon the yield of which is measured in terms of millions of tons of TNT equivalents.

Minuteman: A three-stage solid-propellant second-generation intercontinental ballistic missile equipped with a nuclear warhead, designed for deployment in a hardened and dispersed configuration and in a mobile mode on railroad trains. It is a simpler, smaller, lighter missile than earlier intercontinental ballistic missiles and is designed for highly automated remote operation.

Missile: A non-manned delivery vehicle which can be guided after having left the launching base, during part or the whole of its trajectory. Strategic missiles are classified as follows: Intercontinental ballistic missile (ICBM); intermediate range ballistic missile (IRBM); medium-range ballistic missile (MRBM); submarine launched ballistic missile (SLBM); and modern large ballistic missile (MLBM).

MK-12A: A higher yield, more accurate warhead designed to replace the MK-12 warhead first deployed on Minuteman III missiles. MK-12A warheads may also be deployed on MX ICBMs and Trident II SLBMs.

Mobile Missile: Any ballistic or cruise missile mounted on and/or fired from a movable platform, such as a truck, train, ground effects machine, ship, or aircraft.

Modern Large Ballistic Missile: An intercontinental ballistic missile (ICBM) of a type deployed since 1964 and having a volume significantly greater than the largest light ICBM operational in 1972 (the Soviet SS-11). The United States has no MLBMs.

Multiple Aim Point (MAP): A term for basing a force of ICBMs among a larger number of protective missile shelters. See Multiple Protective Shelter.

Multiple Independently Targetable Reentry Vehicle (MIRV): Two or more reentry vehicles carried by a single missile and capable of being independently targeted. A MIRVed missile employs a "bus" or other warhead dispensing mechanism. The dispensing mechanism maneuvers to achieve successive desired positions and velocities to dispense each RV on a trajectory to attack the desired targets. Thus the reentry vehicles are aimed at separate targets over a large geographical area called the MIRVed missile's footprint.

Multiple Protective Shelter (MPS): A term describing a basing mode for land-based missiles in which missiles are deployed among a large number of hardened structures. These are designed and distributed to provide protection against nuclear weapon detonations.

Mutual Assured Destruction: A condition in which an assured destruction capability is possessed by opposing sides.

Mutual Deterrence: A stable situation in which two or more countries or coalitions of countries are inhibited from attacking each other because the casualties and/or damage resulting from retaliation would be unacceptable.

National Technical Means of Verification (NTM): Technical intelligence information collection systems which are under national control for monitoring compliance with the provisions of an arms control agreement.

Parity: A condition in which opposing forces possess capabilities of certain kinds that are approximately equal in over-all effectiveness.

Payload: The weight of the weapons or any penetration aids carried by a missile.

Polaris: U.S. submarines that carry the first generation of submarine-launched SLBM missiles. Each submarine can carry 16 missiles. Expected to be phased out in the early 1980's.

Reentry Vehicles (RV): That part of a ballistic missile designed to re-enter the earth's atmosphere in the terminal portion of its trajectory.

SALT: An acronym for the bilateral negotiations between the United States and Soviet Union on the subject of Strategic Arms Limitation Talks. SALT I refers to the agreements concluded in May 1972 including the ABM Treaty and the Interim Agreement on Strategic Offensive Nuclear Weapons.

Sea-launched cruise missile (SLCM): A cruise missile capable of being launched from a submerged or surfaced submarine or from a surface ship. The U.S. SLCM under development is sized for launch from standard submarine torpedo tubes, and thus could be carried by SSBNs or SSNs. The SLCM is to be developed in both strategic and tactical variants, the former being able to carry a nuclear warhead about 1500 nm. The latter will be designed to be launched from surface ships as well as submarines, primarily as a non-nuclear antiship missile with a range of up to several hundred miles. The SLCM will have a low cruise altitude flight profile and will have a high accuracy. The Soviet Union currently has SLCMs of a shorter range deployed on both nuclear- and diesel-powered submarines and surface ships.

Second Strike: A term usually used to refer to a retaliatory attack in response to a first strike. A high-confidence second-strike (retaliatory) capability is the primary basis for nuclear deterrence. To provide this capability U.S. forces have been structured on the basis of well-hedged assumptions regarding force survivability following an enemy first strike and the level of retaliatory destruction needed. Options for second strike include attacks on cities, industrial facilities, and military installations.

Second-Strike Strategy: The employment of strategic nuclear weapons only in reprisal for a nuclear first strike by the enemy. This strategy implies a capability sufficiently large and invulnerable to sustain an enemy first strike with residual forces available to inflict unacceptable levels of destruction.

Silo: Underground facility for a hard-site ballistic missile and/or crew, designed to provide prelaunch protection against nuclear effects.

Single Integrated Operational Plan (SIOP): The strategic nuclear war plan of the United States.

Smallsub Underwater Mobile (SUM) Basing: A concept for the deployment of MX missiles on small submarines proposed by Sidney Drell and Richard Garwin.

Soft Target: A target not protected against the blast, heat, and radiation produced by nuclear explosions. There are many degrees of softness. Some missiles and aircraft, for example, are built in ways that ward off certain effects, but they are "soft" in comparison with shelters and silos.

Strategic Bomber: A multi-engine aircraft with intercontinental range, designed specifically to engage targets whose destruction would reduce an enemy's capacity and/or will to wage war.

Strategic Nuclear Weapons Systems: Offensive nuclear weapon systems designed to be employed against enemy targets with the purpose of effecting the destruction of the enemy's political/economic/military capacity; and, defensive nuclear weapon systems designed to counteract these systems.

Strategic Sufficiency: A force structure standard that demands capabilities adequate to attain desired ends without undue waste. Superiority thus is essential in some circumstances; parity/essential equivalence suffices under less demanding conditions; and inferiority, qualitative as well as quantitative, is sometimes acceptable.

Submarine-Launched Ballistic Missile (SLBM): A ballistic missile launched from a submarine.

Throw-weight: Ballistic missile throw-weight is the maximum useful weight that has been flight tested on the boost stages of the missile. The useful weight includes weight of the reentry vehicles, penetration aids, dispensing and releasing mechanisms, reentry shrouds, covers, buses, and propulsion devices with their propellants (but not the final boost stages) which are present at the end of the boost phase.

Time-On-Target Control: The ability to control the time at which several nuclear weapons arrive at a particular target.

TNT Equivalent: A measure of the energy released from the detonation of a nuclear weapon, or from the explosion of a given quantity of fissionable or fusionable material, in terms of the amount of trinitrotoluene (TNT) that would release the same amount of energy when exploded.

Triad: The term used in referring to the basic structure of the U.S. strategic deterrent force. It is comprised of land-based ICBMs, the strategic bomber force, and the Polaris/Poseidon submarine fleet. The U.S. Triad of forces evolved from an allocation of national resources and priorities in order to meet certain strategic objectives, the most important of which was the capability to deter nuclear conflict. Each element of the Triad relies on somewhat different means for survival; hence, an enemy's potential for a successful first-strike attack is severely complicated. Bombers rely on warning, fast reaction, and ground or air-borne dispersal for survival; ICBMs are placed in individual hardened silos for survivability. SLBMs depend on the uncertainty of location of the submarine to enhance survivability.

Trident Submarine: A very large nuclear-powered submarine being deployed by the United States which carries 24 missiles and 240 warheads.

Verification: The process of determining the degree to which parties to an agreement are complying with provisions of the agreement.

Warfighting strategy: A strategy designed primarily to fight any kind of war at any level in the conflict spectrum (as opposed to deterrence strategies, which are designed to prevent wars).

Warhead: That part of a missile, projectile, torpedo, rocket, or other munition which contains either the nuclear or thermonuclear system, high explosive system, chemical or biological agents or inert materials intended to inflict damage.

---

*The definitions for these terms were taken from three sources.
a) Wolfram Hanrieder, *Arms Control and Security: Current Issues* (Boulder, CO: Westview Press, 1980), pp. 341-59.
b) U.S. Office of Technology Assessment, MX Missile Basing (Washington, DC: G.P.O., 1981), 331-35.
c) The Arms Control Association, "Glossary of Armed Control Terms."
Arms Limitation: An agreement to restrict quantitative holdings of or qualitative improvements in specific armaments or weapons systems.

INDEX

285

Ford administration 5, 22, 30, 37, 45, 47, 48, 68, 83, 96, 133, 135, 139, 148, 216
Foreign Relations Committee 136, 137
Foley, Representative Thomas 236
Foster, John 131
Fratricide 60, 80
Freedom of Information Act (FOIA) 6, 7, 34, 190, 207, 208
Friends of the Earth 241

Gephart, Representative Richard 236
Garn, Senator Jake 55, 74, 89, 146, 161, 167, 168, 169, 176, 192,
General Accounting Office (GAO) 105, 153, 163, 198, 257, 258
Ginn, Representative Bo 174
Goldwater, Senator Barry 146, 147
Gore, Representative Albert 235, 236, 237, 239, 241
Graham, General Daniel 55
Gray, Colin 47, 48, 73
Great Basin MX Alliance 104
Great Basin of Nevada and Utah 97, 98, 99, 101, 107, 112, 119, 127, 154, 161, 162, 166, 167, 168, 170, 179, 180, 183, 187, 190, 191, 194, 196, 199, 204, 207, 208

Halperin, Morton 12, 17, 139
Hammond, Paul 12, 16
Hanson, Representative James 176, 178
Hart, Senator Gary 144, 241, 257
Hatch, Senator Orrin 161, 167, 169, 192
Hatfield, Senator Mark 162, 174, 225, 228, 234
Heady, Douglas 110
Hercules 99, 161
Heritage Foundation 55
Herschler, Representative Larry 225, 257
Hilsman, Roger 12

Historic Preservation Act 207
Hubbard, Carroll Jr. 227
Humphrey, Senator Hubert 37, 137
Huntington, Samuel 12, 16, 139
Hydra 72

ICBMs (Intercontinental Ballistic Missiles) 46, 50, 52, 54, 55, 57, 66, 88, 123, 124, 130, 131, 157, 159, 233
Ichord, Representative Richard 155, 160
Initial Operational Capability (IOC) 133, 175, 176
Indians 33, 99, 103, 108, 119, 208
Inner-layer, of procurement activities 21-23, 25-27, 29
Intergovernmental Coordination Act of 1968, 118
Interim silo basing, Minuteman 180, 216-21
Interior and Insular Affairs, House Committee of 187

Jackson, Senator Henry M. 55, 56, 84, 137, 146, 147
Jackson, Jesse 257
Johnson, Representative James P. 160
Johnson, President Lyndon 36, 48
Joint Chiefs of Staff 23, 157, 158, 227, (365)
Jones, General David 140
Jones, T. K. 90

Kansas 96, 99, 154, 160
Kanter, Arnold 17
Kemp, Representative Jack 55
Kennedy administration 45, 46, 47
Kennedy, Senator Edward 37, 55, 137, 225
Keyworth, General George 234
Kincade, William 61
Kissinger, He ᵗ 22, 87
Korean plane incident (KAL007) 240
Krulitz Doctrine 207

30 455 D
M

Strat-X, study of strategic systems 66, 67, 70
Strategic Air Command (SAC) 45, 46, 55, 124, 125, 126, 129, 130, 132, 223, 234
Strategic issues, questions, influence on MX debate 45-62
Submarine launched ballistic missile (SLBM) 52, 55, 61, 72
SUM (Shallow Underwater Missile) 71
Supreme Court, federal courts 112, 113, 114

Texas 98, 99, 104, 154, 160, 210
Theater Nuclear Weapons 83, 91, 92
Thiokol Chemical Corporation 99
Titan 108, 216
Tonopah 208
Tower, Senator John 55, 36, 137, 146, 147, 181, 193, 220, 223, 224, 240
Townes Commission 172, 180, 222
Triad of strategic forces 72
Trident Missile 49, 53
Truman, President Harry 16
Tsipis, Kosta 61
Turner, Admiral Stansfield 145
Two-layered model, assumptions of 18, 19, 20

Ulsamer, Edgar 55
Union of Concerned Scientists 104
U.S. Air Force Association 55
Utah 97, 98, 99, 106, 107, 115, 127, 154, 160, 161, 162, 166, 168, 176, 179, 183, 191, 194, 196, 200, 204, 205, 210
Utah Mining Association 103
Utah Wilderness Association 104

Vance, Cyrus 88, 145, 155, 157
VanCleve, William 55
Vessey, General John 227
Vietnam 1, 33, 34, 35
Vladivostok Accords 88, 135

WS 120 Program 125
War-fighting Doctrine 45, 47, 54, 56, 57, 61
Warner, Senator John 181
Watergate 33, 35
Weinberger, Casper 9, 55, 70, 89, 171, 172, 175, 182, 194, 208, 221, 236
Western Solidarity 257
Wheat Grower's Association 97
Wisconsin 160
Wohlstetter, Albert 47
Women Involved in Farm Economics 97
Women's League For Peace and Freedom 104
Woolsey, James 234, 240, 242
Wright, Representative James
Wyoming 104, 209, 257

Yates, Sidney 227

Zieberg, Seymour 140, 144, 146, 170

289